Don't Tell:

Stories and essays by

agnostics and atheists in AA

Edited by Roger C.

AA Agnostica

Don't Tell:
Stories and essays by agnostics and atheists in AA

Published in Canada by AA Agnostica

aaagnostica.org

Library and Archives Canada Cataloguing in Publication

Don't tell : stories and essays by agnostics and atheists in AA / edited by Roger C.

Issued in print and electronic formats.
ISBN 978-0-9917174-4-6 (pbk.).--ISBN 978-0-9917174-5-3 (epub)

1. Alcoholics Anonymous--History. 2. Alcoholism--Religious aspects.
3. Alcoholics--Rehabilitation. 4. Drug addicts--Rehabilitation.
5. Agnostics--Mental health. 6. Atheists--Mental health. 7. Twelve-step programs. I. C., Roger, 1950-, editor II. AA Agnostica

HV5278.D66 2014   362.292'86   C2014-902142-9
                                             C2014-902143-7

Table of Contents

Dedication

This book is dedicated to Wayne M. At the age of 57, after decades of boozing and several visits to rehabs, Wayne quit drinking, having resolved that it was never too late and that he did not want to die a drunk. He would have nothing to do with the "God bit" in AA and so his home group since it was founded in the fall of 2009 was an agnostic AA group called "Beyond Belief." His story, *A higher purpose*, is included in the "In the rooms" section of the book. Wayne died on March 21, 2014. He did not die a drunk.

Acknowledgements

Every one the stories and essays in this book was first posted on the AA Agnostica website. We are grateful to all of the women and men who share their "experience, strength and hope" with the readers on AA Agnostica, a website that is meant to be "a space for AA agnostics, atheists and freethinkers worldwide." For those whose articles are included in this book, thank you once again. Our mission, of course, is to be a proactive part of AA in realizing our primary purpose, which is to lend a helping hand to "anyone, anywhere who reaches out for help" in her or his recovery from the affliction of alcoholism. Thus our profound gratitude towards those who have chosen to tell their stories on AA Agnostica and in this book as well, with its rather poignant and ironic title, Don't Tell.

Foreword

By Ernest Kurtz and William White

Alcoholics Anonymous (AA) is the standard by which all recovery mutual aid groups are judged. It has earned this distinction by its longevity, its growth and worldwide dispersion, its influence on the professional treatment of addiction, and its widespread adaptation to other problems of living. Beyond AA's well-known Twelve-Step *program*, at least as impressive is its unique structure as a *fellowship*, protected by its Twelve Traditions. Both have contributed to the history of ideas, engendering an unending stream of research studies, books and articles.

The twin challenges faced by any recovery mutual aid group are to define a program of personal recovery and to define how it will operate as an organization, including its membership boundaries. Alcoholics Anonymous achieved these through its Twelve Steps and Twelve Traditions. Since their initial formulation, the Steps and Traditions have been continually re-interpreted in light of changing personal and cultural contexts. As historians of AA and similar movements, what we find most significant in recent decades are the growing varieties of recovery experience within and beyond AA. It is within this context that the history of AA Agnostica and its newly released book, *Don't Tell*, are best viewed.

Since the founding of Quad A (Alcoholics Anonymous for Atheists and Agnostics) in January of 1975, a wing of unconventional believers has grown within AA. There have been other efforts of members who broke from AA to form secular recovery support organizations (e.g., Women for Sobriety, Secular Organizations for Sobriety), but Quad A was a milestone in that it sought to establish a non-theistic approach to alcoholism recovery within AA. At the same time, others have sought to advance a more Christianized understanding of Alcoholics Anonymous and its history. Both movements will exert a significant influence on the future of AA as a program and fellowship of recovery. Where these diverse branches meet is the testing ground for AA's future. This is why *Don't Tell* is an important book for anyone interested in the future of Alcoholics Anonymous and the future of alcoholism recovery -- as well as for those looking to read some fascinatingly different stories of "what we used to be like, what happened, and what we are like now."

They go by many names: "freethinkers," "agnostics," "atheists," "humanists," "secularists," "unconventional believers," but each also claims the names "alcoholic" and "AA member." All are represented within the pages of *Don't Tell*. Since its 2012 founding, AA Agnostica has emerged as the voice of these pioneering dissidents who are seeking space and legitimacy within Alcoholics Anonymous. In the pages of *Don't Tell*, readers will find their stories, their ideas, their concerns about their exclusion from Intergroup listings and even from some AA meetings, and their frustration at the lack of a more substantive – some would say "more Christian" – response within Alcoholics Anonymous to the non-believer seeking recovery from alcoholism.

What do we think, as long-time students of AA's rich story? The essence of Alcoholics Anonymous as *fellowship* is the practice of the Twelfth Step of its program: carrying its message to another alcoholic. This is how AA began, William Griffith Wilson seeking out Dr. Robert Holbrooke Smith so that he himself would not take a drink that warm May afternoon in 1935. This is how AA grew, Wilson haunting the corridors of Towns Hospital in New York City, Smith using various diagnoses to smuggle a rag-tag bunch of drunks into Akron's St. Thomas Hospital. Now, over 75 years later, in an age when an ever greater percentage of young people answer "None" when queried about their "religious affiliation," an Alcoholics Anonymous that refuses fellowship to those unconventional in belief would seem to be gravely endangering its future: to whom will it carry its message? And, more importantly, *who* will carry its message to coming generations of alcoholics?

Many individual AA members have experienced defining moments that tipped the scales from active addiction to sustained sobriety. Alcoholics Anonymous itself, *precisely as fellowship*, has faced and continues to face defining moments that test its character and fate. We believe that AA's current response to efforts to widen the doorways of entry into AA by non-believers constitutes such a defining moment. *Don't Tell* is must-reading for anyone invested in the outcome of this potentially historic watershed.

In reading *Don't tell*, we were reminded of earlier periods in which Alcoholics Anonymous faced challenges, reminded also of some of the carefully wise words of AA co-founder Bill Wilson about the future of AA as a fellowship and organization:

> *The process [trial and error] still goes on and we hope it never stops. Should we ever harden too much, the letter might crush the spirit. We could victimize ourselves by petty rules and prohibitions; we could imagine that we had said the last word. We might even be asking alcoholics to accept our rigid ideas or stay away. May we never stifle*

progress like that! (Wilson, Twelve Suggested Points for AA Tradition, AA Grapevine, April, 1946)

We have to grow or else deteriorate. For us, the "status quo" can only be for today, never for tomorrow. Change we must; we cannot stand still. (Wilson, The Shape of Things to Come, AA Grapevine, February, 1961)

Let us never fear needed change. Once a need becomes clearly apparent in an individual, a group, or in AA as a whole, it has long since been found that we cannot stand still and look the other way. (Wilson, Responsibility is our Theme, AA Grapevine, July, 1965)

Alcoholics Anonymous, like its predecessors and its current alternatives, must define as a fellowship how to distinguish between changes that help fulfill its ultimate mission and changes that in retrospect will be understood to have been a diversion from that mission. If that mission is, as its Twelfth Step suggests and its own story affirms, carrying its message to other alcoholics regardless of their race, gender, sexuality, religion or lack thereof, or any other accidental quality, AA has in living its Third Tradition – "The only requirement for membership is a desire to stop drinking" – consistently chosen to risk erring on the side of inclusion.

Once upon a time that Third Tradition read "The only requirement for membership is an honest desire to stop drinking." Set forth for the first time in the 1939 "Foreword" to the book *Alcoholics Anonymous*, the wording was changed and the term "honest" dropped only in 1949, at the time of the first publication of the "short form" of the AA Traditions. The official explanation given for that change just might also apply in its own way to present concerns over unconventionally believing members:

> *As AA has matured, it has been increasingly recognized that it is nearly impossible to determine what constitutes an "honest" desire to stop drinking, as opposed to other forms in which the desire might be expressed. It was also noted that some who may be interested in the program might be confused by the phrase "honest desire." Thus . . . the descriptive adjective has been dropped.*

Broadening, welcoming change, as the story of its key Third Tradition suggests, is of the essence of Alcoholics Anonymous.

Ernest Kurtz, Author, *Not-God: A History of Alcoholics Anonymous*
William White, Author, *Slaying the Dragon: The History of Addiction Treatment and Recovery in America*

Introduction

You can't solve a problem if you don't first admit that it exists.

That's just about the first thing we learn in recovery.

Almost forty years ago, in July 1976, a report was presented to an AA trustees' committee suggesting that agnostics and atheists in the fellowship were often made to feel like "deviants" rather than "full, participating members in the AA Fellowship without qualification."

That's the problem.

Agnostics and atheists often don't feel comfortable or even welcome in the rooms of AA.

It's a problem that has been around for a long time.

And nothing – repeat, nothing – has been done about it.

Well, nothing positive anyway.

There are Intergroups across North America that actually bar agnostic groups and won't include them on the regional meeting lists. As for example in Lafayette and Laytonville, California, Des Moines, Iowa and Portland, Oregon.

And in Canada, groups have been booted out of Intergroups and off of meeting lists in both Vancouver and Toronto.

The first agnostic AA groups ever in Canada – Beyond Belief and We Agnostics – were also the first agnostic groups ever to be booted out of an AA Intergroup, and that was in Toronto on May 30, 2011.

Two weeks later, a website appeared on the Internet, AA Toronto Agnostics. At first it was meant only to provide the locations, dates and times of the two agnostic meetings. It quickly became much more than that and a year later morphed into AA Agnostica, "a space for agnostics, atheists and freethinkers worldwide."

And that's where this book comes from.

It contains a total of 64 stories and essays mostly by agnostics and atheists in AA originally posted on AA Agnostica, most often on Sunday mornings, over the last almost three years. These were written by over thirty men and

1

women from almost as many cities, states, provinces and counties within three countries, the United States, Canada and Great Britain.

It is a diverse and eclectic sampling of writings by women and men for whom sobriety within the fellowship of AA had nothing at all to with an interventionist God.

Nothing at all.

The stories are broken down rather naturally into ten categories. The first, "In the rooms," deals with what it feels like to be a non-believer at church basement AA meetings. Another category consists of reviews of books that have been found to be helpful for We Agnostics and FreeThinkers (sometimes referred to as "WAFTs") in AA. There are several articles under the heading of the 12 Steps. And, not to list all the categories, there is a special one for the two founders of the very first AA meeting to be called We Agnostics – Megan D. and Charlie P. – because we are so thankful for their historic efforts to accommodate non-believers in the fellowship: efforts that would no doubt have been deeply appreciated by the co-founders of Alcoholics Anonymous.

Just a very few of the writers – in the "Many Paths" section of the book – do not identify as members of Alcoholics Anonymous. It is important to share, however, that as AA members we respect and celebrate all of the paths to recovery. Thus this important section of the book.

Alright, back to the beginning.

We started by suggesting that you can't solve a problem until you acknowledge its existence.

The discomfort that nonbelievers experience in the rooms of AA was first officially raised as a problem in the mid-seventies, some forty years ago.

It was at that time that efforts began to get the General Service Conference to approve a pamphlet specifically welcoming, and respectful of, agnostics and atheists in AA. The stories of those efforts are told in a section of this book. All of these efforts were ignored or rejected, year after year, decade after decade, by the de facto "group conscience" of AA.

Here's why.

There is an unofficial but coercive "Don't Tell" policy in the rooms of AA. If you are an atheist, agnostic, humanist or secularist you had best keep your lack of belief in a deity to yourself.

In this sense, AA is a bit like a cat trying to catch its own tail. You can't solve a problem if talking about it isn't even allowed. If you insist on pretending it doesn't exist.

Thus the AA Agnostica website. Thus this book.

It is no longer possible to pretend the problem doesn't exist. The question now is simply whether or not the fellowship of AA wants a solution.

I. In The Rooms

The "Don't Tell" Policy in AA

By Roger C.

There often seems to be an unofficial policy in Alcoholics Anonymous especially for nonbelievers at AA meetings: "Don't Tell."

It is a policy imposed by just a few but rarely challenged.

If you are an atheist, agnostic, humanist or secularist you had best keep your lack of belief in a deity to yourself. (And yet, according to Bill W., AA is officially for everyone "regardless of their belief or *lack of belief*").

Here's an example of the problem: John M tells about how easily everyone accepts it when an AA speaker says, "I owe this to my Higher Power whom I choose to call God."

"No problem here!" John writes, and he continues:

> However, a long standing sober member of my home group once told me that when she was sharing at a closed meeting she spoke of her higher power "whom I choose not to call God." The looks she got, the raised eyebrows, the shuffling of fannies in the chairs indicated to her that her declaration was a problem for many in the room. At that moment, it felt to her as if she had uttered a blasphemy.

"Don't Tell." That's the policy for nonbelievers in AA.

There are three main ways to be "outed" as an agnostic in Alcoholics Anonymous:

1. By sharing, as John's friend did.

2. By removing the word "God" from the 12 Step program of recovery. In 1939 the words "as we understood Him" were added to "God" in the suggested 12 Steps. Today, for many nonbelievers, that compromise is not enough. The word "God" is removed while the intent of the Step is maintained.

3. By declining to recite the Lord's Prayer at the end of an AA meeting.

Some readers will be familiar with the "Don't Ask Don't Tell" policy which was for some time the official United States policy on homosexuals serving in the military. The policy prohibited discriminating against or harassing closeted homosexual or bisexual service members, while barring openly gay or lesbian persons from military service.

The "Don't Tell" part of the policy meant that if you didn't let on that you were a gay or a lesbian then you could still be a member in good standing of the armed forces. If you admitted you were a homosexual, however, then you were kicked out.

The "Don't Ask" part meant that nobody could ask you if you were a gay or a lesbian. Or even a bi-sexual. And the top brass couldn't investigate to find out; they couldn't go to your home, ask your friends or follow you to bars or meetings.

There doesn't appear to be a "Don't Ask" part in this policy in AA.

A rumour circulated in the Toronto area that there was a new AA group in Richmond Hill which, although it read the traditional 12 Steps of AA, also shared an interpretation of some of the steps without the "God" word.

Four self-appointed AA police officers decided to investigate and showed up at a Widening Our Gateway meeting on Sunday, November 20, 2011, and sure enough, they concluded, there was evidence of tampered Steps.

A month later, on December 20, one of these detectives presented a motion at Intergroup that Widening Our Gateway be suspended from Intergroup membership for changing the Steps.

Meanwhile back in the United States military, the "Don't Ask Don't Tell" policy finally came to an end on September 20, 2011. It took a while for the new rules to take effect but on December 21, in an article headlined "Gay Navy Couple Torpedo Don't Ask Don't Tell with First Kiss," the San Diego News reported on an historic moment. Petty Officer Marissa Gaeta and her partner Citalic Snell became the first gay couple in Navy history to share the "first kiss" moment when the navy ship USS Oak Hill returned from Central America.

The News further reported that Gaeta told a gaggle of reporters: "It's something new, that's for sure. It's nice to be able to be myself. It's been a long time coming."

Will the "Don't Tell" policy at AA meetings ever come to an end?

Of course.

AA as a fellowship will meet this new challenge or, as Joe, a founding member of an agnostic AA group put it: "My bold prediction is that if AA doesn't accommodate change and diversify, our 100th anniversary will be a fellowship of men and women with the same stature and relevance as the Mennonites; charming, harmless and irrelevant."

Remember, everything is always impossible until, well, it turns out to be both possible and normal. Look at the picture of Marissa and Citalic again.

It's been a long time coming but nonbelievers will yet have a place in the rooms of AA.

In the meantime, for God's sake:

"Don't Tell."

Six Shades of Nonbelievers

By Joe C.

The nonbeliever world is a hexagon shaped world, according to a University of Tennessee finding. Christopher Silver and Thomas Coleman III derived their six types of nonbelievers based on an analysis of interviews across the United States.

Well, let's see. Do you fall into one of these subgroups?

1. Intellectual atheist/agnostic: Well read, eager to engage in debate or any social intercourse that will stimulate them intellectually.

2. Activist atheist: This unbeliever isn't content with just disbelieving in God; they speak to the dangers of theism and the religions that preach theistic dogma. Politically engaged, the activists bring their brand of scientific realism to causes from minority rights to the environment.

3. Seeker-agnostic: "I don't know and can't know—and neither can you." Divinity, if it exists, is beyond human understanding. These seekers, although searching, are skeptical that any of the book-based messages from God are anything other than political/cultural, man-made fiction. Doubt is a greater state of enlightenment than certainty. Type 3s don't see themselves as undecided, rather, they are firmly committed to middle ground.

4. Anti-theist: Being "diametrically opposed to religious ideology," anti-theists view religion as promulgating ignorance and delusion in a way that is socially detrimental. This group feels that theirs is the more enlightened and superior worldview. Confronting belief and opposing religion is a duty.

5. Non-theist: This group is apathetic. Rarely giving the matter any thought, this smallish group wouldn't care about the truth or fiction of a Divine creator any more than someone from New York would care about what day of the week that trash was collected in Beijing. Non-theists don't feel part of a team nor do they find the great worldview debates entertaining.

6. Ritual agnostic/atheist: "Don't throw the baby out with the bathwater," would be a theme for these nonbelievers who still find cultural connection to their religion of birth or worthy philosophy from religions as a whole. Secular Jews, Baptists, Muslims or Hindus might not worship God, Allah or Shiva or be invested in an afterlife but they feel a connection to the community that religious rituals offer. Even a priest could be an atheist but fulfill his role in a community of adherents. Some who check off, "Protestant," in a survey might not believe the Jesus fable or virgin birth myth but they identify with their cultural background.

The authors of the Tennessee study agree that any of us may identify with more than one of the six sub-types although nonbelievers have a primary sub-type. Even in a college town, this type of study in the bible belt will draw a range of attention from, "Finally," to "You better not have spent my tax dollars on this blasphemy!"

Silver says, "One of the main purposes of this study is to start a conversation and raise awareness of the diversity of the nonbelief community. Tommy and I both accept that there are other academic researchers out there with far more psychometric and methodological sophistication. Certainly these researchers may be able to explore the community in greater detail, shedding light on aspects of the community not detected in this study. We welcome others to explore the diversity of nonbelief and share their data and conclusions."

The infamous Pew Forum on Religion and Public Life in America separated their respondents as claiming to be a member of a named Christian or other religion and if they didn't fit in one these numerous categories, there was "atheist," "agnostic" or "none" left to choose from. Silver and Coleman try to expand on who this growing category of nonbelievers really is.

How might each of these six sub-types fit in to a Twelve Step fellowship?

1. The intellectual atheist/agnostic will know our history, from Jim Burwell to the official endorsement that the first Buddhist AA groups received to re-write a God-free version of the Steps from Bill W., to how many agnostic groups are found in the world directory and where to find and quote Warranty Six in Concept XII of the AA Service Manual:

> Much attention has been drawn to the extraordinary liberties which the AA Traditions accord to the individual member and his (or her) group; no penalties to be inflicted for nonconformity to AA principles; no fees or dues to be levied—voluntary contributions only; no member to be expelled from AA — membership always to be the choice of the individual; each AA group to conduct its internal affairs as it wishes—it being merely required to abstain from acts that might injure AA as a whole; and finally, that any group of alcoholics gathered together for sobriety may call themselves an AA group provided that, as a group, they have no other purpose or affiliation.

Type 1 wouldn't shun or discourage theistic devotion. However, she or he would prefer lively debate over everyone keeping to themselves regarding worldview issues.

2. The activist atheist may feel strongly not only about the erroneous conclusions about a sobriety-granting loving Father but some of the other AA dogma, too. Can the religious morality be purged from the Twelve Steps? Along with sexism, Americanism, and canonization of the founders, the activist might ask that we remain open-minded about the disease, allergy and incurability model as it makes us look like rigid religious crackpots if we seem fearful of studies that try to debunk our most heart-felt tenets about addiction.

3. The seeking agnostic might get more heat from other nonbelievers in the rooms than the more religious God-conscious members. "Stop fence-sitting! 'Half measures avail us nothing.' How could you still think an interfering/intervening deity might be keeping you sober? There's no Zeus, no Santa, no Unicorn, no God." This might be the grief Type 3 gets from their fellow none so righteous as the recently converted apostate 12 Step member. While, to the deeply devoted, anyone on the search is a legitimate 12 Stepper. To them, the searching agnostic hasn't found God YET!

4. The anti-theist will quote Jim Burwell, "I can't stand this God stuff! It's a lot of malarkey for weak folks. The group doesn't need it and I won't have it." Type 4 will always be ready in a meeting to counter someone's fear-mongering proselytizing such as, "You might as well leave if you aren't going to believe in God, because you're going to get drunk anyway!"

The most dogmatic of all nonbelievers would be the anti-theist. Seeing oneself as the voice of reason or sober, second thought, the anti-theist is ready to pounce with his or her own script and AA verse about the wider tent, suggested program and Bill's own words, "The wording was of course quite optional, so long as we voiced the ideas without reservation." (Alcoholics Anonymous, p. 63.)

Of course, many Type 4s won't stay. They really think AA would be better off without the God talk because atheists are superior. Many will migrate to SMART Recovery, SOS or another secular recovery fellowship where they are in the company of only like-minded folks.

5. Non-theists might not stay too long in the rooms either. If everyone is so sure of what they believe why don't they just shut up and get on with it? All the description of how God is working in each of our lives is really boring to a non-theist. There is so much more about recovery to talk about — why focus on what we believe when the material world has all the awe and wonder we need. One day at a time, don't pick up the first drink, stick with the winners, personal inventory, making amends, meditation: these are things the non-theist will be heard talking about. They are real and concrete and what living sober is about.

6. Type 6 Twelve Steppers enjoy camaraderie and the idea that faith in something bigger than self-will alone helps keep us sober. The power may not be ethereal. The esprit du corps felt in the rooms is powerful enough. The **ritualistic atheist** might even be heard saying the Serenity Prayer or telling us how they turned their life over to God, not because that's what they believe — they are going along to get along. Ritualistic atheists might be closet agnostics. Either they are sure or they aren't sure but they want to fit in — not take a stand. If it's all bull shit, what does it matter saying "God could and would if He were sought?" Who knows how many of our 12 Step members are closet atheists who want to speak, chair meetings and get elected to service positions so they say what people like to hear. "What about rigorous honesty," you ask? "Except when to do so would injure them or others," is their response. Why make waves?

So what number are you? Some of us evolve from one type to another. I was a closet-atheist 6 for years of my sobriety, an anti-theist 4 during my recently converted phase when I first came out. I was suddenly offended by the blatant and sometimes bullying pro-theism. Today I think I am a Type 1, self-proclaimed "post-theist." Maybe one day I will be non-theist # 5 and grow bored of the whole discussion.

I don't think there is a right type of nonbeliever to be; "to thine own self be true." The Twelve Traditions ensure that there is room for you and me and everyone. Even before the Twelve Traditions were ratified by the membership, co-founder Bill Wilson was expressing the need. In The Grapevine (July 1946), in an article called, "The Individual In Relation to AA as a Group," Wilson writes:

> So long as there is the slightest interest in sobriety, the most unmoral, the most anti-social, the most critical alcoholic may gather about him a few kindred spirits and announce to us that a new Alcoholics Anonymous Group has been formed. Anti-God, anti-medicine, anti-our Recovery Program, even anti-each other — these rampant individuals are still an AA Group if they think so!

Like other types of inventory it is worth exploring our own beliefs, the evolution of our thought process and our gut feelings. Tommy Coleman talked to me about categorizing ourselves, "Now in terms of individuals looking to find out which type they are we say that due to the nature of all typologies, you may see yourself in more than one. However, we ask that you pick what describes you best as most people usually have one type that fits them better than the rest."

For me, the better I know myself, the more apt I am at understanding my triggers and preferences. It makes me less reactive and more self-aware. So bravo, U of Tennessee; thanks for keeping the discussion going. (Of course a Type 1 would say that).

Joe C. was one of the founding members of the first agnostic AA group in Canada: Beyond Belief. He is the author of the book, based on the same name: Beyond Belief: Agnostic Musings for 12 Step Life.

Perry Street Workshop

By John L.

Thousands of people, now living all over the world, have found sobriety in a storefront room in New York City's Greenwich Village: the Perry Street Workshop. For me Perry Street will always be Alcoholics Anonymous, my home base no matter where I am. In 2008, as Perry Street celebrated its 50th anniversary, members created a website and a brochure, *The Perry Street 50th Year Anniversary Booklet*.

When I revisited Perry Street last year, time stood still. I saw the exact spot where I had sat at my first AA meeting, 46 years ago. Almost nothing had changed. The podium; the chair arrangement; the hand-lettered Steps, Traditions and Serenity Prayer, were the same. The only thing missing was cigarette smoke.

I remember my first meeting very well, a Thursday beginners meeting in early January 1968. I was in bad shape, having almost died in terminal alcohol withdrawal. My friend Andy and another AA member helped me walk across town, from my apartment in Manhattan's East Village. When I sat down, I was very weak and shaking violently, my teeth were chattering, and I was unable to focus my eyes. People said I should go immediately to a hospital, but I refused, saying that I was there for the meeting — so they covered me with overcoats and set an electric space heater in front of me. I identified completely with the speaker, a man in his thirties. Everything came together. I experienced hope and an intense desire to live. If the others in the room had survived, then so could I.

That weekend Andy had a relapse and disappeared, but I was not alone. I had a meeting list and phone numbers. Although Andy never did achieve lasting sobriety, he saved my life. He was the only sponsor I have ever had. In those days, at least at Perry Street, sponsors were regarded as optional, intended mainly to help the newcomer in early sobriety. They were not, as now, supposed to be long-term, all-purpose counsellors or therapists.

I'll pass over the story of my physical recovery and concentrate on memories of my first year — what in AA has changed and what has remained the same.

In 1968, as now, almost all meetings at Perry Street (except beginners meetings) were closed — for alcoholics only. This lends them a sense of candor and intimacy that is lost when meetings are open to the general

12

public. Anything a recovering alcoholic discusses, in the company of other alcoholics, can be relevant. I remember a small afternoon meeting at Perry Street — most of us newcomers — where one young man shared that, in the euphoria of his new sobriety, he had gotten a $15 haircut. We laughed and identified completely. (For perspective, that $15 haircut in 1968 would cost many times that much now.)

Sometimes discussions led into what I call "recreational arguments" — energetic, but good-natured. Some of the bones of contention were doctors, the Steps, and religion. Those who preened themselves on their piety, or even worse, "Higher Power, whom I choose to call [dramatic pause] God", would likely be answered by someone who hated religion, especially the Catholic Church, which had blasted his life. At a meeting of the New Day group in Greenwich Village, my friend Bruce responded to an egregious display of piety by saying, "I'm in AA to be sober; I'm not here to be good."

As pungently free as discussions could be, the Perry Street meetings were orderly. It was believed important to maintain a tone conducive to sobriety. Meetings never ran over the time allotted; if a meeting was supposed to end at 9 p.m., it did, even if someone was cut off in mid-sentence. "No souls saved after Midnight." People did not interrupt each other, although people were tactfully prevented from speaking too long or running off the rails.

Active alcoholics were welcome at meetings, but only so long as they behaved themselves; if they created a disturbance, the chair would tell them that if they did it again, they would be escorted from the meeting. They usually remained silent. I remember one occasion when "escorting" was necessary; it was done, gently but firmly, by a man who had been a professional bouncer before sobriety.

I had been sober for perhaps two months when a thoroughly disreputable old man showed up. In those days people didn't arrive from detox centers, but sometimes right from the Bowery. He was not only ragged and dirty and unshaven — he smelled bad, and people moved away from him. Vaguely believing that I could do a 12th Step, I spoke to him and did my best to carry the message of sobriety. Week after week he would show up, and I always spoke to him. Then one day he showed up: clean, shaven, well groomed, wearing a new suit, and looking many years younger. He looked so proud! I think I was never happier for the happiness of another human being.

It wasn't always sweetness and light. Beginning in 1965, I was heavily involved in the antiwar movement, until my activism was curtailed by physical collapse in the final year of drinking. In August 1968 the Democratic Party

13

convention was held in Chicago, with two peace candidates: Senators George McGovern and Eugene McCarthy. The Chicago police, under the direction of Mayor Daley — violently hostile to the antiwar movement — rioted, attacking protesters, photographers, reporters, and bystanders. In the morning of 29 August 1968 the police invaded the campaign headquarters of Senator McCarthy, destroying equipment and brutally striking campaign workers with their nightsticks. Some of the workers were even dragged out of bed before being beaten. At this time I had been sober for half a year, and was horrified. At a meeting, with tears streaming down my face, I shared my distress — but for less than a minute. All hell broke loose, as soon as people realised that I was against the war in Vietnam. They furiously shouted me down, and some of them leaped from their seats to attack me. Two older women led me outside, and then to their apartment, which was nearby. Perhaps a half dozen others also left with us, and we held an alternate AA meeting there. They comforted me, and I realised that I had friends — but also realised that there are limits to AA discussion, politics being one of them.

Another newcomer in the Village groups was a retired army colonel. No matter what he started out talking about, he always concluded by saying that we had to have Victory In Vietnam. No one ever objected. I would remain silent, wishing that he and everyone else in the room would stay sober, but not sure I'd mind watching him walk in front of a truck. Live and Let Live!

Perry Street members were heterogeneous, although, as expected for Greenwich Village, there were writers, artists, intellectuals, gay men, lesbians, political radicals, and sundry nonconformists.

On the whole, there was an absence of religiosity. Some used the Steps, but others ignored them, and some actively hated them. On the wall were hand-lettered Steps and Traditions; the header of the former read: "12 Suggested Steps" — where the central and longest word is Suggested. The significance of this occurred to me only recently, when viewing the Perry Street brochure. All other versions of the Steps that I've seen on AA walls omit the most important word of all: **suggested**. I would guess that most of the Perry Street members back in the 1960s and 1970s rejected the "suggestion" and simply ignored the Steps.

All meetings ended with the Lord's Prayer, which bothered me as I began to heal, physically and psychologically. In retrospect, I think that most members had no enthusiasm for the LP, but simply thought that AA meetings had to end that way. I and a handful of others defiantly remained seated when the others got up to recite the LP. Years later I wrote and circulated *A Proposal to Eliminate the Lord's Prayer from AA Meetings*.

14

All Perry Street meetings, as well as the midnight meetings held on West 23rd Street, stressed the 24-Hour Plan, staying away from the First Drink. In my first year I must have heard thousands of times, "Stay away from the First Drink." "It's the First Drink that gets you drunk." "Don't drink, no matter what." Most importantly, "You don't have to drink!" These are what I needed to hear.

On weekend evenings, people from meetings all over Manhattan would go to a restaurant near Perry Street — Spiro's, a large restaurant on 7th Avenue. Spiro's would then be virtually all AA. There was a very long table that could seat perhaps 30 or more, and many smaller tables and booths. It was the custom that anyone could sit at the long table, as though already introduced to the others. The booths would be filled by those with common interests, including freethinkers, gay men, and those who qualified for Mensa.

A good friend during my first few months was Bob, a freethinker, gay man, and hemophiliac. We and like-minded guys spent many dozens of hours in booths at Spiro's — talking about all kinds of things. We sometimes made fun of the Steps or Big Book religiosity, but always respected sobriety and the Fellowship. One day it was announced that Bob had begun bleeding uncontrollably and was in St. Vincent's Hospital. In the next two days more than 80 AA members donated blood to help him. I did myself, although I was still so thin that the nurse wasn't sure she could get a pint out of me. But it was too late: he bled to death. There was no Factor VIII then. Although Bob had despised religion, he was given a Roman Catholic funeral, well attended by AA members.

Death was a constant companion in recovery. I remember announcements of people who died in relapses, and others who died sober of old age. In my first year I frequently went to weekend midnight meetings, which I liked because the people there were fighting for sobriety, not dabbling in "spirituality". A young man, who had been in for a few years, always talked to me, and we were getting to know each other. Then one night I was told that he had died — which hardly seemed possible, since he was strong and vigorously healthy. He was a classic periodic drunk, someone who can stay away from a drink for a long time, but for whom a First Drink means immediate disaster. The man who told me put it: "He drank until his heart stopped." Less than three days.

The worst thing about the Perry Street meetings was the smoke, especially at crowded evening meetings. They were gas chambers. Just being in the room meant inhaling the equivalent of a half pack of cigarettes. Perhaps this is why I don't recall going through nicotine withdrawal, even though I stopped smoking at the same time I stopped drinking. As my sobriety progressed, this

15

bothered me, for a reason that is seldom discussed. We stay sober by not picking up the First Drink. But being in a smoky room is like puffing on the First Cigarette plus several more, thus triggering a craving for one of the most addictive substances known: nicotine. Although I didn't entirely stop going to Perry Street meetings, I increasingly went to meetings where there was less smoke or none. According to the 50th Year Anniversary Booklet, it wasn't until the 1990s that Perry Street finally banned smoking.

At Village meetings, an announcement was made: "If you have had a drink today, or a mood-changer, we ask that you not take part in discussion — but please stay around and talk to someone after the meeting." I'm not sure those were the exact words, but they are the gist of it. On this issue, AA was far ahead of the medical establishment, which maintained that the new generation of tranquillizers (Valium and Librium) were not addictive, and had none of the terrible toxicities of the old tranquilizers (like Miltown). We knew better, because we had heard one person after another describe the harmful effects of Librium or Valium, and the sheer hell of breaking addiction to them. Obviously, this is an area of controversy. My own sobriety entails the avoidance of all mood-changing drugs, whether street or pharmaceutical, whether prescribed by a physician or not. I think it's deplorable that many alcoholics are now put on psychiatric drugs before they even leave detox.

Some things change, and some remain the same. Perry Street and most AA groups no longer allow smoking and have replaced the Lord's Prayer with the Serenity Prayer (or something else or nothing). That's good. I personally think some of AA's intimacy and intensity was lost when boisterous practices from California spread across the country in the 1970s: frequent applause and the shouting of greetings and various interjections. You can't listen and applaud at the same time. To me, the emotional commitment of saying: "I'm John, and I am an alcoholic." is lost when the rest of the room yells, "Hi-ya, John!"

I am no longer young, and no longer middle-aged, but I'm still in AA and still sober. Thank you, Perry Street!

My Name is Marnin

By Marnin M.

My name is Marnin and I'm an alcoholic and an agnostic/atheist. Marnin is Hebrew for he who brings joy, a singer of songs. In my youth I was embarrassed to have such an unusual name.

I have been sober for 42 years, since my first AA meeting on October 27, 1970, in Brooklyn.

AA saved my life, and I am forever grateful for the opportunities it has provided me. Because of the AA program and therapy, I try to live as full and as emotionally satisfying a life as possible.

What It Was Like

I was born in 1935, the only child of parents with poor nurturing skills. I was nervous as a child and my parents sent me to a Jewish private school. I felt like a square peg forced into a round hole then, and for the rest of my life, before AA.

My father rarely ever spoke with me. When my mother divorced him, my father blamed me for the breakup. I felt abandoned by my parents. To this day I often feel like an orphan and find it hard to remember that I had parents.

I muddled through high school and college socially inept and feeling lost.

The first time I felt "normal," like one of the boys, was in the Army. I liked that the army, my "Uncle Sam," was taking care of me. For the first time someone cooked for me on a regular basis.

I found the perfect place to work when you have little self confidence and self esteem – the garment industry in downtown New York.

At the age of 28, I got my own apartment and sort of accidentally threw explosive floor shavings into the incinerator. As a result of the explosion, I was rushed to King County Hospital.

It was at this time that my doctor, who was familiar with my family history, got me into therapy. I was a very angry young man. The only emotions I was in touch with with were anger and fear. I went into therapy a college graduate, a virgin, non smoker, non drinker, and fearful that I might be gay.

17

And it was in therapy that I began to drink. I discovered how angry I was with both my parents, particularly my mother. In order to quell the anger I would go from the doctor's office to a bar (Yaeger House) and meditate about what I was learning in therapy over a stiff martini.

I now had my magic solution to life's problems – therapy and alcohol. Within a year I was in a relationship and, with enough alcohol in me, lost my fear of intimacy. No longer a virgin at age 28 I had to make up for lost time. In my mind I set out to be a Jewish James Bond of the garment industry.

After being in therapy for seven years, a serious relationship with a girl I wanted to marry ended suddenly. I was crushed and crashed. I experienced the feelings of abandonment from this relationship that were part of my life as a result of my parents.

I became a full blooded alcoholic, drinking 24 hours a day. I drank the way they describe in country music songs. I showed up for business trips without my air line tickets and all the other things that you hear in AA. Blackouts were frequent. I shudder at the thought of going through the Brooklyn Battery Tunnel often in blackouts and getting up at 2 a.m. to look for my car and be sure that their was no blood or damage from an accident I did not remember.

In 1969 I met a Jewish young lady and married her in ten days. My orthodox Jewish family had considered me dead because I had been living with a Christian girl. So I was married to a Jewish woman by a Rabbi and I was now kosher in their terms. The marriage was a disaster. I was in a blackout at our wedding because I knew I had made a terrible error.

I had my first detox soon after at Freeport Hospital in Long Island. They used the 12-Step program of AA at Freeport. I heard the Steps for the first time and decided they were Christian in nature and not for me. Needless to say I continued drinking. My therapist says that if you can't kill yourself, you marry someone who will do it for you. My wife literally tried to murder me and I went off to Mexico for a quickie divorce.

What Happened

My end came in October 1970 as a result of a suicide attempt that involved drinking, marijuana and thorozine. The thorozine had been prescribed because I had developed alcoholic neuropathy. I was having trouble walking without alcohol in my blood stream.

I had a terrible drunk/trip which ended with a vivid hallucination and "spiritual experience." I hallucinated Jesus on the cross bleeding all over me. Turns

18

out it was my own blood. I heard Jewish music coming out of the walls. I lay there and realized that I was crucifying myself and that I did not want to die!

I called AA in New York. I told them AA wouldn't work for me because "I'm Jewish and a college graduate." The volunteer at Intergroup responded with "Maybe we can help you anyway."

I joined AA on October 27, 1970. AA was only lifeboat around so I climbed aboard.

My first home group was the Brooklyn Heights group. Coming into the rooms of AA, I perceived it to be a religious program and that is still how I view it. I looked for answers in the 12 Step program and, not believing that God intervenes in human affairs, I put the whole God thing aside and followed my own secular version of the Steps.

AA was my "religion." When I was two or three month's sober an Episcopalian Minister in Brooklyn Heights defined religion as the three B's and it saved my life: **Believing** that AA will help me stay sober; **Behaving** as a responsible person, going to any length to stay sober and **Belonging** to a fellowship that rooted for me to stay sober.

In the 1970s, it was thought that Jews couldn't be alcoholics. The same Minister pulled out a Jewish copy of a Biblical proverb and I knew then I could be Jewish and have a disease from the Old Testament:

> Who has woe? Who has sorrow?
> Who has strife? Who has complaining?
> Who has wounds without cause?
> Who has redness of eyes?
> Those who linger long over wine.
> Those who go to taste mixed wine.
> Do not look on the wine when it is red,
> When it sparkles in the cup and goes down smoothly;
> At the last it bites like a serpent
> And stings like an adder.
> Your eyes will see strange things
> And your mind will utter perverse things.
> And you will be like one who lies down
> In the midst of the sea, on top of a mast.
> They struck me, you will say, and I was not hurt.
> They beat me, you will say, but I did not feel it.
> When will I awake?
> So I can seek yet another drink.

AA was my home base for sobriety. Most of my life I've fought the feeling that I was not good enough. This feeling sometimes overwhelmed me and it is what precipitated my final drunk. I found in AA what I had been looking for in the bottle: I was welcomed by total strangers and experienced from them the warm feelings and concern that most children receive from loving parents. Nurturing: this was what I had been looking for in the bottle. I found it in AA.

The "B" of Belonging means to me being active in AA, sharing, attending and chairing meetings. Sometimes even going to a meeting when I don't want to.

Because of how I work the program I have not always been the most popular person in AA, and some have told me that I am not doing it the "AA way."

It's not surprising to me then that when members first choose to come out of the closet about their real beliefs about GOD they whisper it to me like they are guilty of a great sin. I share this message today partly in the hope that other nonbelievers will find strength in knowing that they are not alone and can still, as I did, find sobriety in AA.

I went to any length to stay sober and immersed myself in AA. I was assured my life without alcohol would change dramatically and it did!

What It's Like Today

It was only after joining AA that I started using my real name, Marnin. Having escaped death I felt free to use my real name. I was no longer embarrassed by a unique name. Sober in AA I felt I had earned the right to be me. For my first anniversary instead of a medallion I had an ID bracelet made with my name engraved on it in Hebrew.

Since sex without alcohol was new to me I acted like a tomcat. I had another spiritual awakening this first year and discovered I could no longer act like this and live with myself.

I met my wife Fran at Grossingers Resort singles week in the Catskill Mountains in my first year of sobriety. The previous year we had both been there but I was on a seven day drunk and met no one. We have a daughter Lisa who is still finding her self. Unfortunately she eats like I drank. Since I identify with her addiction I want to "fix" her. I am learning that we are powerless over her illness and all we can do is be there for her and be loving, nurturing, supportive parents.

My years of sobriety are the happiest I have ever had. AA's 12 steps, as I have understood and worked them, have provided me with a tool box for living that allows me to try to be the best Marnin I am capable of being, one day at a time. When we left New York and moved to Florida in 2003, I had been very active in the Promises Group in Nyack, NY. I booked institution talks for my group and was very active getting members to speak. I still sponsor and correspond with my AA friends back in New York. I've also created an AA speakers CD library for the group and for Open Arms, the local half way house.

I am presently an active member of the Sunday morning Tequesta, Florida Beachcombers Group Meeting. I am known at the CD man, always pitching portable sobriety in the form of AA and Al-Anon speaker CDs. Some call this my "ministry." I call it part of my twelfth Step.

During my years of sobriety I've tried to be open and honest and to practice the 12 Steps in all my affairs. Many have told me that I talk about things that should not be talked about. I say "malarkey." If it is part of my story, I talk about it!

I have answered phones at Stuart Intergroup Office for almost ten years, since I first arrived in Florida. They know here that I am an agnostic and don't care. I guess they must think I am doing something right.

From my first day of sobriety, Alcoholics Anonymous has been my loving, accepting family.

Thank you. My name is Marnin.

———

Thirty-five years ago an aspiring writer in group therapy with Marnin wrote this wonderful poem about him:

> Like a sailor ashore after a long and stormy voyage,
> Marnin walks with exaggerated care,
> expecting the earth to roll and toss him off balance.
> He scans the sky looking for thunderclouds to brighten his day,
> and shivers in the sun.
> Prepared for tempests, he stows his joy and battens down his life,
> so he won't be washed away.
> But the sea change has rooted, the gales passed.
> It is the calms Marnin must weather, to avoid drifting
> into whirlpools of anticipation.
> Fear-fogged, snug in his own cool shadow,
> only the heat of his passions can melt the mists in which he hides.

Faye's Story

By Faye P.

My name is Faye and I am an alcoholic. Like everyone else who has made this admission, it was not supposed to be this way...

I began drinking at the age of 14 and from my first, planned drink with friends, my only purpose was to get as drunk as I possibly could. I grew up with a lot of alcohol around me and it seemed like it was my birthright to continue the tradition. From my warped understanding, alcohol made you happier, stronger and prettier. It was only when people like my dad were dry, that they were miserable and sad. Aggressive, abusive behavior seemed to be flare up at any time, whether alcohol was involved or not. At least if I was drunk, stoned or caught up in a fantasy, I was less likely to get hurt.

I drank and did drugs throughout high school, skipping class whenever possible. If I thought that I already knew what the teacher was teaching or if I found the material difficult, I was "out of there." I loved to learn, but since it didn't seem to be cool, I pretended that it didn't matter. Somehow, I finished high school and got accepted at a university music program, studying piano.

The day that I arrived at university, I realized that I didn't belong and that I was not like everyone else. They were talented and could play instruments because they had practiced. I had to keep my inability to perform to myself and the only way that I could look and act normal, was to secretly binge drink whenever possible. No one, except me, knew how I craved alcohol. It was the only thing that I needed to keep going. I had absolutely no self confidence.

Fast forward to a family and career life which on the outside seemed pretty wonderful. I had a remarkable career, a beautiful son and a successful husband. From all outside appearances, life was great. It wasn't enough for me so I continued to drink whenever possible. Since the time that I was eighteen, I was a daily drinker. I drank to get drunk at least two days of seven. Looking back, I realize that I was pretty miserable, but I had stopped feeling since I was about sixteen.

During my forties and leading into what seems to be the longest mid-life crisis on record, things started to fall apart. My marriage broke up and I was going through an incredibly stressful time at work. I started to run marathons because I figured that no marathon runner could be an alcoholic. I also needed a way to burn the excess calories. After about three weeks of training, I created my 'run and drink' schedule, which now proves to me that alcoholics can be marathon runners. We can do anything.

At the end of my forties I lost my job and I crumbled. I wanted to kill myself because I did not want to go through the pain of getting to know myself. For someone who had blocked all feeling, the desire to die was pretty compelling. The only purpose for me to go outside was to look for a bridge from which to jump. I figured that I would keep drinking until I had the courage to end it all. My greatest fear was waking up in a hospital where someone might try to help me. I had to do it without fail.

As I was preparing my finances for my son and preparing lists for him, I kept thinking that these thoughts and actions were ridiculous. How could this happen to me? I kept trying to drink it away, but nothing was working. The only person who I was talking to on the outside was my landlord and he was starting to ask about all the bottles.

The morning when it seemed like it was time to take action, I decided that I would check out AA. I walked into a meeting that night and I felt like I was home. There was a 21 year old kid who was telling my story. I somehow managed to keep the facade going for a much longer time than him. My only hope was that he would find happiness before I did.

At first, I didn't care about all the references to God in the program because in Brooklyn we were a very diverse mix of religions and cultures. Then I moved to Fort Erie, where the references to God were much more traditional and pronounced. AA was still the only thing that I could count on so I tried to let the God references slide. With my strong Unitarian Universalist beliefs, this was a great challenge. While I seek worship and ritual ceremonies, I do not believe in praying to God or to a Higher Power. I don't feel like I am a chosen one and I don't believe that any power sends me anywhere. While I love the lessons from my Christian faith and Christian friends, being open to nature and meditating works better for me at this point in my recovery. I like the idea of being connected to nature without something in between.

I am now the town agnostic and I try to learn from my Christian friends. Some are becoming interested in a non-theist approach and it is not negatively affecting their sobriety. I am trying to stay true to myself by sharing what is working for me in an honest and compassionate way. I have to remember that I go to AA meetings to stay sober and to live a more meaningful life. It doesn't matter what I or anyone else believes. It is how one is humbled and practices the steps, which is important.

AA is extremely important to me and sharing the gift with others is crucial. It's not easy. I am grateful to my sponsors and my fellow members for showing me how to live a life that I never thought was possible. I don't know as much now as I did when I was drinking, but now the journey is actually interesting and for the most part it is fun. After a period of not wanting to face all of those who I assumed were more capable than me, I am back working in the industry that I love. I used to hate many of them, but now I like almost everyone, even those who are more successful than me. I am passionate about what I do and I can show that I care. Learning new things and accepting that I do not know everything has brought me incredible joy. I used to think that sobriety would be horrible and that it was only for losers. I now know differently and I am glad that I have come out an isolated shell which made me miserable and nearly killed me. I want to share this gift with everyone, without barriers and rules.

And When We Were Wrong…

By Frank M.

I wanted to do this thing right. I wanted to do it by the Big Book. In fact I was pretty sure I needed to, because I appeared to be dying. When you relapsed, I was told, it was either because you had not been doing the Steps or doing them incorrectly. Well, I'd relapsed twice in recovery. I had recently been released from a lockdown ward after a suicide attempt. I had to get it right this time.

I'd been trying to use "God as I understood Him" for my Higher Power and even "God as I don't understand Him" (as someone had suggested). It wasn't working. I thought I might need a more accessible and tangible source of strength and direction.

What did the Big Book say? I really, really wanted to do this right.

After much study, and digging deep into AA history, I saw something that made my heart sink. It appeared that some of the conservative views out there on the Big Book's directions regarding finding and utilizing a Higher Power were more or less accurate. Using your own limited understanding to approach God is not the same as substituting anything bigger or stronger than you for God. The second is AA lore, but not a solid read of the literal instructions taken in their full context.

I made a heartfelt plea one morning in my home group. I wanted to follow the Big Book, but my naturalistic higher power ideas weren't really in there. They looked a lot more like what was described as not working. Like moral and philosophical convictions.[i]

"What do I do?" I said.

"More will be revealed," an old-timer said gently. "They didn't know everything."

He was right. And eventually I saw clearly that more had in fact been revealed. And astonishingly it contradicted one of Big Book AA's three main ideas. So why wasn't I hearing about that from AA itself? Why did I have to go searching on Internet boards and outside literature to find it?

TO (b) OR NOT TO (b)

On page sixty of AA's basic text a bold statement appears that fairly circumscribes what the Big Book suggests can work effectively as your Higher Power -

> (b) That probably no human power could have relieved our alcoholism.[ii]

That's not the group, nor is it AA as a whole, if we're being honest. Whatever it is, the woo factor is pretty high. Some folks I knew in recovery had adopted various new-agey ideas that fit the bill and skirted the personal God issue. That wasn't going to do it for me. Ditto pantheism, the other popular way out of this little trap. But there was, in turned out, a far more direct route around all this.

They were wrong.

They were just wrong here. We know today that secular sources of truth, direction and strength, "higher powers" that are fully natural and fully human also work just fine. These too can break down the walls of alcoholic insanity in conjunction with the actions of the Steps. Tens of thousands of non-theists have achieved long lasting recovery in AA stretching over decades. No honest assessment of our ranks can miss this fact. Proposition (b) on page sixty of the Big Book is simply incorrect.

WHY DON'T WE JUST FIX THIS?

There are a number of factors involved. First there is the mistaken idea that because using God really works (and it does), proposition (b) is not incorrect. After all, before AA and God-based recovery nothing else had treated alcoholism. Besides being historically incorrect,[iii] this is like saying that since penicillin was the first antibiotic to successfully treat bacterial infections, it is therefore the only effective antibiotic. This kind of thinking might be funny if it weren't so often fatal in our Fellowship.

But perhaps chief among the reasons we don't fix this critical mistake in our message is the idea that AA isn't broken. And for most theists this is essentially true. AA even works pretty well as is for non-believers who are able eventually to become believers. This is all wonderful. For them. But AA has always striven to be available to every alcoholic regardless of belief or non-belief in God.

So to the extent that AA doesn't fully support non-theists, and to the extent that they fail as a result, AA is not working just fine.

WHAT ABOUT THE NON-THEISTS WHO SAY IT IS?

I must admit, I find atheist apologists in AA even more difficult to stomach in some ways than the God-botherers. They go to any length to try and demonstrate how the traditional AA Program, exactly as written, is completely available to the principled atheist or agnostic. They pick through the literature like corporate lawyers, checking the fine print for secular loopholes.

Suffice to say this all amounts to a desperate and somewhat pathetic attempt to show how the Big Book gives them permission to work their secular programs. (More on that in a moment.)

Personally, I would rather be up front about the Big Book's pervasive theism and the fact that these are instructions for how you are supposed to connect with a mystical God. I would rather not deny the Big Book's supernaturalist orientation. I would rather not whitewash and deny the Big Book's obvious antagonism toward non-theists. I would rather be honest about it all than argue how the words are squishy enough for non-believers to edge their way in on the margins.

Yes, being a Big Book apologist might help me fit in more smoothly, but it's selling out the non-theist newcomer. It's wrong. It's selfish. It's really just dishonest.

WHAT ELSE IS THE NON-THEIST TO DO?

The way to defeat all arguments about the legitimate approach to the Steps is not to argue (incorrectly and in a convoluted manner) that the Big Book is not really theistic or God-centric. It is to admit its deep and sincere theism, and then to deny the authority accorded to the Big Book that it doesn't even claim for itself.

The way for the non-theist to fit in to AA is not to chop off our philosophical principles like bloody limbs and leave them outside the door. No, there's a much better route.

A BIGGER TENT, NOT JUST A WIDER DOOR

Bill Wilson wrote how men like James Burwell widened the door to AA.[iv] What this really means is that AA is available to non-theists only to the extent that they are *willing to become something like theists once they get inside the tent.*

It's time to do better than that. What we need is not a wider doorway but a bigger tent.

And like always, it will start with honestly admitting our mistakes. First that we were wrong about proposition (b). More has been revealed that contradicts this early and never universal view.

Next we have to be honest about what keeps us wedded to any outdated or unnecessarily limiting idea we find in the Big Book. It is an insidious need to feel certain and sanctioned. To feel we're right, and validated. I had wanted to do this thing "right" and "by the Big Book." and what I learned eventually was that *these two ideas are not the same*. The right way to do the Steps, if you choose to do them, is the way that activates the recovery potential in them for you. There's only what works and what doesn't. Nothing more matters.

What's generating conflict in AA today is not just one side or another saying their approach is the only legitimate one. It's our failure to see that there is no such thing as a "legitimate" or "authorized" or "permitted" approach to the Steps. Let it go. It was never important.

It's time, as a Fellowship, we did a long overdue Tenth Step on this matter of just what is our best understanding of workable higher powers (by our collective experience). And of how that's represented today in our literature, not just our rooms. If we can't bring ourselves to do this, what hope have we of ever amending AA's message to something more helpful and inclusive, and making ourselves of maximum service to all alcoholics?

All that's needed to begin is more realistic and humble attitude toward our basic text, and perhaps a simple footnote to proposition (b)*

> *Over the years we have found that God and many other sources of strength and wisdom, some of them fully human, can help you. If you're willing to go to any length.

It's nothing more or less than the plain truth. Let's honor it.

---

[i] Alcoholics Anonymous – p. 62

[ii] Ibid. – p. 60

[iii] The Washingtonians achieved roughly the same success.

[iv] Alcoholics Anonymous Comes of Age, p. 167

My Path in AA

By life-j.

The path was not easy for this agnostic in AA.

I was an atheist when I got sober, as arrogant as most people with staunchly held beliefs. Sober, I have still never felt the presence of a god, but I have come to be open-minded to accept that if other people think there is one, that's fine and none of my business, so long as they don't try to make me believe there is. But for a long time well meaning old-timers did, and of course I tried to believe them. I wanted to work this program right. Took more than ten years before they quit pestering me, and another ten before I could speak my mind freely about it.

The chapter "We Agnostics" in the big book at least acknowledged that there were people like me, but then it forged right ahead with arguing for the existence of god, and the assumption that surely sooner or later I would find god too. It was only a matter of staying sober a little longer and coming to my senses.

And I read the Big Book and even Came to Believe, but I never did.

I found a humanist meeting which I attended, and later I found another meeting where there was no "Lord's Prayer" at the end. It always offended me to have this piece of Christianity imposed upon me. The closing prayer was the one time during an AA meeting where I would feel truly alone, unless I spotted someone else in the circle with their lips sealed. Then we'd smile at each other and not feel so alone any more.

————

So I'm going to write about how I stayed sober without a higher power, and developed a spirituality which helped.

When a person comes into AA with even some inclination toward accepting a Christian-like god, there is already a well laid out program for them. Most of our literature is focused on this god, even with the caveat "as we understood him," but when the God concept remains completely foreign to us, we have to develop a spirituality all on our own. The kind of help that I could accept was scant and far between in the beginning. Finding a sponsor who wouldn't harass me about finding a higher power was real difficult.

29

One of the reasons that I don't like the higher power concept, and that the religious people are so insistent on it, is that it creates a continuum intended to sneak god in the back door. I can let the group be my higher power they say, but the idea is they aren't really content with that. Sooner or later they expect me to find the real god who isn't just any higher power, but the boss of all higher powers.

I could have the group as my higher power, but why? True, I depend on the group to help me stay sober and grow, and with the help of the group I can do things I likely could not do on my own, but why does that have to make it a higher power?

We all accept the saying that two heads think better than one. So does that mean that the two heads together now become a higher power to the individual heads? Why is it not just two heads thinking together?

Or, like an AA friend of mine says, try lifting a heavy sack alone. It can be tough. Now try two of you together, it gets easier, now try four, of course it gets still easier, and the four of us together can lift something much heavier than one person can all alone. Where exactly does the higher power concept become needed to explain this? This is all the group does, lifts a burden together. We are doing together what we could never do alone. I simply see it as a level field, and no higher power needed to explain how this program works.

The group is not my higher power, nothing is my higher power, and just because I don't have a higher power, does not mean that I am playing god, and just because I figure that there is no god in charge, does not mean that I am, or think I am, or that I am trying to be god.

Maybe this "playing god" was a problem for the high powered Type A professionals and businessmen who started this program, but my problem was fear, not a big ego. If it sometimes looked that way, maybe it was because of fear of losing territory, fear of losing respect, or love or money or whatever, sometimes fear of not getting what I wanted. I had two ways of dealing with it: Try to control the situation, or drink my feeling of failure away when it was obvious I couldn't control it.

So now sober, I couldn't stop trying to play god like they told me to because I never had to begin with. I had only done whatever it would take in the moment to not feel whatever I was about to feel, usually fear, and a poor choice which would take that bad feeling away right now was better than a good choice which would have solved the problem in five minutes.

Of course when I was drinking I was arrogant, self-centered, and self-serving, and it caused me all sorts of trouble. But is it not possible to find a way out of self-centeredness and self will without putting it in relation to the will of a god? Either it is my will, or god's will, they say, but where does god really fit into this? Can I not simply stop imposing my selfishness on the world with the help of other recovering alcoholics? With careful consideration of what sort of results self-centeredness got me, and compared to what sort of results a courteous, considerate, helpful manner of living gets me? Why is a god needed to explain that one works well, and the other doesn't? Isn't simple, common sense enough?

So finally I came to a place of some humility. And here we need to talk about surrender.

This can be a hard concept to swallow at first, because we suspect that probably it again means surrender to a "higher power," or even a god. But is not surrender possible even without it being "to" anything? All it means is to say, "OK, I give up being selfish, self centered and self serving. I become teachable, service minded, and as generous and kind as I am able to be without opening myself to being deliberately taken advantage of by anybody." Isn't that enough? Why do I have to offer myself to a "thee"? I am offering myself to my fellow alcoholic, and my fellow man at large. AA is about one alcoholic talking with another, not about talking with god.

Surrender requires acceptance. And acceptance is not required because "nothing absolutely nothing happens in god's world by mistake," but rather because without first accepting myself as I am, I have no honest self appraisal on which I can base change. I wasn't playing god, I was just hard-headed. God or no god, acceptance is just to gain peace, to have a starting point from which to move forward.

I have learned that I don't need to have answers to all the world's big questions, nor let anyone else impose them on me. That I can't explain how the world came to be, or don't think a god made it does not mean that since I can't explain it, someone who can explain it with that god did it is more right than me. As far as I'm concerned, saying god did it is no better explanation than that nothing did it. All that religious conviction just seems arrogant. But maybe there is a god who did it, I don't know, and I don't need to know, and I don't care, in the end.

If I were an astrophysicist I might be pondering where the universe came from, but as a lay person and as an alcoholic it is sufficient for me to know that it is there. I don't need to make it any more complicated than that. The universe is there. And all the things in it are in it. And regardless of how much it is a wonder that the sun rises and bumblebees can fly, it is simply not my business to know whether it came to be this way because god made it so, or because of inherent laws in the universe, or by some infinitesimal chance it came to be so out of complete chaos. The bottom line still is I'm not in charge, and have every bit as much reason to be humble either way! Can I change the natural laws? Can I control chaos? I wasn't playing god. I just thought I had to do it all alone, and now I know I need help, and it's ok to ask my fellow recovering alcoholics for it.

But I have had to rewrite the whole program for myself, mostly by myself, and it has not been easy. I think it is finally coming together. God or no god, this is a spiritual program but let's keep it simple. It just consists of honesty, open-mindedness, willingness, humility, service, and living by the golden rule. It means doing the right thing, and if I work my program diligently, I will know what the right thing is, whether I pray for the knowledge for God's will for me or not, and if I do the right thing I will have no reason to drink, because I will be ok with me.

I have had to rewrite the steps for myself. I have to have faith that somehow this program will work for me, but that is all the justification for steps 2 and 3 that I have found. Some sort of personal inventory, and sharing it with another person is necessary, steps 4 and 5. The three elements of early AA, confession, restitution, and service, together with self examination are really the only essential elements in my program. And though they are rather Christian of origin, they work for me too, because and I am part of that Christian culture whether I believe in its god or not. Thinking along Christian lines comes easy to me since I grew up with it.

Self reflection does not come easy, though it is a prerequisite for growth. To actually come to think about what makes me tick, and if everything I think and do is right and just and for a good purpose in the greater scheme of things. Not just for my own selfish ends, but whether it makes the world at large a better place. It starts out a bit like the big question in the movie American History X: Has anything you have done made your life better?

Sure the AA fellowship has saved this alcoholic's life, though not because it is a higher power, but simply because of the love and help of the people in it, because together we can do what we could never do alone, like they say in another program's Unity "Prayer."

Sure I have seen a lot of people with a God who have had a much swifter recovery than me. Picking up the "ready made" toolkit has many advantages. However, having walked my own paths in this program I have had to turn every stone in my search for a spiritual life. And being forced to grope around on my own, spiritually – and that has largely been the case for many years – looking back at it I think I have probably grown more, and in ways I otherwise never would have, if I had just taken on some sort of ready made Christian god concept and gone with it. All the answers and concepts a Christian can take for granted in this program, I have had to ponder deeply, and that, like any spiritual exercise, has given me much good growth. So I'm quite content with the course of my own recovery. I'm very grateful for all I have learned within or from AA these last 25 years.

————

The last few years have been real different.

First thing that happened was that the girlfriend left. She later came back, and the time I had on my hands to ponder what made for a good relationship has helped. She has since joined one of the programs, and it's good to have a common spiritual framework.

Feeling sorry for myself while I sat alone out here in a mountain village, I discovered AA online.

It was way better than nothing at all, but people were just hanging out, flirting, or talking about guns, sports, TV, and hating socialists, or being obnoxious in some other manner. Hey, I guess there has to be an online place for all that, too. But when they took time for newcomers it was usually by throwing the Big Book and god at them – go read the doctor's opinion and pray. And it was all done with AA scripture lingo: If you aren't ready to go to any length, just go back out and try some controlled drinking. But rarely did the newcomers get more than two minutes of attention from half the room. I started to not like old-timers anymore.

Luckily I got to hook up with several people along the way who felt like me – that these online chat rooms should be about helping the newcomers – and eventually we found a place to set up a room we call the *Living Sober Room*, a place where we drop everything when newcomers show up, and help them all we can.

Another thing that happened over the last year was an initiative at the Conference level to develop AA literature acknowledging that alcoholics and agnostics can stay sober in AA. We know how that ended: *The General*

Service Conference Stumbles. The backlash against non-believers in AA that I have observed in recent years, including the White Paper, has made me realize the extent to which AA has become fossilized.

We as a fellowship need to take inventory, and when we are wrong promptly admit it. Instead the Big Book has become scripture, and the god people resist any change. For most of my time in AA I lived by a *Don't Tell* policy, but I have had to come out of the closet, as it were, and say out loud I'm an agnostic, and I'm now working on putting together a freethinkers meeting here in my area. I'm meeting more closed-mindedness and unwillingness every step of the way.

The bright spot in all of it is that I have once again, like when I first got sober, found others like myself – this time at the AA Agnostica website, and books and other support material to go along with it. I once again no longer have to feel alone. It is giving me the courage to pick up the responsibility I have toward all the alcoholic non-believers that come into AA to let them know they can stay sober in spite of the god stuff, if they just keep showing up.

My first sponsor, incidentally a devout catholic, told me two things, that I heard, anyway: One was don't ever stop going to meetings, and the other that service work will keep you sober when nothing else will. Sometimes my program is reduced to that, but it's nice and uncluttered, and it worked up to now.

---

life-j got sober in Oakland in 1988. He moved to a Northern California coastal mountain village in 2002 and helped wake up the sleepy AA fellowship there. He's been involved in service work of every kind all along, but now thinks the most important work is to help atheists and agnostics feel safe and welcome in AA. He's spent parts of his life as a building contractor, part as a technical translator, and has dabbled a bit in art work and writing. life-j is now semi-retired on a five acre homestead together with his sweetie, and his dog, chickens, garden, and apple trees.

God and Diet Pills

By Steve B.

I have come to believe that God is to sobriety what diet pills are to weight loss.

The diet pills I'm referring to are the over the counter supplements you see on non prime time commercials on cable TV or obscure channel infomercials. As a rule, these supplements have little pharmacologic value for weight loss.

Nevertheless diet supplements are promoted as essential ingredients for weight loss. So you plunk down some hard-earned cash to get this miracle product. The pills arrive in the mail along with a brochure. It tells you these supplements are meant to work in conjunction with an exercise and food restriction program. So the simple math is Eat Right + Exercise + Diet Pills = Weight Loss.

In AA the equation is Go to Meetings + Participate in Fellowship + Believe in God = Sobriety. In the diet pill analogy the food restriction and exercise are the essential components of weight loss and the diet supplements are basically functioning as placebos. Placebos can be effective. Nearly half of people who take what they think is a pain pill will report a reduction in pain. If you think a diet supplement will decrease your appetite you may actually experience a reduction in appetite. Moreover, when you pay money for some diet pills you are more likely to be compliant with all aspects of the program. So, in that sense, the supplements are working.

For many in our society belief in God is much more deeply ingrained than the belief in pharmacology that results in the placebo effect. Functional MRI studies have shown that, in a believer, the areas of the brain affected during prayer are the same areas affected when interacting with another person. So God is real in the praying persons brain if you're a believer. The non-believer does not activate these areas of the brain if saying the same words to himself. I've commented to my home group that the religious person probably does have an advantage in maintaining sobriety in AA. The religious person who comes to AA is very likely to believe that the God in AA is the essential ingredient in sobriety. This attitude is held to as tightly as religious beliefs are in general and is fostered by the AA literature and the sharing at most meetings.

This poses a challenge for agnostics in AA.

For most agnostics fellowship, participation, and being of service are the essential components to sobriety in AA. Yet at the same time our personal philosophical outlook makes us less likely to relate to the group and to be shunned.

One solution is to have "We Agnostics" meetings. AA sanctions several other speciality meetings and a few agnostic ones, although some agnostic meetings have been delisted. I'm fortunate to have one agnostic meeting near me but it's still a 40 mile drive and only once a week. I also participate in a Life Ring meeting, but that is also only once a week and about a 40 mile drive. I live in a densely populated area. There are hundreds of AA meetings a week within that 40 mile radius of my house. Most AA members do not have the option of attending an agnostic oriented meeting.

Another thing that can be done is the agnostic can talk about her or his belief or lack of belief with shares and in one-on-one sessions with other alcoholics. When I am open and honest about my opinions with shares in meetings people may not agree but they can't stop my words. For every five or six people who shuns me someone will come up to me after a meeting and thank me for my share and may say something along the lines of "I'm agnostic too but I just don't talk about it." I think there are more closeted atheists and agnostics in the fellowship than we realize, although data on this is obviously hard to come by.

The fifth tradition of Alcoholics Anonymous states: "Each group has but one primary purpose – to carry its message to the alcoholic who still suffers." I've done an informal survey of several AA members asking if my contrarian sharing is violating this tradition. Am I poisoning the message with my shares? Everyone, even the majority of religious members, seem to think I'm not in violation. Diversity of opinion may not be completely welcome but with the attitude of "take what you need and leave the rest" the primary purpose is not violated. Believers are free to ignore my sharing.

I've been in 12 Step programs since 1990. I made the mistake of not sharing my opinions and keeping silent about my atheism while I went to meetings for about 12 years. I therefore was dishonest with the group and not participating in the fellowship. I'm not blaming AA or claiming I was victimized by the fellowship. I was dishonest. I dropped out of meetings but managed to stay sober for about five years before relapsing. I'm now back in the program and have about 20 months sobriety. I'm not being silent this time around. I'd much rather be rejected for who I am than accepted for someone I'm not. I'm in the rooms of AA to stay sober, not to make friends. But, by being open and honest, the friends have materialized.

36

I encourage agnostics, atheist, freethinkers, and skeptics to share openly at meetings. I know this may be more of a challenge in red states versus blue states and in smaller towns with less diversity. Even there though are people who will relate to you and those are the ones you want to be friends with or to have as sponsors. I believe there are many people in AA who don't feel comfortable going along with mainstream Big Book philosophy. By letting them know it's OK to not be an AA mainstreamer in order to stay sober you are being of service to a substantial minority of people in the room. As one AAer told me, "I've seen a lot more people leave AA because of all the God stuff than leave because of all those damn atheists in the group."

Unless the Alcoholics Anonymous WSO amends the Third Tradition to read "The only requirements for membership are a desire to stop drinking and a belief in God," they can't kick you out.

Steve has been in recovery since 1990. Presently retired and living the good life in sunny southern California, he has a particular interest in the neuroscience of addiction and how this affects treatment programs. He is also interested in the neuroscience of religious beliefs and non-critical thinking. He has just finished reading "The Believing Brain" by Michael Shermer. Another one of his passions is comics, from the Golden Age to contemporary off the shelf. He is active in the Facebook group: Agnostics and Atheists in AA.

My Last Binge

By Laurie A.

My wife thought I would get up and walk out from my first meeting of Alcoholics Anonymous. The meeting started with a recitation of the 12 Steps suggested as a programme of recovery and six of them mention God or "Him" or "Power."

I was a surly, cynical agnostic and my wife, sitting beside me, thought, "This won't work." But I was a week away from having attempted suicide. I'd survived by the skin of my teeth and was in no state to engage in theological wrangling. I listened with laser-like attention to anything that would keep me alive, and staying alive meant not drinking.

My last binge had not been that spectacular; in fact I thought I deserved a pat on the back for arriving home before the pubs closed. But my wife took one look at me as I reeled through the front door and fled out of the back door with our daughter. As they drove off into the night I cursed them for being so unkind. I then turned the place upside down, wreaking my frustration and resentment on the furniture.

The next morning as I surveyed the wreckage I knew this could not go on. I'd never smashed the place up before and was appalled and horrified.

It finally dawned on me that while I kept on drinking my life just got more chaotic. Despite all my well-meaning and strenuous efforts I could not stop drinking. I couldn't face another ten, 20 or 30 years of that living hell so I decided to end it all. As an alcoholic, loneliness was a way of life. I felt despised and rejected, shunned like a leper; I despised and rejected myself. But that morning I felt as though the cosmos itself had rejected me. I no longer belonged here. The pain of being alive was impossible to bear. Words diminish it.

As I left the house, my wife and daughter arrived home. I muttered, "They shoot mad dogs, don't they?" and pushed past them.

I went to a chemist's (pharmacy) and tried to decide how many aspirins would do the job, 25, 50 or 100. I bought 100 just to be sure, along with a bottle of orange juice. I walked into nearby woods, left the path so I wouldn't be found, sat under a tree and gulped down the aspirins in handfuls. I then lay down and waited to die.

I was saved by luck and ignorance. I thought I would swiftly lapse into unconsciousness and the oblivion I craved; I didn't know how long the tablets would take to work. I was aware of an insect scratching away next to my ear. I felt woozy but that passed, as did the ringing in my ears. I watched the sun passing through the branches. At one point I began to panic and struggled to get up. But I forced myself to stay there and told myself I had to go through with it.

Baffled that nothing seemed to be happening, I thought, "You haven't killed yourself but you haven't done yourself any good so you'd better get help." A cynic might say, "Well, why didn't you put your head on a railway line?" I don't know the answer to that. All I know is that I was confused and bewildered – I wasn't thinking straight; maybe the instinct for self-preservation had kicked in.

I walked back into the town and gave myself up to the police. Two young Police Constables rushed me to an Accident & Emergency room with the car siren blaring and lights flashing. One of them said, "Don't you be sick in our car." He added, "You're not going to like what they're going to do to you." I found out what he meant when I was pumped out. I really did think then that I was going to die.

My wife refused to visit me; here was yet another disaster caused by my drunkenness. The kids persuaded her to come but she just sat at the end of the bed, quivering with rage, refusing to speak to me.

Before I was discharged a psychiatrist told me, "If you'd left it any longer before getting help, all they could have done was watch you die." I didn't plan to cut it that fine; I just wanted off the planet. He told me I would need to arrange psychiatric aftercare with my doctor – and suggested I attend AA.

I'd turned my nose up at AA years before but now I was terrified that if I drank again I would die; and I just knew I would drink again because that's what I always did. In AA I often hear members say they lacked the courage to commit suicide. It seems a perverse sort of courage that enables someone to die but not to live. I didn't want to die but didn't know how to live; I lacked the courage to live. I've seen suicide described as a supremely selfish act. In my case morality didn't come into it; I just couldn't take any more. Depending which statistic you believe, a third of male suicides are drink-related.

When I got home I phoned AA and my doctor. He encouraged me to go to AA and arranged an appointment with the consultant psychiatrist at a National Health Service addiction treatment centre. That evening two AA members visited me and told me their stories. They invited me to an AA meeting, which

I went to with my wife. She had put me on probation. She thought going to AA was just another one of my "tricks"; I was always making solemn promises not to drink again.

At that first meeting I got hope that my alcoholism was no longer my unique problem; that there was help if I was prepared to use it. A few days later I met David Marjot, the psychiatrist at St Bernard's hospital, West London. He listened to my story and said, "Well, I confirm the diagnosis. You're a chronic alcoholic and from now on things can only get worse." I thought, "I've just tried to kill myself – how much worse can it get?"

He went on, "I've seen hundreds of men like you. You're in your mid-40s, still employed and married – it will all be gone if you carry on drinking, and with your pattern of binge drinking you're in danger of having an oesophageal haemorrhage and bleeding to death." He offered me an inpatient bed but said there was a seven-week waiting list. He added, "I'll keep a place for you but in the meantime keep going to AA."

That was in September 1984. I still have his letter of appointment; I hope I never have to use it.

In AA there's a saying which I found immensely consoling: "I'm not a bad person trying to get good – I'm a sick person trying to get well." I always blamed myself for not being able to control my drinking. I didn't realise I was very sick. The illness theory is controversial but I find it a useful metaphor. If not scientifically exact it works for me as experiential verification. And it doesn't let me off the hook. I had to try to put right the damage and hurt that I'd caused others in my alcoholic descent.

As soon as I felt well enough I went to the police station and thanked the two PCs who had rushed me to hospital. I wrote to the hospital and thanked them too. Those people saved my life. I've tried to be the husband to my wife that I'd denied her while in my alcoholic wilderness. I've made amends to our lovely kids.

The AA group that I began attending met at a Quaker meeting house. There was a poster on the notice board that said: "A silent Quaker meeting for worship can be a quiet process of healing and a journey of discovery." I plucked up courage one Sunday and went to my first Quaker meeting. I was not judged for my belief or lack of belief and welcomed.

I was attracted by the similarities between Quakerism and AA. Here in Britain both are practical, non-hierarchical, egalitarian and non-creedal.

Unlike some Quaker meetings in North America, British Quakerism has no priests or pastors, nor liturgy, sermons or hymns. Meeting houses are unconsecrated and bare of ornament. Meetings for worship are held in silence from which arise occasional, spontaneous, spoken contributions which anyone present can offer if so moved. When AA began in Britain in the late 1940s British members discarded the Lord's prayer. Most meetings end with the Serenity prayer, but it's optional and as an agnostic I stay silent.

Both Quakerism and AA say the spiritual life is not a theory – we have to live it. I am more open-minded and tolerant than I have ever been and I'm still an agnostic.

I thought the worst thing that could have happened to me was to become an alcoholic; it turned out to be the best thing. If I hadn't found AA and the Quakers I would never have found myself. I drank for limitless expansion, but that thirst was never satisfied.

Today it is one day at a time.

Laurie A. is a retired national newspaper and BBC journalist in the UK. His sobriety date is 8/10/84. He served on the Great Britain AA literature committee and edited Share, the British fellowship's national magazine, and Share and Share Alike, a book celebrating 60 years of AA in Britain in 2007.

First AA Meetings

By Thomas B.

A couple of years ago, my wife Jill and I were visiting my daughters and grandkids in Frederick, Maryland. We found an open Big Book meeting listed on the Internet at a nearby Methodist church. Held in a classroom, neither the window shades for the 12 Steps or Traditions were in sight. No slogans either. A small book of Christian meditations, The Upper Room, was at each seat. Before the meeting started, I asked the chairperson if this was an AA Meeting.

Rather arrogantly he replied, "Absolutely, this is AA the way it was supposed to be."

"Excuse me?" I queried.

"Yes, we follow the original format used by the Akron Oxford Group as developed by Dr. Bob and his wife, Anne."

"What do you mean?" I further inquired.

"We all surrender on our knees in prayer to Jesus Christ. Then we read from our meditation book and seek guidance in quiet time for 15 minutes. We then share with each other the guidance we receive from our Lord and Savior, Jesus Christ."

Jill and I were appalled. We quickly left the meeting.

This incident made me most grateful for my first AA meetings.

———

It was the dreary, drizzly evening of Thursday, October 19, 1972, when I went to my first meeting. It happened I took my last drink the previous Saturday. I didn't go to AA to stop drinking – I went to get my second wife back. You see, one night I flew into a drunken rage sloppily carving the chicken I had cooked for Debbie and me to have for a romantic candlelight dinner after her first day at a new job. It kept burning my fingers! She insisted I had thrown it at her. I hadn't. I had just screamed in frustration and thrown it into the faux fireplace beside our dining table. Nevertheless, she fled our Manhattan apartment in terror.

Unemployed, I drank, per usual, around the clock for several days, desperately seeking Debbie. I couldn't find her, so I made several pitiful, drunken attempts to kill myself. My last attempt was an hour or so before my last drink while driving to my mother-in-law's apartment in New Rochelle, NY. Driving along a parkway, I saw a wide expanse of curving concrete wall before me. I revved up my car, a dilapidated Opel Stationwagen, and aimed straight for the gray-white concrete rushing towards me. I could feel the bumps and rattles as I drove onto the shoulder, chugalugging a can of Colt . 45.

BLACKOUT!

I came to several minutes later, aimlessly driving around an upscale neighborhood. This was my moment of "pitiful and incomprehensible demoralization." I was a complete and utter failure – I couldn't even properly kill myself! I drove to my mother-in-law's hoping to find Debbie. She wasn't there. Yelling obscenities, I slammed out the apartment. There were two unopened 16 oz. cans of Colt .45 on the front seat. My intention was to drink them, buy another case of 16 oz. cans, and continue to drink until I killed myself.

Just as I have no explanation why I ended up not smashing into the concrete wall, I have no explanation as to what happened when I got into the car. I did not open a can of beer. I drove in a fugue-like state through a blinding rainstorm back to Manhattan. I spent the first night in several years without drinking my self into a stupor. I tossed and turned, shaking horribly with night terrors, but I did not drink again.

I desperately wanted to get my wife back, and thought that maybe, if I stopped drinking and went to AA, she would come back. So, I called AA Intergroup. I had a hazy concept of AA being something about broken-down old men who were 60 or 70. I was 29 years old. My second wife had left me. I was an utter and total failure. I couldn't even f—king kill myself.

I remember little about that first AA meeting, but incredibly, I didn't drink and went to the same meeting the following week. The first speaker I could identify with was Stanley Stancage, who spoke at the third meeting. A chronic relapser, he usually got violent and ended up in an emergency room or jail. A couple of years older than me, he was highly educated, quoting Marx, Camus and Nietzsche in his qualification. He waved his huge hands about, gesticulating like an Italian fishmonger, while spewing a plethora of F-bombs. I was riveted by his qualification and thought, "Shit, if this asshole can stop

43

drinking, maybe I can too." I heard he tragically alcohol-poisoned himself several years later chugalugging a quart of 100 proof vodka.

After that meeting someone approached me, asking if I had a meeting list.

"Meeting List?" I replied, "What's that?"

"A listing of AA meetings in New York City."

I was dumbfounded. "You mean this isn't the only one?" I really was quite mocus when I first came around.

"Oh no," he replied, reaching into his back pocket, "There're some 500 meetings a week in the City. Here, take my list."

I saw from the meeting list I could go to meetings practically around the clock. Since I was unemployed, that's what I did. I didn't drink, and I went to meetings. I had no difficulty identifying as an alcoholic. I accepted I was virulently addicted to the liquid, legal drug, Colt.45. What I did deny was the hope that I could recover – I could see that the program worked for others. I just wasn't sure it would work for me. Nevertheless, I didn't drink and went to meetings. That's all that I did. I didn't get a sponsor, I didn't work the steps, I didn't read any literature. I just joined the Fellowship of AA.

I wanted my wife back.

———

After being sober eight months, Debbie let me move into her apartment. Just as soon as I did, I darkly fantasized she had a lover. Every Tuesday evening she had a group meeting with her therapist. She would stay out until the wee hours the next morning. Her story was that the group lasted until about eleven o'clock. One rainy night I crouched behind some garbage cans across from her shrink's office, waiting for her to leave with a lover. About eleven o'clock the group members came out and walked to a nearby coffee shop. I had to take a taxi home to get there before she did.

I continued not to drink and to go to meetings. I celebrated my first sober anniversary.

A couple of weeks later, I came home early from a midnight meeting and found Debbie in bed with Tom, a co-worker. After he left, we argued, while I hastily packed a suitcase. I was devastated, distraught, inconsolable. I didn't know for certain what I was going to do. Nevertheless, sitting forlornly in Stuyvesant Square Park, as the rosy-fingered dawn brightened the New York City morning, I knew only one thing for certain. I did not want to drink! Debbie had taken me back, but she had betrayed me. However, because I had gone to lots of meetings and did not drink between meetings, I surprised myself – I did not want to drink!

———

A couple of weeks later, I met Peter, who became my sponsor, but mostly a dear friend, for the next 33 years. I chose him for a sponsor because when he discovered his second wife having an affair, he got drunk. I did not want to get drunk, so I began doing the steps with Peter. I had no problem with the first step. I knew alcohol made my life unmanageable. I had a bit of hesitation at the second step because no way could I accept any "power greater than myself" being some kind of distant god somewhere unknown. I did not, however, have a problem with being restored to sanity – I accepted I was sometimes crazy as a loon.

"So," Peter queried me, "Can you stay sober by yourself?"

"Uh, probably not," I hesitantly replied. "I know I need meetings."

"So, there you have it," Peter said.

"Huh," I puzzled, " Have what?"

"Your higher power is the group of drunks, g-o-d."

Made sense to me! Peter also made the third step easy for me. He pointed out that I don't turn my life and will over to some nebulous big daddy in a sky far, far away. He taught me that I turn my life and my will over to the care of a higher power, in my case the group of drunks. I could readily accept that I was cared for, certainly by Peter, as well as by other men and women in the rooms of AA.

In short order, I did a 4th and 5th step with him. Then, we just stopped doing the steps formally as sponsor and pigeon. There was no black and white decision to do this. We just morphed into peers, co-equals sharing recovery together. We related with each other. We meditated together. We talked about our experiences, what we were reading and thinking about. In other words, we shared our "experience, strength and hope" with each other. We also shared our anger, resentment, frustration, fear and despair! No matter what, though, we stayed sober. I experienced with Peter a level of trust and unconditional acceptance that is the essence of intimacy: into-me-see, and equally he let me see into him.

I threw myself into the fellowship of AA, getting active in service work. I co-chaired the first New York City Young Peoples Conference in 1978. I became a licensed professional in the field of addiction, from which I retired in 2006. I married for a third time – Sara birthed a son now 33, who shares recovery with me. I continued not to drink and to go to meetings. I've attended meetings all over the world, several in languages I didn't understand, but felt deeply our shared language of the heart. I continued to help others whenever possible.

———

In full retirement, I now live on the coast of Oregon and am once more happily married. In my 41st year of recovery, I don't consider myself "recovered." I trust explicitly the dictum in the Big Book that "we experience a daily reprieve contingent on the maintenance of our spiritual condition." I remain dogmatically anti-religious, but continue to be a devout spiritual seeker. I deeply respect and learn from the wisdom traditions around the world.

I am ever so grateful my fate had me experience the gift of recovery in New York City. I don't believe I could have gotten sober in a fundamentally Christian environment, such as Jill and I experienced in Frederick, MD. I believe that IF fundamentalist Christian influences in AA succeed in forging the principles of the 12-step recovery process into a ritualized, Bible-oriented dogma, then AA shall wither on the vine of it's own self-inflicted demise.

The dynamic between evangelical Christians and humanist, secular, freethinking members has been ongoing since AA's earliest beginnings. The collaboration between Oxford Group Christians in Akron and several agnostic/atheist members in New York resulted in an organization, which for most of its 78 years has been all-inclusive.

But we all know that there is currently a fundamentalist trend within AA.

Nevertheless, I am greatly relieved by the growing freethinking, humanist and secular initiatives within AA. A day at a time, we shall continue to help each other stay sober in recovery. I humbly accept I am powerless to change AA but I am grateful I can choose to speak my truth of 41 years of continuous sobriety, a long-term recovery not based on the Christian religious beliefs I often hear about at AA meetings. I will continue to carry the message of spiritual recovery not based on Christianity or any other religion or "God:" just one sober drunk / clean drug addict talking to and working with another, one day at a time.

The Bird in Your Hands

By Ivan K.

A salesman was traveling from Toronto to London and got lost. He stopped at a farmer's place to ask directions, and this is the conversation between the two of them: Salesman, "Do you know the directions from here to Woodstock?" Farmer, "Nope." Salesman, "Do you know the directions to St. Thomas?" Farmer, "Nope." Salesman, "Do you know the direction to London?" Farmer, "Nope." Salesman, "Mr. Farmer it seems you don't know very much." Farmer, "Nope, but I sure ain't lost."

That is me in a nutshell. I don't know everything, but I sure ain't lost.

My name is Ivan K. I am 81 years young, and on August 30th, 2012 at 2 p.m. I celebrated my 59th year of one-day-at-a-time sobriety.

Step 1 says "We admitted we were powerless over alcohol – that our lives had become unmanageable," and I believe that I was born with the disease of alcoholism.

This is how I look at Step 1: my life was always unmanageable, and when I took a drink I became an alcoholic.

My father had a bad drinking problem. He kept the wine in the kitchen pantry, and I would lay in bed, and when I believed everyone was asleep I would sneak into the pantry and take a couple slurps, and go back to bed.

I started smoking when I was 9 years of age by picking butts off the sidewalks.

There is a book written by Robert Ringer named "Winning Through Intimidation." I knew the secret years before he wrote the book.

Listed are a few of many examples.

My mother knew I smoked, and she would search me before I would go skating. When she found cigarettes, she would say, "You are not going skating." I would answer, "You don't like me. You wish I was never born. I am going to the basement, lie on the floor, get sick, and die, and you will be happy."

I would go to the basement, and my mother would come down with tears flowing like Niagara Falls, and Ivan would go skating.

I used hammers. If I could not get my way I would stand in front of the China cabinet, my mother's pride, with a hammer and tell her I would break it. We had a Rodger Majestic Radio and I would tell my father that when he was at work I would take a hammer and break the glass on the dial. All day at work he would worry about the radio.

About 40 miles from Brandon, Manitoba where I was born there was a place called Clear Lake. We used to hitchhike there every weekend in the summer, and we did some drinking. One Saturday I did more drinking then usual, and Sunday morning I woke up sitting in a chair back at home, and that was my first blackout.

Fast forward to 4 p.m. December 27, 1949. I took my Oath of Allegiance to King George the VI of the British Empire as a new member of the Royal Canadian Air Force (RCAF). I can remember this part of my story as if it was yesterday.

The recruiting officer said, "Congratulations, young man. You are now a member of the greatest air force in the world."

Less than a month later I left by train for two months of basic training at the RCAF base in Aylmer, Quebec. By the end of the training they were going to release me. My shoes were not shined properly. I was late for parades... I drank too much.

The man that was to make the final decision was squadron leader McNee, a WWII Fighter pilot, with two tours of duty and a chest full of medals. I put my uniform in the drycleaners, get a new shirt and tie and shined my shoes until anyone who looked at them too hard would go blind.

I marched in front of the squadron leader and saluted. He looked me all over, and it felt like an eternity.

Finally he said, "Airman, I have been in the RCAF for many years, and have seen many airmen, and in my opinion you are the sharpest airman I have ever seen. The problem here is I believe someone is picking on you."

I stayed in the RCAF another 20 years to protect Canada.

I was transferred to RCAF Beaver Barracks in Ottawa as a food service attendant to work in the kitchen.

My drinking escalated. I drank every night. Most days I was late for work. I was confined to the barracks many times.

In September, 1952, a friend and I were given 27 days in army detention (jail) for being drunk and wrecking my living quarters.

On January 31, 1953, I was once again in front of my CO for being drunk, and behaviour unbecoming of a good airman, and received 14 days in RCAF detention.

When I got out I phoned this beautiful woman and asked if she would like to go to the Valentines Day dance at the barracks and she accepted.

At the dance I started to drink, and continued to drink. The evening of Sunday, April 12, 1953, I left her apartment took a cab back to the barracks. The next thing I remember I woke up late for work, my shorts covered with blood. When I went to urinate out came blood. I counted 12 bowel movements in one hour. I was admitted to the RCAF Hospital and stayed 33 days. Dr. Doyle, my civilian doctor, sat at the edge of the bed, and said: "Young man you came into the hospital with almost an ulcerated bowel. Tomorrow you are being released, and I strongly advise you to quit drinking."

"Well, can I have a few beers?" I asked.

His answer was no and when I asked why not, he said, "You will be back in six months, and we will measure you up for a wooden suit."

I stayed sober and went home to Brandon on my annual leave. I started to drink, and Saturday, August 29, 1953, at 22 years young I was drinking in the Legion. All the time what was running through my mind was Dr. Doyle's message: "If you drink you will have a tailor-made wooden suit."

I looked up at the wall clock. The time was 2 p.m. I said Ivan drink up, stand up, walk through the door, and you will never drink again.

I drank up, stood up, walked through the door, and the rest is history.

What has happened since then?

I was promoted a year later to corporal. I became a cook and transferred to England in 1955. In 1957, I went to RCAF Clinton, Ontario, to take an advanced cooking course, met the most beautiful woman in London and married her the next year. On March 24, 1959, my wife gave birth to our son, and I have two daughters also.

On Wednesday, April 29, 1959, I attended my first AA meeting. I told a fellow corporal in the air force how I had drank in the past and how I had been sober since August 30, 1953. He told me he was a member of AA and invited me to an AA meeting.

49

The speaker at the meeting was a man by the name of Don who had been a Spitfire fighter during WWII, and now was a helicopter pilot with 12 years sobriety. Guess what: he was telling my story. At the end of the meeting I said Ivan you should have come to AA the day you quit.

I was told AA is not a religious program, but a spiritual program, and I bought it.

It was many years later when I started to think for myself that I said, Ivan, God is mentioned more times at an AA meeting than at church. Why is it some AA members pray to God and get drunk while some atheist and agnostic alcoholics do not pray to a God, and yet stay sober?

Bill, our founder, died from smoking. If prayer could keep him stay sober, why did prayer not help him to quit smoking?

I have been alcohol-free since 1953, nicotine-free since October, 1961, smoking between 20-40 cigarettes a day, and caffeine-free since 1961, and the God of the Bible had nothing to do with it.

On December 28, 1969, I retired from the RCAF with 20 years of service.

When I retired I sold mutual funds and life insurance for three years. In 1972, I started to sell home improvements. In 1975, I started my own home improvement company called Honest Ivan's Home Improvement Co.

In June, 1976, at 39 years young my wife died of cancer.

In 1979, I went bankrupt, lost my business, my home, my Lincoln and had to send my children to their grandmother's.

A friend of mine in AA had a home improvement company. I went and sold for him, and stored my furniture in his warehouse. I would work selling home improvements, and at 1 a.m. I would pull into the Ramada Inn parking lot, go to sleep, wake up at 6 a.m. I would wash, put on a clean suit, shirt, tie and look like I walked out of Esquire magazine.

I was not a happy man.

One day in September, 1979, I was driving down one of the streets feeling poor and depressed when I hit a red light, and there crossing the street in front of me was a man crawling on all fours, like some chimpanzee.

I had never seen him before. But as I was watching him I said, Ivan, you are an Idiot. Why do you say so, I asked myself. Because I bet that man would change places with you in a flash of a second.

50

The light turned green, I put my foot on the accelerator, and I haven't had a bad day since.

Over 20 years ago I was at a London AA convention and Clarence S. spoke. He said you need to work Steps 1 to 9 but once to the best of your ability, and then you stay sober one day at a time on Steps 10, 11, and 12.

An AA joke: A cop stopped a juggler. In the back seat of his car was a bunch of knives. The juggler said they were for his juggling act and the cop asked him to prove it. The juggler took out the knives, and started to juggle them. A man going to an AA meeting said, Boy am I glad I quit drinking. The roadside tests are sure getting tough these days.

In 1985, I found the phone number for Dr. Doyle. I phoned him and told him my name was Ivan and in 1953 I had been admitted to the RCAF Rockliffe hospital with a bad alcohol problem. You doctored me back to health, I told Dr. Doyle, and the day prior to my release you gave me a prescription to stop drinking. I told him I had been following that prescription ever since and thanked him. He cried, and I cried, and that was a great spiritual experience.

In closing I want to tell the story of the wisest man that ever lived. One day a young lad said the man is not that wise and I will prove it. With a bird in his hand he knocked on the door, and when the wise man answered the young lad asked, "Wise man I have a bird in my hands. Is it dead or alive?" Now being a wise man he thought, if I say the bird is alive he will squash it and kill it. If I say the bird is dead he will open his hand and the bird will fly. Being the wise man that he was, his answer was very simple, "Today the bird is in your hands."

AA friends, remember that sobriety is in your hands, and no one else's.

II. 12 Steps

An Atheists Guide to 12 Step Recovery

By Frank M.

You're a thoughtful and well considered atheist.

And you've noticed recently that you might be dying from the crap you put in your body. A little. Maybe that's just the hangover or the dope-sickness talking, but the dirt has been hitting the fan a lot lately and drinking and/or drugging is playing a leading role in all the drama. You've heard of 12-step recovery and you want to try it out. You know there are other programs but this one is everywhere and it's free.

You've also heard this AA stuff has something to do with God. Having given the God hypothesis a fair shot over the years, you found it doesn't fit your honest experience of the world. You'd kind of like to believe it, it would make some things much easier, but you know in your heart that the universe doesn't hear or answer prayers. Not the way most religious people you've ever met think of it anyway. You may have played around a bit with Buddhist ideas, but never very seriously. You were busy getting loaded and trying always to feel better than – well, than however you might have felt at the moment. Good bad or indifferent. It's tough work and it's been keeping you fairly preoccupied.

You figure you can fake your way through the God part and get to whatever's actually useful, so you make a call and get a meeting time and place for the program that seems to deal most directly with your favorite mind-altering hobby.

The second you walk in **God is everywhere. God is on the walls. God is in the opening prayer**. God is in the book. God is in the steps. They even close the thing with the Lord's Prayer. What the hell?

It's okay. You can do it without the God concept. Many have. Many are.

So how do you approach this 12-step thing as an atheist?

First of all, expect that you probably won't be well understood by many of your fellow AAs, NAs, CAs, whatever. Not all of them will know you're an atheist, of course, unless you insist on wearing your "God is dead" Nietzche T-shirt to every meeting. But simply by being honest in your speech you'll reveal yourself often enough. You'll frequently be put in a box marked "UNWILLING TO BELIEVE," and all the ingredients are listed on the outside:

CONTENTS: close-mindedness, self-will, arrogance, resentments against God, too smart for own good.

Many of the most orthodox 12-stepper you meet – the ones who have memorized dozens of quotes and their associated page numbers in the literature – will feel no need to look inside the box. At you. It's all on the label, after all. Often as not you'll get a condescending "Keep coming back," with an unspoken, "You'll eventually get it if you don't die first," from these sorts. In that ubiquitous blue book they use there's a whole chapter dedicated to describing what lunkheads some alcoholics had been (and by extension, you are now) for resisting the quite logical idea that there's a God running things. The man who wrote that chapter fancied himself something of an Aquinas at the time. Forgive that, he's really not a bad guy. He was just doing the best he could, same as you.

Despite all this, you will – if you look around a bit and stay open – find someone unbigoted enough to accept your sincere atheism without judgment. And you will discover in that person a caring friend who will show you the ropes. There are people like that here. Also, you will learn that being fully understood and accepted by everyone is not the be all and end all of life. That's a lesson that could help immeasurably as you move on without the old numbing tools, the ones that helped take away the sting of unfair judgments. Life's not fair. Life is all sorts of things that aren't pleasant. That has not been the problem.

Why hang out with these starry-eyed believers?

You're not expecting to have some kind of conversion experience and suddenly find that God has lifted away your obsession to get loaded (after all, AA's very religious co-founder spent his first two and a half years sober craving a drink). And, of course, you're not asking God to fix you either. Hell, even the people here who do believe in intercessory prayer and who've asked Him to take away their various human frailties fully accept that for reasons unexplained, He can't quite pull it off. That particular aspect of the program, the part about the so-called defects of character, requires a lifetime of constant work. There's a lot of trust in Allah, but tie up your camel going on there.

So what's the point of being here?

They have something, these people. You can feel it, and you can see it in the smiles of the best of them. Some of their stories are a lot worse than yours, and they're fat and happy now. They have a solution to this endless, insane habit of eating yourself alive for emotional sustenance until you're gnawing away at your own heart. They're not getting loaded and they're not white-knuckling it. They just don't need it anymore. You're pretty sure there's no God up there, so what in the world is at work here?

Here's the nut of what they have going on in a quote from their literature:

> This is the how and why of it. First of all we had to quit playing God. It didn't work.

They stopped playing God.

You don't run the world, so stop trying. You can't alter the law of cause and effect, especially when the cause is a drink or a drug, and the effect is the need to drink and use even more. Wishing, hoping, pretending that you can change the things you can't – this could be described poetically as "playing God." The folks here have quit that position. It was a suck job anyhow.

I'm referring only to the people that are actually practicing the principles represented in the steps. There are plenty of poor bastards here too who are just following their herd instinct and are staying dry because they couldn't bear the disapproval of their new friends. For the most part they're a miserable lot. Some of these people will get loaded again and eventually die of their addictions because they can't bear to come back through those doors minus the badge of however many years they had without a drink or a drug. That pride in their clean and sober time was in essence their new drug. They're not your concern.

But the people who really have decided to stop playing God, they have something you need. They have a willingness to live life on life's terms. And the most important of those terms is that if you're an alcoholic or an addict, you can't get loaded recreationally. For people like us the consequences of getting loaded are disastrous. Jails, institutions, death – they will tell you –and you can see it's true from the arc of your own experience.

Most of these people gave up playing God because they came to believe there is a God – and so of course they accept that they can't possibly be Him. Perfectly logical. You can do it for the simple reason that it just doesn't work. That's enough, isn't it? Maybe it's time to say enough of doing what doesn't work. That you're not God means quite simply that you don't dictate the laws of reality. It doesn't really matter who or what does. That's what the 12-step program has for you.

You can accept reality as your Higher Power.

You'll be told you can choose your own Higher Power. In the AA literature this is very clearly just a placeholder for God, a way to get started on the path to finding Him. But in the rooms things are generally much more lax. You can accept as your higher power the reality that you can't get loaded safely, no matter how much you wish you could. The reality that your actions have consequences are never divorced from consequences. The reality that whatever you feel or think this moment about getting loaded must come after the certainty of what always happens when that crap gets in your body. You may have seen the truth of this quite clearly at times in the past, but there was always something lacking in your relationship to that truth. That was the problem all along. Putting yourself above the truth. Playing God. You'll be hearing a lot about humility in these rooms. This is what they're talking about.

To accommodate using reality as your higher power, you will have to bend the steps some from their current and now canonical wording. You can't pray to reality, but you can form and express your intention to live by its rules. And you can meditate in order to cultivate mindfulness of what's real. This won't necessarily please all those orthodox 12-steppers, but then it's unrealistic to expect literalists to be open-minded. And getting real is the whole idea here.2

How about the inventory stuff? Sounds like the confessional.

Yeah, that's what it started as in the Oxford Groups, from which early AA took its original steps. Confession and restitution, they called it. But the principles involved are practical and ethical, not religious. Before you can set off in the right direction, you need to know where you are just now. Even a compass and a map won't help you without the "YOU ARE HERE" part. And then practicing some form of ethical living is a better painkiller in the long run than what you've been using. It all goes to clearing up much of the crap you used to get loaded over. Consider this part of the program a kind of navigational tool to steer you away from creating more wreckage in the world. Because the heartbreak of that wreckage is just goddamn impossible to bear sober.

For the atheist, those twelve steps on the wall and in the book represent four things in essence:

   1. A recognition that you haven't been able get loaded in anything approaching moderation and without consistently creating havoc.

55

2. A surrender to the fact that this is a kind of law of nature for you, and that fighting it has been insane.

3. A willingness to let reality be the guide of your actions henceforth in this and in everything else.

4. A commitment to try and stop hurting yourself or others, and to help where you can.

It does get better along this path. Your chances improve if you keep at it with some kind of daily practice that keeps you mindful of reality – especially the reality of your addiction – and of your place in it. Service from within a sober community helps immeasurably there. That's my personal experience and that of many other atheist drunks and addicts who are walking up this road as best they can. You'll find them in the 12-step rooms and other recovery networks and they can show you what words can't teach.

---

1 Alcoholics Anonymous pg. 62.

2 Keep in mind that AA was midwifed by a small group of men who believed in mystically revealed wisdom. But those men were also humble enough to admit that their book should be suggestive only, and to predict that more would be understood over time. With the continuing recovery of many non-theist AA's over the years, this prediction has been realized.

Personalizing the 12 Steps

By Neil F.

On the 13th of April 1986, during a drive from Montreal to Toronto, I broke into a cold sweat and started shaking. I felt like I was losing control of my mind and my body. It was all I could do to resist the temptation to curl up into a little ball and cry. I could no longer stand the pain of living this way but did not want to die. Something had to change.

I decided to try the same changes that had seemed to work under similar circumstances in the past; I would stop smoking tobacco, I would stop drinking to reduce the likelihood of smoking and I would start an exercise program to regain my physical health. With this approach, I gained short term relief from my problems and I avoided admitting that alcohol was the real problem. In retrospect, this was denial and was always the source of my downfall. When I regained my health, I always went back to drinking as I was convinced that I had to be able to drink to be normal. Alcohol was a part of my business and social life and was to be protected at all costs.

While this approach had seemed to work in the past, this time was different. A week later I was bouncing off of the walls and the ceiling and really needed a drink. In a moment of desperation, I reached out for help; I attended my first AA meeting. Thanks to the fellowship of AA and the recovery process of the 12 Steps I have not had to pick up a drink since.

Thus began my struggle with the Twelve Steps. I really wanted the recovery that AA seemed to offer, but I didn't believe in God. As a result, I was hung up on the second and third steps. Despite the platitudes of a "Higher Power" and a "God of Your Understanding," when I read the Big Book and the 12 & 12 it was clear to me that the expectation was that if I did the steps I would come to my senses and convert to a belief in a personal God that sounded very much like the Christian God. For some time I tried the "fake it till you make it" approach but the truth is that I couldn't just decide to believe what I didn't believe. Pascal's wager would not work for me.

Over time, I have come to accept the Twelve Steps as a template for a recovery process. This template can be tailored to be compatible with the beliefs and needs of each alcoholic. If I were a christian I could use the original template without modification. If I were a muslim, I could substitute Allah in the place of God. If I were a theravadan buddhist, I could edit the template to replace God with the Dhamma, the teachings of the Buddha. For an agnostic, or an atheist the tailoring might be more extensive but it is still possible.

After many modifications over the years, the following is my current, personal 12 step process:

1. We admitted that we suffer from a seemingly hopeless state of mind and body.

2. Came to believe that we could recover.

3. Became open to changes in how we approach and respond to life.

4. Made a searching and fearless inventory of ourselves.

5. Reviewed our inventory with another human being.

6. Became entirely open to change.

7. Humbly affirmed our desire to change.

8. Made a list of all persons we had harmed and became ready to make amends to them all.

9. Made direct amends to such people wherever possible.

10. Continued to take personal inventory and when we were wrong promptly admitted it.

11. Sought through meditation to improve our understanding of ourselves, our program and our progress.

12. Having changed as the result of these steps, we tried to carry this message to alcoholics, and to practice these principles in all our affairs.

This process addresses what I believe are the core requirements of each of the steps and guides my recovery and daily living. This is how I understand the steps and this understanding informs any discussion I have with another alcoholic or any contribution I make in an AA meeting. I don't try to convince others that the wording of the steps needs to be changed, I just talk about what each step means to me and how I practice the step.

In Step 1, I do not admit to being powerless over alcohol or to having an unmanageable life. The first step as worded in the Big Book seems to influence the newcomer to conclude that only God can bring about the required change. I do not believe that it is necessary to believe in God to recover from this seemingly hopeless state of mind and body. When I came to AA everything seemed to be hopeless but by working this process my life today is anything but hopeless. By following the process of the 12 Steps I remained an alcoholic but I recovered from the seemingly hopeless state of mind and body.

In Step 2, I came to believe that I could recover. This came about by reading the stories in the Big Book, by listening to what other members had to say during AA meetings and by talking to other members over coffee after the meetings.

My way of approaching and responding to life before coming to AA always led to drinking. I believed that I had to drink to be normal. I believed that I needed to be in control of all aspects of my life. I believed that what was important was success. Success would lead to happiness and success was measured in terms of money, position, power and prestige. When I did not get what I wanted, I responded to life with a lot of anger, resentment and fear. In step 3, I decided to take another look how I approach and respond to life to see if some changes might reduce the likelihood of my picking up a drink. I didn't actually look at what needed to change in Step 3, I just made a decision to take a look and be open to change.

In Step 4, I made a searching and fearless inventory of how I approached and responded to life. This is the step where I really got to know myself. I explored resentments, anger, fears and relationships. I understood which actions and reactions have negative and which have positive impacts on me and others. I identified what leads to lasting happiness and what to unhappiness. In this step, I tried not to judge myself or others. This step was about getting to know myself; not about moral judgement.

In Step 5, I gained additional insight by reviewing my Step 4 with another person. An individual with more experience in the program was able to help ensure that I had an understanding of how I had approached and responded to life and the impacts that this had on me and others.

My step 6 required a lot of action. I needed to examine each inventory item and come to some conclusion about whether it led to happiness or unhappiness for myself and others. Then I looked at each item that led to unhappiness for myself or others to consider the impact of letting go of that approach or response. Invariably what I concluded was that letting go of negative approaches or reactions would lead to more happiness and that this in turn would reduce the likelihood of me picking up a drink.

In Step 7, I affirmed my desire to let go of my negative approaches and reactions. This is a step that I took on completion of step 6 but it is also a step that I revisit on a daily basis as a part of Steps 10 and 11.

At this point, I had identified changes that would improve my life and reduce the likelihood of my picking up a drink. I concluded that this would provide great benefits going forward but I was still bothered by my past. I wanted to be able to walk down the street and look everyone in the eye. I did not want to be worried about who I might meet. I wanted to be able to answer the phone without being concerned about who might be on the other end of the line. To accomplish this, I needed to clean up the wreckage of my past. To this end, in Step 8 I made a list of all persons that I had harmed and became ready to make amends to them all. To become ready to make amends required that I look at each situation and decide how I might best address any harm that had been done.

Having prepared to make amends in Step 8, in Step 9, wherever possible, I approached each person on the list to correct any harm that had been done in the past. My objective was to perform a reset. As much as possible, I tried to return the situation to the state that it was in prior to any harm that I had done. In some cases an apology was sufficient, in others money owed needed to be repaid and in some cases just being an engaged, supportive member of the family was all that was required.

In Step 10, I try to be mindful of what I am thinking, saying and doing on a continuous basis throughout each day. I try to look at how I am impacting myself or others and if I find myself engaging in my old approaches or responses I try to point myself back down the path I affirmed in Step 7. I find it most important to watch what I am thinking. If I can catch myself as soon as my thinking starts to go off of the rails, I get get myself pointed back in the right direction before doing vocal or physical harm. The more I practice being mindful on a continuous basis, the more likely this becomes. If I have gone beyond thinking and actually harmed someone else, I try to make amends right away.

Step 11 provides guidance for my daily living. In this step, at the beginning of the day I review how I want to approach and respond to life. During the day, I practice Step 10. If I remain frustrated when I try to reorient myself, I find it helpful to take some time for meditation. The meditation can be used to calm down, refocus and remind myself of how I want to live. At the end of the day, some quiet time to review my day is beneficial. It is a good time for ongoing self examination. At this time, I review what I am trying to accomplish, what progress I am making, what seems to be working, what seems not to be working. If I have missed something during my day, I can make note of any amends that still need to be made. I also use meditation on an ongoing basis to explore the working of my mind, my body and the relationship between the two.

In Step 12, I recognized that I have changed. While I an still an alcoholic, I no longer suffer from a seemingly hopeless state of mind and body. I am able to live a normal life. I have become a useful member of my family, Alcoholics Anonymous and society. I try to carry this message to other alcoholics and to practice these principles in all aspects of my life.

The preceding is my personal process. It is what I have used to guide my recovery and day to day living. It has worked for me. If you feel this process can work for you please feel free to use it. If not, please feel free to personalize it. If it is way off, please feel free to start again from the original template so that you have a process that you are comfortable with and that works for you.

May you achieve sobriety. May you remain sober. May you be happy.

Over a long and diverse career, Neil has lived in six provinces and two states. Now retired, he and his wife live on an acreage outside of Stony Plain, Alberta. He struggled with the religiosity of the Big Book and the 12 Steps, eventually discovering a lot in common between the teachings of the Buddha and the AA 12 Steps. He found that the steps could be tailored to a wide variety of spiritual beliefs and developed his own personalized 12 Steps, based upon the core principles of the original 12-Step template. In recovery for the last 26 years, Neil works his personalized 12 Steps, helps others in the fellowship in their recovery and is active in AA Service. His new way of life has led him out of despair to a life filled with hope and happiness. Neil and his wife enjoy camping and hiking in the Canadian Rockies.

You Cannot NOT Interpret the Steps!

By John M.

Last May 14th I attended the annual Toronto Round Up which featured three speakers, two from Ontario and, the other, the headliner, a long standing, highly respected member of AA from California. Well known to many from AA conferences across North America, he was also the featured dinner speaker at the 2009 Ontario Regional Conference held at the Royal York.

In the morning, he presented a highly regarded talk on the story of AA and how we are all to "pass it on" (which was the theme of the Round Up). In the afternoon, he answered questions from the "ask-it basket" and after dinner he shared with us his experience, strength and hope. The speaker has a remarkable story to tell. He is very entertaining and quite humourous and, at the same time, he delivers an inspiring message of recovery.

As many of you are aware, the impending Toronto Intergroup vote on whether or not to delist two groups, Beyond Belief and We Agnostics, was to be decided at the end of May at Intergroup so it was no surprise that the following question from the "ask-it basket" was forwarded to the speaker: "What is your opinion on agnostic groups taking God out of the 12 Steps?"

The speaker responded (and I am summarizing from the CD recorded at the event) that he was "very much opposed to that whether or not my feeling about God has anything to do with it." He explained his position on the issue as one of accepting the AA program as a package and if we were to take God out of the Steps then where do we stop? Do we take the inventory out? Do we take the amends out? Any reference to God in the Steps is like our inventory and amends; "it's part of the package."

One cannot but respect the speaker for taking a stand and providing the reasons why he holds this opinion. One can disagree with him but at least we know the reasons for his opinion.

Perhaps with this question in mind and/or perhaps on learning at the Round Up about the possible delisting of the two AA groups (who have indeed taken any reference to God out of the Steps they read at their meetings), when he was delivering his own story in the evening about his battle with alcoholism and his subsequent recovery, he spoke about the meaning of the Steps in his life. When he came to Step Two he said the following (and here I quote verbatim from the CD):

I guess what the Second Step means—much to my surprise, the Steps all came to mean what they said. To this day I cannot sit through a weekend where people are interpreting the Steps, or even a meeting, for goddamnit they're simple. They mean what they say. And the Second Step means you have to come to believe that there is some power here that will make it unnecessary for you to drink alcohol. That's all! No big deal!

Of course, he is right! He has captured the essential meaning in the freeing action of our program of recovery. And what he said can certainly be what Step Two means: that is, it is one of the things Step Two can mean. But it is not what Step Two says. As we know, it is written as follows: "Came to believe that a Power greater than ourselves could restore us to sanity."

As soon as a speaker (or writer) begins by saying what a statement means, he/she is eo ipso engaging in interpretation unless he/she quotes verbatim from the statement. The speaker tells us that he cannot sit through a weekend or meeting where people are interpreting the Steps (for "the Steps mean what they say") but he then engages in the very act of interpreting the Steps which he indicates he disdains.

It is not my sole intention here to point out the speaker contradicting himself but instead to highlight that the speaker in fact spoke profoundly and meaningfully precisely because he captured the spirit of Step Two. His interpretation violates nothing in the Step (from what is literally written) and his interpretation quite simply expresses an essential truth of the Step.

So what do we take from this? Let's at least acknowledge here that even an experienced, long term, very active member of AA will find it extremely difficult not to interpret the Steps. When we interpret words or phrases we do so to make them deeply meaningful to our lives and to the lives of others. Otherwise they are mere words written down in the pages of a text.

Let's shift the perspective a little, however, and assume that there are those who wish to adhere strictly to the literal, uninterpreted words in AA literature. Since we are dealing with the question of whether or not two groups can interpret the Steps and remain as members of AA, let's look at what Bill W wrote in the 1946 Grapevine (the quotation here is from the essay "Anarchy Melts"):

> In fact, our Tradition carries the principle of independence for the individual to such an apparently fantastic length that, so long as there is the slightest interest in sobriety, the most unmoral, the most anti-social, the most critical alcoholic may gather about him a

few kindred spirits and announce to us that a new Alcoholics Anonymous Group has been formed. Anti-God, anti-medicine, anti-our Recovery Program, even anti-each other–these rampant individuals are still an AA Group if *they think so!* (Bill W's italics.)

What could be clearer? If taken literally then, Beyond Belief and We Agnostics should still be listed members in Toronto Intergroup literature with full voting rights on the floor of Intergroup. The members who disapprove of these two groups interpreting the Steps have themselves interpreted Bill W's words to mean something else in order to support the motion to delist. (By the way, the quotation above by Bill W. was read to the members on the floor of Intergroup prior to the vote.)

Further, Tradition Four reads: "Each group should be autonomous except in matters affecting other groups or AA as a whole." The literal meaning of "Each group should be autonomous" is also clear and therefore decisions at the group level are the sole business of the group, as the group conscience. So it cannot be here that these two groups have violated anything from the standpoint of Tradition Four.

The other part of the Tradition, however, may have been (for many who voted to delist) the key to their decision (despite what Bill wrote in the Grapevine). They too have based their decision on their own interpretation of Tradition Four. I was the Intergroup representative at the time for a group just north of the city and nowhere was anything presented to the members which demonstrated, with any kind of supporting data or from any reported uproar from other groups or "confused" new comers to AA, that Beyond Belief and We Agnostics negatively affected "other groups or AA as a whole." Some supporters of the motion to delist said that there could be mixed and confusing messages to new comers to AA if there were other versions of the Steps other than the original. But this was their interpretation of only <u>possible</u> consequences not current, existing ones.

Some may point out, however, that the qualifying phrase used in the 12 Steps, "God as we understood him," allows us the freedom to interpret God or Higher Power in any way we please. So why remove God from the Steps? Many of us who claim to be atheists, agnostics or free thinkers, in fact, do this on a regular basis and the word "God" does not deeply offend us. But if we remove God from the Steps, this does not necessarily imply that we do not believe in power(s) greater than ourselves; without God, we are not necessarily left isolated and riotously self-willed. The strength we gather from the spirit of our program of recovery is greater than any one word (which in at least one religion there is a tradition that maintains that an infinite deity cannot be expressed in one word without falling into idolatry).

Other nonbelievers on quite reasonable and modern grounds simply confess that God has no meaning (except negatively) for them and therefore other more secular words and phrases can express quite profoundly that AA is not a "solely-about-me" recovery program but is rather all about the power of some form of "otherness."

There are finally those who have been so emotional scarred by a religious upbringing that any reference to God creates an inexorable barrier to 12-Step recovery. Of all people, alcoholics should be sensitive and compassionate toward the alcoholics of this type. We all know how naive and insensitive the advice is by non-alcoholics to "just stop drinking" or the "just say no" campaign: the alcoholic knows that our illness occurs at a deeper level than the level of conscious free will. We are therefore acting like these very same non-alcoholics offering this advice of "just say no" when we tell the religiously scarred alcoholic to "just get over" his/her abhorrence to God references. (And if there are any alcoholics who do not believe other alcoholics suffer in this way from previous religious wounds, I would ask that they go out and share their stories at the "you just lack moral character" forum of public opinion to see how much sympathy for their woundedness they get!)

It is especially this type of alcoholic (as well as other non-believing alcoholics) that the agnostic interpretation of the 12 Steps and the rest of the AA program can help to remove the final barrier to those seeking recovery. This point is nicely noted by atheist Marya Hornbacher, author of Waiting: A Nonbeliever's Higher Power:

> The subject line of an email to me said, 'You have taken away my last excuse for not going to AA.' That cracked me up. Many do stay away from AA because they feel like they are going to have to believe in a certain type of spiritual platform.

Or, on hearing about the result of the Intergroup vote to delist Beyond Belief and We Agnostics, a church going member, with over 50 years of sobriety in AA, despondently remarked to my wife and me: "Why do we continue to place barriers in the way of people who are just trying to get sober."

There is an almost hidden, subtle bias in AA even as we claim that we are a spiritual not a religious program. God becomes AA's default setting where everything said must somehow return to God's grace. Note how easily everyone accepts a speaker's declaration at meetings when he/she says, " I owe this to my Higher Power whom I choose to call God." No problem here!

However, a long standing sober member of my home group once told me that when she was sharing at a closed meeting she spoke of her higher power "whom I choose not to call God." The looks she got, the raised eyebrows, the shuffling of fannies in the chairs indicated to her that her declaration was a problem for many in the room. At that moment, it felt to her as if she had uttered a blasphemy.

Finally, some argue that the delisting of the two groups is not about the God-issue per se but that this is all about the Charter of Alcoholics Anonymous such that to change or amend the 12 Steps requires the written consent of three quarters of AA groups worldwide; the Charter acts to protect the group conscience of AA as a whole. Here, an interpretation is key. Some take this at face value. Others interpret this to mean that indeed this is the case (wisely and democratically so) at the level of AA publications ("Conference approved") and in AA policies and procedures to ensure AA unity and harmony but that deviation from the suggested (page 59, Big Book) Steps of recovery can occur at the level of group autonomy.

Returning to the featured speaker at the Toronto Round Up, recall his interpretation of Step Two even though he claimed not to be able to sit unperturbed through an AA meeting when others interpret the Steps. His interpretation of Step Two rings so true to us even though it is his interpretation of Step Two: "And the second step means you have to come to believe that there is some power here that will make it unnecessary for you to drink alcohol." Right on!

The spirit of interpretation in AA is deeply engrained in our history. Note Dr. Bob's approval of the interpretation of the 12 Steps in Ed Webster's The Little Red Book, Bill W.'s own interpretation of the Steps in the Twelve Steps and Twelve Traditions and, of course, at many meetings, one member is asked to share his/her interpretation of the slogans. In short, one cannot not interpret the AA program of recovery. It is a key to living sober, keeping words and phrases alive in our own experience so that we can stay vigilant, not rest on our laurels, and, happily, not succumb to the sinister singularity of that first drink.

The Silver Tongued Devil and I

By Joe C.

"Keep me safe in the company of those who seek the truth and safe from those who profess to have found it." I don't know who said that but with this in mind I want to say that I am still learning about the Twelve Steps. I enjoy Step Meetings for the wealth of experiences of other alcoholics. I wanted to write a bit about my personal experience with Step One. By my experience I mean what I have filtered, attempted and worked out in my own unique way. There has been a wealth of ideas and instructions I have gleaned from other peoples' life stories in AA.

Admitting that I am powerless and that my life became unmanageable was a process not an event. I didn't always disappoint myself or others, I didn't always embarrass myself when I drank and I hadn't given up on the idea that I could drink like a gentleman. I wanted to be a drunken gentleman. I thought that it was a cruel joke that alcohol (and drugs in my case) presented itself as the answer to life that I was looking for and then it would tempt me, turn on me, get me in trouble and leave me the blame. Kris Kristofferson has a song lyric that describes the Dr. Jekyll and Mr. Hyde aspect of addiction that I loved to sing and still do:

> I sat me down by a tender young maiden,
> Who's eyes were as dark as her hair.
> And as I was searching from bottle to bottle,
> For something un-foolish to say.
> That silver tongued devil just slipped from the shadows,
> And smilingly stole her away.
> I said: "Hey, little girl, don't you know he's the devil.
> He's everything that I ain't.
> Hiding intentions of evil,
> Under the smile of a saint.
> All he's good for is getting in trouble,
> And shiftin' his share of the blame.
> And some people swear he's my double:
> And some even say we're the same.
> But the silver-tongued devil's got nothing to lose,
> I'll only live 'til I die.
> We take our own chances and pay our own dues,
> The silver tongued devil and I."

Still, I thought that getting the good stuff from drinking and not having to suffer any of the bad, was a labyrinth in chemistry. If I could find the right mixture of this-and-that, I would be like Thomas Edison – doubted by everyone, after 14,000 tries he finally invented the incandescent light bulb. By ass-mossis more than osmosis – sitting my ass down and listening – I gradually accepted that my thinking was flawed. I understood what was meant by, "A pickle never becoming a cucumber again."

Still, I would often feel entitled to a largely imaginary past-glory. If there was a pay-day from drinking I had cashed that check and spent it – another one wasn't coming any more that Santa Claus had a bag of toys for me. I was powerless. I lacked the power to choose if I would be good or bad once I started drinking. I came to understand that my intentions weren't the measure of a manageable life, my actions were.

It's true – I was better than the heart-breaking drinking me. Step One was taking ownership of that. Instead of demonizing "bad Joe," I accepted that I couldn't shift my share of the blame. The cause and the blame were no-longer the issue. Debating if it was my genes or my circumstances that made me an alcoholic were infinitely futile. The question now was who was going to do something about it? The answer was that I was going to do something about it, with help. I was one of these alcoholics who had tried to stop drinking and I had failed. My dilemma wasn't stopping – I had done that before. My dilemma was staying stopped.

In Montreal where I got sober there was an ad that ran in the personals of one of two daily English papers at the time. It said, "If you want to drink and can, that's your business. If you want to quit and can't that's our business. Call Alcoholics Anonymous." It was followed by Montreal's English Intergroup number. I couldn't drink and I couldn't quit on my own. I was a good candidate for AA.

My sobriety was shaky then. I didn't have faith in myself. I did have faith in you. You were proof that sobriety was possible. I wrestled with thinking I was different; I still do sometimes. But your sobriety was evidence that if I wanted to stay stopped, I could. Just for today my sobriety is a prized possession. "Sobriety is mine and you can't have it," is how I feel about it today. You can threaten me, you can treat me badly but I know now that you can't make me drink. I took ownership of my alcoholism and I take ownership of my sobriety today. Because I said, "My name is Joe and I am an alcoholic," there was no indication that I had won the game of life there and then. Step One was a beginning.

How I navigated the rest of the Twelve Steps is a story for another day. I did not have all the honesty, integrity, open-mindedness and willingness that that the Steps require. I would have to learn and I would have to grow new muscles. It didn't happen all at once and there was never a time when I knew I was home-free. The rest would take faith. I had faith that staying stopped was your business and you could teach me. It wasn't rationally certainty; it was a gut feeling. I trusted that feeling and so far, so good. I am grateful to say that I am an alcoholic and a proud member of Beyond Belief Agnostics Group of Alcoholics Anonymous.

A Higher Purpose

By Wayne M.

I am an alcoholic and have been sober for over nine years. I am also an agnostic/atheist who attends AA on a regular basis.

Many people have asked how I as an agnostic can stay sober in AA even though I reject one of the fundamental premises of AA, that being a required belief in God or a Higher Power.

To put it simply, my sobriety depends not upon a "Higher Power" but instead is based upon a "higher purpose."

I will explain that in a moment but first let me tell you a little about myself.

My problem with alcohol was so bad that between 1992 and 2004 I was in four different rehabs in the Toronto region.

The first two rehabs were not AA-based and that was why I went to them. I had gone to a few AA meetings and was appalled at the not too subtle religious overtones at them. I could not buy the God thing, or a Higher Power as an alternative. Sorry folks, same thing.

After three months at Halton Recovery House (October 1997 to January 1998) I managed to stay sober for a year and a half. I picked up a drink and the next thing I knew five years later I was in a psych ward. It was 2004 and I was jobless, homeless and friendless. Even my brother would not take a phone call from me.

It was there I decided that I did not want to die a drunk.

I knew I needed treatment to get started – again – and I chose Renascent.

My sobriety date is Sept 30, 2004. In November I entered Renascent and completed treatment.

Now, my higher purpose.

In the last two rehabs I discovered that I was self-obsessed, with no concern for other people. As Bill Wilson said, "The primary fact that we fail to recognize is our total inability to form a true partnership with another human being." This is a brutal fact and one that would have been fatal for me, unless I took action.

My higher purpose is about as simple as I can make it (which is no small feat for an alcoholic). It is simply to be there and to share the experience of being human with other people. Even if I can't do anything to help, I need to be there if someone needs me. If I am using, I am not there for myself, let alone anyone else. This obviously requires I interact with others. I strongly believe that isolation in its many forms is one of the primary reasons we use and especially why we relapse.

I acknowledge that I am dependent on others for my sobriety. To do that on an ongoing basis, I must always endeavor to do the right thing.

AA was – and continues to be – my first line of defence against isolation. I know I can be honest and talk about real things in that environment. AA is not the only place where I can relate to others but it was a start. I also have people in my life outside of AA.

Now I am a part of, not apart from. So now that I am a part of the human race, how do I act and what do I do in this strange arena of the real world?

I believe we can't think our way into good behavior but we can behave our way into good thinking. What is good behaviour? It is doing the next right thing regardless of what I may feel like or think. This can be where the second use I make of AA can come in. For me the Steps are sign posts and guides on how to behave as a normal human being. They also act like idiot lights on my dashboard of life. If in a certain situation one of those steps keeps popping into my head, I know I need to look at something I am doing. For example, if I become resentful or angry I need to look at what my part is in this (Step 4) and if I am wrong I need to apologize and try to make it right (Step 10).

After being sober for more than a year, I started volunteering at Renascent.

As time went by and I always showed up and did well at what they gave me, they started offering me paid shifts. I was offered a full time job in 2007. It was to assess people that wanted to attend our treatment program. My job was to interview them and determine if they were a fit for us and, more importantly, if we were a fit for them.

To say I loved it would be the understatement of all time. For the first time in my life, I had a job that was not a job. It was what I did when I woke up. I could not wait to get there in the mornings.

You see, it was an ideal way for me to live my higher purpose. That way I could be a useful part of the human race.

Everything at my job was going more than well until 2010 when I checked myself into the hospital with crippling stomach pain. Operations (two within a week) found colon cancer which was removed.

No reprieve however. In February 2013, I was back in the hospital due to extreme hip pain. The diagnosis was lung cancer, which had spread to my pelvis area and taken away most of the bone structure on the left side of my hip. Hence the pain and for which there is no cure, only, hopefully, control. Renascent literally sent me home one day because they could not stand seeing the pain I was in trying to get around. I went home and again checked into St Mike's Hospital. That was last February, a year ago. Since then, I have gone through radiation therapy and several rounds of chemo. I just started another one recently.

I have had thoughts and even discussions of going back to work. No one can know how much I miss it.

You see this work is all about my higher purpose.

I can remember the first time I mentioned this higher purpose when I spoke at a meeting. I was surprised at how many people came to me after wanting to know more. This is still my core belief. It has a lot to do with recognizing the existence of others, not just my own.

Way back in a psych ward in 2004 I decided I did not want to die a drunk.

And I won't.

Because I have something new to me in recovery: a purpose.

Wayne died on Friday, March 21, 2014, twelve days after sharing this article on the AA Agnositca website. He kept his commitment: with nine years and five months (3,459 days) of continuous sobriety, he did not die a drunk.

A Higher Power of My Understanding

By Gabe S.

I first encountered Alcoholics Anonymous when I found myself in rehab in December 2010. I had, after many months of resistance, followed the advice of my psychiatrist and my good friends and turned myself in. I had not known that it was a Twelve-Step rehab. I had no idea what the Twelve Steps were. I thought I was in for the best, scientifically-valid treatment for addiction in the world.

I very quickly learnt a little bit about it. It seemed to involve a bunch of rather trite touchy-feely sorts of therapies, readings from an absurd little book of starry-eyed design-stance banalities and fabrications, called 'The Promise Of A New Day,' and readings from the Big Book of Alcoholics Anonymous. On the first day, when I met my therapist, I said to him: "I have to get out of here: it is the God squad!"

I attended for four weeks. I looked at the Big Book. But I didn't like it. I was horrified by the chapter called "We Agnostics." This chapter seemed designed to convert atheists and agnostics to believers in God. A refusal to consider the possibility of such a Being, it was indicated, was vain and illogical. Atheists and agnostics who do not yet believe can begin to work on the Twelve-Step program of recovery using the group as their higher power, but in order to recover fully, a belief in God would eventually be necessary. The Big Book as a whole seemed to be riddled with God talk. And this put me right off.

I emerged clean and sober. I attended a few AA meetings. I had a sponsor but I never called him. I was fine. I had no cravings, no obsession. I needed no help. Then one day I became stressed out. With no mental defense, I had a drink to calm me down... and I did not stop drinking for about a month. I went back to rehab for a week's detox. At the end of the week I was fine. There was no more problem with my disease. Every one of my peers at the clinic said to me: 'Don't leave. You are not ready'. I didn't listen.

On the way home I bought a bottle of vodka. And I continued to drink as before, all the time. I descended into that pit of despair: the more depressed and anxious I became, the more I needed to drink to try to escape from the inner horror. The worse the horror became, the more I needed to drink: a pit of swirling blackness from which there was no escape. A drunkard's dream if I ever did see one.

A very good friend was looking after me. She would visit every day, for hours. Sometimes she would stay the night if I was afraid to be alone. She now reports that I resisted returning to the clinic mainly on the 'God' grounds. I was not going to participate in what seemed to me to be a faith-based program of recovery. I looked at the Steps. If I were to participate then my higher power would have to be other people. But that would not work. Other people would give inconsistent advice and I would end up having to make my own decisions anyway. Nothing, existent or non-existent, could be My higher power.

But my psychiatrist was in my ear. I was at serious risk of brain damage. I had to go back to rehab. By then my anxiety was crippling. I was delighted to be given a huge dose of Librium to get me out of the withdrawal-drink cycle. I was delighted to be in a comfortable place where I could not get at any bottles of gin or vodka.

My disease had beaten me all ends up. I could not face alcohol any more. I did not know it, but at that moment I took Step One. I was in rehab. Perhaps these people could help me. That was Step Two.

I had known that I was insane for some time, although realizing just how insane, took me a long time. I decided that I might as well really give this recovery malarkey a good go. I would do everything my therapists said – as long as it didn't involve talking like a believer or acting like a believer. My atheism runs deep, as does my integrity. I do not believe in any God and I will not represent myself as a person who does. So I will not talk or act like a believer. Some tell me this is pride, resistance to authority. Perhaps there is some element of unhealthy pride involved. But, however that may be, my integrity does not allow me to present myself as something I am not. So, aside from saying 'God' in a manner that would misrepresent my beliefs, I decided to do to my best ability everything that my therapists recommended. That was Step Three.

At that point, other people became my "higher power." My love of language prevents me from calling them 'God.' I made a decision to turn my will and my life over the care of my higher power. And it worked. I am experiencing a new freedom and a new happiness.

My atheist therapist gave me a secular version of the Steps when I started out. Since then I have collected others. Now I enjoy working from my own version, which reconstructs my route to a psychic change and maintenance of psychic good health.

My higher power is very important to me. I have a large group of very wise people who know me well. Most of them are fellowship, but not all. All my life I have been self-reliant because I am oh-so-clever. I always knew best. But in the end I could not manage my own life or my own mind at all. Now if I have to make any big decision, or just need help managing any aspect of my mind or my life, I just ask my higher power. In fact, the different components of my higher power very rarely disagree among themselves. And when they do, then it is ok for me to make the final call. My initial argument against the possibility of others being my higher power held no water at all. Now, when my higher power delivers a view, I follow its guidance without question. Collectively they are far wiser than I am. And turning over to them takes the load of stress and responsibility off of me.

The Big Book and Twelve Steps and Twelve Traditions are part of my higher power too. All I had to do was remove all references to God and replace them, where this made sense, with references to a higher power. What remained was a wonderfully insightful description of the alcoholic mind, and a carefully crafted and targeted recipe for the development of good mental health.

Once God is removed, many aspects of AA's program in the Big Book and Twelve Steps and Twelve Traditions can be seen to be focused on stress-management: building a realistic self-image, boosting self-esteem and avoiding guilt. The approach echoes that of the Stoics. AA makes much of the Serenity Prayer: "God grant me the serenity to accept the things I cannot change, courage to change the things I can and wisdom to know the difference." It is often remarked that the prayer echoes a central theme in the work of such thinkers as Epictetus, Seneca and Marcus Aurelius. The Stoics are thought by some to have originated cognitive therapy. Both the Stoics and AA hold that problematic emotions can be dealt with, in part, by the application of intellectual analysis.

With anger-management, for example, AA bids a member to consider how he himself contributed to a situation in which he became angered, and what it is about himself that fuelled his angry reaction. Seneca bids us not to dwell on a perceived wrong that has been done to us, and not to focus on a justification for revenge (letter to Novatus). Seneca and AA differ in that AA accepts that in general a certain amount of emotion is natural, inevitable and a good thing, while the Stoics held that, with work, emotions could be entirely eliminated by intellectual means. Both note that in being angry, one allows

75

another to disturb one's serenity. Both want that particular emotion eliminated. In this context, Seneca writes: "human life is founded on kindness and concord, and is bound into an alliance for common help, not by terror, but by mutual love." while AA writes (Twelve Steps and Twelve Traditions p. 48). "Courtesy, kindness, justice and love are the keynotes by which we may come into harmony with practically anybody."

By following the advice of others and taking the Steps — understood from an atheist point of view — I found my higher power. With a higher power like that, who needs God?

Gabe was born in 1959 in the leafy area of Hampstead, London. His parents were decent and kind and he describes his childhood environment as "peaceful and secure." He went to University College School, a liberal secular school, and eventually studied philosophy at University College in London. Philosophy suited him, and he pursued a career in it. He got his PhD from MIT. He taught first at the University of Madison, Wisconsin, then moved to King's College, London. Eventually, in 2010, alcohol got the better of him and he was dismissed on grounds of ill-health. He recovered and was rescued by the University of Reading, where he now teaches part time. Semi-retired, he does research on addiction, helps alcoholics and works on creative writing projects.

The Program

By John L.

Several years ago, at a meeting of the Boston Crossroads group, a speaker said: "Alcoholics Anonymous is a fellowship — of people working their individual programs."

This got me thinking. There can be "My Program" as well as "Your Program" and any number of other programs. But what about "The Program", which we hear often enough at AA meetings. From a bit of questioning I've found that by "The Program" many members mean pretty much everything — the total AA experience. But others take "The Program" to mean specifically the 12 Steps, perhaps along with the 12 Traditions.

Alcoholics Anonymous World Services has this to say:

> The relative success of the AA program seems to be due to the fact that an alcoholic who no longer drinks has an exceptional faculty for "reaching" and helping an uncontrolled drinker.

> In simplest form, the AA program operates when a recovered alcoholic passes along the story of his or her own problem drinking, describes the sobriety he or she has found in AA, and invites the newcomer to join the informal Fellowship.

> The heart of the suggested program of personal recovery is contained in Twelve Steps describing the experience of the earliest members of the Society.

Accordingly, "the program" means sober alcoholics helping others to achieve and retain sobriety, with the Twelve Steps at the heart of recovery. However, the third paragraph is simply untrue. The Twelve Steps, far from being based on group experience, are a concoction of Bill W., who cribbed the ideas from the Oxford Group. AA was getting off the ground and doing well, having broken from the Oxford Group, when Bill W. came around peddling his Steps. They were not well received. But he persisted, and in time the Steps became holy dogma. The main thing here is that, on empirical grounds, the Steps are not a necessary part of recovery, since many of us have achieved long-term sobriety without them — or at least without them as written by Bill W.

The basics of *my program* are:

1. A day at a time I stay away from the first drink. (24-Hour Plan)
2. I try to help others — be a part of the Fellowship.
3. I try to be in good health: diet, exercise, no cigarettes, etc.
4. I don't take other psycho-active drugs.

In addition there are many other things, perhaps peculiar to myself, which I believe enhance my well-being in sobriety. Early in sobriety I was diagnosed with severe hypoglycemia, which is strongly related to alcoholism. This means I need to follow a diet which eliminates sugar and sharply reduces carbohydrates. So long as I follow this diet, which I have done for about 90% of my 44 years of sobriety, I am healthy and happy.

For exercise I go to a gym, where I do calisthenics and use the various machines. At home I use a rebounder, which is one of the best investments I ever made. I make my own yogurt and kefir. About once a week, especially in cooler months, I take a sauna. In nice weather I take long walks.

I try to have an intellectual life. Much of my life is spent in libraries, and last year I published two books (early 19th century translations of Aeschylus plays, done by Percy Bysshe Shelley and his cousin, Thomas Medwin).

I play the piano. The world may be going mad, but Bach is always logical.

Such as they are, these are the main elements of my program.

Can we speak of "the program"? I think we can. It's the part of AA that works: the 24-Hour Plan (or Program), the AA Fellowship, and the Twelve Traditions (which really are based on group experience).

The AA Preamble states:

> ALCOHOLICS ANONYMOUS is a fellowship of men and women who share their experience, strength and hope with each other that they may solve their common problem and help others to recover from alcoholism. The only requirement for membership is a desire to stop drinking. There are no dues or fees for AA membership; we are self-supporting through our own contributions. AA is not allied with any sect, denomination, politics, organization or institution; does not wish to engage in any controversy; neither endorses nor opposes any causes. Our primary purpose is to stay sober and help other alcoholics to achieve sobriety.

To me the Preamble eloquently espresses the heart of AA recovery. It's what has worked for me, and for my friends with long-term sobriety.

III. Book Reviews

A History of Agnostic Groups in AA

Reviewed by Chris G.

When the Big Book, *Alcoholics Anonymous*, was being written there was an irritating atheist in the mix: Jim Burwell.

He was responsible for the phrase "God, as we understood Him" in the Steps and for AA's Third Tradition: "The only requirement for membership is a desire to stop drinking." Today, if an AA group dares to take this a step further and call itself "agnostic," or "atheistic," or make any changes to the Steps as published, it risks expulsion from the sacred meeting lists of its local Intergoup. What is going on? Are we here to get sober, or to argue about our religious beliefs?

This story is the subject of Roger C.'s book, A *History of Agnostic Groups in AA*.

From the early beginnings of individual beliefs in opposition to the "god bit," and particularly the western Christian culture from which it came, to the current situation of Intergroups delisting AA groups who find a non-God path to sobriety, Roger takes us along the story of what has happened — so far.

The History opens with "Excommunicated:" the bare facts concerning the delisting of several Toronto groups in 2011 by the Greater Toronto Area Intergroup.

To set the stage, there follows a summary of the Jim Burwell's part in the writing of the Steps, leading to Bill Wilson's 1961 Grapevine article in which he realizes that "his early Christian evangelicism had been a serious problem."

Agnostic groups have been a part of AA since the 1970s. Roger covers the development of these groups in sections on New York, Chicago, Los Angeles, Austin, Des Moines and elsewhere in fascinating detail. He names key names in the development of these groups: Don Wilson who started the first Quad A (AAAA – Alcoholics Anonymous for Atheists and Agnostics) in Chicago in 1975 and Charlie Polachek, who started the first group named "We Agnostics" in 1980 in Hollywood. This is interesting reading, full of quotes showing the juxtaposition of "the literature" to the real world, and how people selectively interpret it.

In the section "Missteps," Roger addresses the conflicts arising when groups, in their group conscience, alter the Steps as published. Has the Big Book become a canon? For some people, you bet it has. The "Misdeeds" chapter can best be summarized as "it got very twisted." In this section Roger explains the ins, outs, and twisted logic by which Intergroups and even the General Service Office (GSO) have interacted with agnostic groups. The traditions are examined and ignored at whim… there is humour here, if you are sufficiently detached from the ruckus.

Roger ends with a brilliant plea for a "Vatican II" of AA. If you are old enough to remember Vatican II, you will remember the furor it caused, and how, in the end, the Catholic Church, that bastion of old, old tradition, remarkably produced the enlightened Declaration of Religious Freedom, from which Roger quotes:

> All men are to be immune from coercion on the part of individuals or of social groups and of any human power, in such wise that no one is to be forced to act in a manner contrary to his own beliefs, whether privately or publicly, whether alone or in association with others.

Does that not mirror the spirit of what AA professes, though not always practices?

Lest you leave this book feeling slightly helpless in the face of the opposition, Roger has supplied some very useful material in the appendices: a non-religious meeting format, a widely available non-theist version of the 12 Steps, and information about a wonderful resource for all things agnostic in AA: the AA Agnostica website. All suggestions, of course.

It is often said that history is written by the winners. This is an important work because it is written by a participant who is squarely in the midst of the struggle. We who are in it do see it as a struggle, but perhaps some years from now the essence of the 12 Traditions and Vatican II will prevail, and there will come a solution with no winners or losers — one of true consensus, in the spirit of our Group Conscience. In setting out the facts as they evolve, Roger can only contribute to such an eventual solution.

The Little Book

Reviewed by Jean S.

This book offers a way forward for the fellowship of Alcoholics Anonymous.

The unstated goal of *The Little Book* is to widen the gateway of AA so that all who suffer might pass through, regardless of belief or lack of belief.

The book presents the 12 Step program of recovery in a way that reflects and respects the diversity of culture, gender, religion and lack of religion within today's worldwide recovery community.

Only 72 pages in length, *The Little Book* is divided into four main parts.

The first part consists of 20 alternative versions of the 12 Steps which were originally published in 1939 in the "Big Book," *Alcoholics Anonymous*.

Want to know how a Native American might understand the Steps? Page 22. How would the man who won the 1972 Humanist of the Year award translate the 12 Steps? You can read B.F. Skinner's version on page 13. Can the Steps be done by a Muslim? Of course! Page 21. Is there a Buddhist alternative to the 12 Steps? At least two of them, on pages 19 and 20.

Want to know which group wrote "Made a decision to entrust our will and our lives to the care of the collective wisdom and resources of those who have searched before us" in Step Three? Page 11. Want to read single-word versions of the Steps? Pages 17 and 18.

And on. And on. There is so much in this book. There is so much on every page of this book!

And there could be so much more. As the author of *The Little Book* writes: "There are about as many versions (of the 12 Steps) as there are alcoholics in AA who use the program to get sober and maintain their sobriety." (p. 1)

In the second major part of the book, four concise interpretations of the original 12 Steps are presented, one Step at a time.

The intepretations run from pages 33 through 44, with one Step per page.

Most of us are aware that there is a Christian interpretation of the 12 Steps. As the author notes in Appendix Two of *The Little Book*: "The word 'God' (or 'Power' or 'Him') appears six times in the (original) Steps and the practices described have historically been designed to win redemption, that is, to satisfy the demands of a judgmental and interventionist deity. That they might also help to allay the cravings of an incorrigible alcoholic seems something of an… afterthought." (p. 52)

But historically there have always been other interpretations and this book continues that lovely, and liberating, tradition.

The first interpretation is by the renowned author, Allen Berger. He has written a number of popular books such as *12 Smart Things to Do When the Booze and Drugs Are Gone*. His interest and expertise is in emotional and cognitive therapies and his approach science-based.

Perhaps the most moving set of interpretations is by Stephanie Covington. She presents a woman's perspective on the 12 Steps. It needs to be noted that the original 12 Steps were not written for women or with women's struggles with alcoholism or addiction in mind. Talking about powerlessness and humility, as the original Steps do, can have a different meaning for, and impact, upon women. Today we also understand that trauma plays a large role in alcoholism and addiction, something not at all grasped by the early founders of AA. In order to deal with these and others issues, Stephanie wrote *A Woman's Way Through the Twelve Steps*, a treasure for women in recovery, from which her interpretations of each of the Steps are culled.

Next comes interpretations by Gabor Maté, author of **In the Realm of Hungry Ghosts**. As a doctor and the staff physician for the Portland Hotel Society, which provides medical care to addicts in Vancouver's notorious Downtown Eastside, Gabor has a unique and contemporary perspective on addiction. It is fascinating to read his book, and his interpretations of the 12 Steps are one of the treasures of *The Little Book*.

We keep hearing that there is a great deal in common between Buddhism and AA's suggested program of recovery, but how would a Buddhist interpret the 12 Steps? Read *The Little Book* and you'll find out! The author of *Mindfulness and the 12 Steps*, and the founder of the Mind Roads Meditation Center, home to Twelve Steps and Mindfulness meetings, Thérèse Jacobs-Stewart shares her interpretations as both a Buddhist and a woman in recovery.

These interpretations are all so insightful and refreshing.

Still, **a favourite part of the book** is the fact that the reader is given a template to write her or his own alternatives and interpretations of each of the 12 Steps. This is so the opposite of "one size fits all" that it makes the heart throb with relief. We all "work" the 12 Steps in our own unique ways so for many of us in recovery this will be an invaluable tool. It also encourages the reader to work harder, to bring her or his own understanding and experience to working each and every one of the Steps and thus to more genuinely tackle the challenges involved in achieving a life of sobriety.

The very last part of the book consists of two appendices. One contains the original 12 Steps published in 1939 and the other is an insightful essay, "The Origins of the 12 Steps."

"It all began in the waning months of 1934," the essay begins and then goes on to describe the contributions of people like Ebby Thacher, Bill Wilson, Dr. William Silkworth and Jim Burwell to the development of AA's program of recovery.

The author pays particular attention to Appendix II of the Big Book, which was added in the second printing of the book in 1941. "The purpose of the appendix is to correct the impression in the Big Book that recovery requires a religious conversion," the author of *The Little Book* said. "Instead, the purpose of the 12 Steps is framed in psychological terms and its goal restated as the pursuit of "a personality change sufficient to bring about recovery from alcoholism."

The book was put together and authored by Roger C., the administrator of the AA Agnostica website.

A former government writer and political organizer and activist, Roger is a member of Beyond Belief, an agnostic group in Toronto. Perhaps ironically, he has a Masters degree in Religious Studies from McGill University. He spent several years there working on his doctorate and teaching ordinands – men and women studying to be ministers in the Anglican, Presbyterian and United Churches. He was known as the "resident atheist" and treated with respect. "In AA, not so much," he reports.

"All our thanks goes to the people and groups whose alternative versions of the Steps are included in the book. Some of these go as far back as the 1980s. And deep gratitude goes to Gabor Maté, Thérèse Jacobs-Steward, Allen Berger and Stephanie Covington for their very generous support both for me and for the book," Roger said. "Their unconditional support for this project was an inspiration and an essential ingredient in making this book a reality."

Asked about the Toronto area Intergroup decision to remove two agnostic groups (including his own group, Beyond Belief) from the official AA list for creating their own alternative 12 Steps, he responded: "Intergroup representatives behaved in a silly and un-AA way."

"The Intergroup representatives are making up rules that are meant to discipline others in an organization that quite deliberately chooses not to have rules," he said. "What is there about 'The only requirement for membership is a desire to stop drinking' that is so hard for them to understand?"

In its inclusivity and unqualified respect for diversity and difference, *The Little Book* paradoxically represents both a challenge to AA while anchored in the very best of its history and traditions.

Ernest Kurtz, the author of *Not-God: A History of Alcoholics Anonymous* calls the book "a beautiful testimony to AA's *living* history."

And William White, author of *Slaying the Dragon: The History of Addiction Treatment and Recovery in America*, refers to *The Little Book* as "a celebration of the varieties of recovery experience."

Indeed, *The Little Book* is a veritable encyclopedia of knowledge and wisdom about the 12 Step program of recovery.

Beyond Belief: Agnostic Musings for 12 Step Life

Reviewed by Carol M.

Finally! A daily reflection book for nonbelievers, freethinkers and everyone, *Beyond Belief: Agnostic Musings for 12 Step Life* offers 365 quips for every alcoholic/addict. Drawing on quotes from writers, skeptics, entertainers, economists, religious leaders, philosophers, psychologists and varied recovery fellowship literature, *Beyond Belief* neither canonizes nor vilifies any school of recovery thought.

Where else would you find Sam Harris followed by Mother Teresa, Bill Wilson followed with Anais Nin, a doctor's opinion by Dr. Seuss or a spiritual perspective from Albert Einstein? *Beyond Belief* takes a secular look at our recovery culture with help from the classic thinkers of the ages and the wisdom in and around the rooms.

"A funny thing happened to me on the way to the new Millennium," writes author Joe C. "I realized I had been a closet Agnostic for most of my recovery." Well a funny thing also happened to 12 Step Groups on the way to the year 2000. We were joined by thousands of people of different ethnic and religious backgrounds in numbers the fellowship had not seen before in North America. A few stayed, but many, if not most, leave because of the dominant theme which insists the alcoholic, addict, or codependent has to one day accept help that is always described in theistic terms.

Many members will say "Our fellowship is very diverse." But when we look around our community and assess its ethnic make-up – and then measure it against the meeting rooms - it never fails: the 12-Step basements are filled with mostly Caucasians and more men than women.

There's a simple explanation which Joe C. says he thought about while putting these daily meditations together; the literature we depend on was created by white men in the 1930s. The book includes a historical reference to the struggle Bill W. recounts when the first two African-American men asked to attend a meeting. Those attending insisted on a group conscience and the result was a devastating, "No."

Beyond Belief: Agnostic Musings for 12 Step Life is not just a great daily meditation tool. It's also a gateway into a program that can still work for those who feel they don't belong because they stand out at their regular meeting. Like agnostic meetings, the theme of this book is, "We don't care what you believe we just want to welcome you and help you stay clean, abstinent, and sober – away from whatever substance or process that's making your life unmanageable."

The true spirit of the traditions is contained in the fact that the book is not Joe C's thoughts on sobriety. It's a mix of what he's heard in meetings for more than 35 years, and that means it includes thoughts from those who have joined us on the road: Hindus, Muslims, Buddhists, Jews – even feminists.

Despite the pitfalls of the Big Book and other literature around 12 Step rooms – the ubiquitous allegiance to Christian ideas - there are golden nuggets buried within the dogma. One is the suggestion to take a few moments of reflection before going out to tackle another abstinent day. This book opens the door for anyone and everyone to practice a ritual that has led to years of sobriety and abstinence. *Beyond Belief* can help you build this practice into your life without offending your beliefs or your current rituals.

Finally, if you're a woman who has experienced trauma you've no doubt been told that what happened to you is intertwined with your addiction. You've also probably been going to meetings and getting more and more confused as you go along. You may have relapsed and you are confused about why the program isn't working for you. Your therapist or counsellor tells you being abused led to your addiction, and people in meetings tell you the opposite.

You really are no longer alone and this book can be a very useful tool. The old literature was written at a time when people didn't understand the link between trauma and addiction. Even though it's well documented these days, Twelve Step devotees sometimes show an aversion to new information. One of the sub-titles of this book is "finally, daily reflections for nonbelievers, free-thinkers, and everyone." For women who are re-traumatized by AA approved literature this could just as easily read, "Finally, a book of daily reflections you won't have to throw at the wall." I know there are a few dents in my drywall from books that carried the message I was responsible for being raped, molested, or abused. This book not only provides new ways to think about our rage and hurt, it also points out how platitudes are harmful. It doesn't even tell you that God planned your demise to build your character. Now there's a turgid little cliché that has sent many a survivor running for the closest exit…

I highly recommend this book to anyone who is struggling with finding their place in recovery, and in the spirit of our traditions – hopefully we'll see you one day at one of our dogma-free gatherings.

Mindfulness and the 12 Steps

Reviewed by Roger C.

There would appear to be much in common between Buddhist thought and the 12 Step recovery program practised by some in AA.

A number of books have made the connection between them.

Three of the more popular ones include Kevin Griffin's work, *One Breath at a Time: Buddhism and the 12 Steps*, published in 2004. That was followed in 2009 by Darren Littlejohn's rather well-known work, *The 12-Step Buddhist*.

And the third is Thérèse Jacobs-Stewart's book, *Mindfulness and the 12 Steps,* published in 2010.

Jacobs-Stewart got sober in 1975. "Now, thirty-five years later, I owe the programs of Alcoholics Anonymous and Al-Anon my life. I've stayed straight and can say I am genuinely happy." She is a psychologist, a counsellor, an AAer and a practising Buddhist.

For Jacobs-Steward and these other writers, Buddhist practice is in sync with AA's 12 Step program.

Buddhist thought holds that craving leads to suffering (the second noble truth). Twenty-five hundred years ago the Buddha taught that snippets of addiction – constantly wanting, ever craving this or that – are the source of all human suffering.

He also taught that this suffering could be reduced and eventually eliminated.

This is where the author introduces mindfulness, which can be defined as self-awareness writ large, built into every moment of our lives, as both a form of behaviour and through the practice of meditation.

Meditation is a mode of mindfulness and leads incrementally towards an "awakening:" an understanding of human interaction in the world that is both craving and delusion-free.

> We have the choice to live an awakened life... This is a choice to be mindful, see our patterns, and recognize the delusions that lead us to act the way we do. In Twelve Step terms, it is the practice of taking inventory, searching out what's driving our actions and reactions, and taking responsibility for it. (p. 52)

It is certainly worth noting that the idea of "mindfulness" as a way of dealing with addictive behaviour that leads to suffering is ever more prevalent in the rooms of AA.

Last week Julie B. celebrated a year of sobriety at the We Agnostics meeting on St. Clair Avenue in Toronto. She chose to have one word, an acronym, on her one-year medallion: S.O.B.E.R.

When we have a troubling thought, or a desire to drink, the mindful approach is laid out this way:

> • **S**top – Pause for a moment and consider what you are doing;
>
> • **O**bserve – Think about what you are sensing, feeling and experiencing, and what events led to the situation;
>
> • **B**reathe – Pause for a few deep breaths in order to assess your situation in as calm a manner as possible;
>
> • **E**xpand – Expand your awareness and remind yourself of what will happen if you keep repeating the unwanted behavior (and how you will feel afterward);
>
> • **R**espond mindfully – Remember that you have a choice, that you are not required to continue the undesired behaviour.

As Jacobs-Stewart puts it, "If we are mindful, we can slow down the reactionary chain of thoughts, feelings, and subsequent actions. We can see the whole cycle." (p. 81)

In 2004 she founded the Mind Roads Meditation Center which is home to Twelve Steps and Mindfulness meetings in St. Paul, Minnesota.

> Each month, we discuss one of the Twelve Steps and how Buddhist thought, meditation, and mindfulness practice can be applied to our life in recovery... Seeking deeper serenity in our lives, (we are) grounded in sobriety by the Twelve Step program, inspired to awaken and live in the present by the practices of mindfulness meditation. (p. xv)

Jacobs-Stewart devotes a chapter in her book to each of the Steps. We shall look at just one of these chapters/Steps.

In the chapter devoted to a discussion of Step Three, she writes that the Buddhist approach to "turning our will and our lives over to the care of God as we understood Him" is to "take refuge."

There are three refuges in Buddhism (also called the three jewels).

The first is taking refuge in the actual practice, which has earlier been described as a process of awakening. It is called taking refuge in the Buddha or in our Buddha nature. "Taking refuge in awakening suggests that many of the self-critical or self-important beliefs we hold are simply overlays, clouding and distorting our conscious contact with the (mind in its fullness)... I think of a carnival, with a loud, neon-lit, mental fun house, filled with mirrors." (p. 32)

The second refuge is *dharma.* These are the teachings of the Buddha, which embody core principles such as the Four Noble Truths and the Eightfold Path.

The third and final refuge is the *sangha*, the Buddhist community.

The reliance on a community or a fellowship will be quite familiar to those of us with experience in the rooms of AA. There are some who, when they stumble onto the third step, decide that "God as we understood Him" is a Group of Drunks, the fellowship itself.

Buddhism places a great deal of emphasis on interdependence (all being and phenomena depend on all other beings and phenomena) – as one will discover reading Jacobs-Stewart book – and thus has no difficulty whatsoever with the principle of "one alcoholic helping another alcoholic," the core mandate of AA.

There are many stories out there, from many diverse perspectives, about recovery from alcoholism that are both inspiring and helpful.

Thérèse Jacobs-Stewart's book, *Mindfulness and the 12 Steps*, is one of those works. If you are interested in how a Buddhist might interpret the 12 Steps, then this is a wonderful book. It is also a landmark document in terms of understanding how the practice of mindfulness meditation can help in dealing with some very severe afflictions, including – and maybe especially – alcoholism.

A Woman's Way Through the Twelve Steps

Reviewed by Linda R.

A Woman's Way Through The Twelve Step by Stephanie Covington was published in 1994 and has become a favorite book for many women in AA. Why do women have their own book? One reason is the effect on women of the religious language used in the original AA literature. And it is important to recognize that the Big Book was written in 1939, when the possibility of a woman being an alcoholic was barely considered.

Although an entire chapter in the Big Book was devoted to women, it was not addressed to them as women alcoholics. Instead, it categorized them as the wives of the men for whom the book was written. This chapter, entitled "To Wives," was written by a male alcoholic, Bill Wilson, who instructed the "wives" on how to behave toward their alcoholic spouse. Many women find this chapter quaint and antiquated, if not downright condescending.

A Woman's Way through the 12 Steps is specifically geared to a women audience, but it may be useful too to men who also live in the modern world; a world which differs significantly from the world occupied by the author of the Big Book. Covington's discussion of "God" should be of interest to all genders. Her treatment of the God topic is non-judgmental and higher power neutral.

Covington acknowledges that on the surface the original AA literature suggests that we can choose our own conception of God, and that AA is not intended to be a religion or a church. However, she points out that while some alternatives to using the word God are provided — The Great Reality, Creative Intelligence, Spirit of the Universe – the text in the Big Book reflects and emphasizes the traditional religious notion of an all knowing supernatural Being. Moreover, there are many references to God as "Him", where "He" is the "Father" and we are "His" children. Language and imagery that depicts God as a male figure can be alienating for women. Reading the original AA literature often replicates the alienation felt by these women through experiencing the same emphasis on God as a male figure in their childhood churches and religions.

Furthermore, Covington does not agree with the viewpoint of the original AA literature which portrays rejection of God as a dangerous rebellion that leads to drinking. She notes that the original AA literature warns of the "belligerence" of the alcoholic who won't believe in God and provides an extremely negative image of the non-believer:

> He is in a state of mind that can only be considered savage. (Twelve Steps and Twelve Traditions, p 25).

Covington reflects that on the contrary, "By staying true to what is right for us, we may actually do better in our recovery." (p. 32)

Stories are provided of women who come to think of God in non-traditional ways that are different from the original AA literature. In addition, stories of women who do come to believe in the traditional "God of our Fathers" are provided too and according to Covington *"There is nothing wrong with the traditional male image of God, though, as long as it is supportive."* (p. 33) But stunningly, Covington includes the voices of women who do not develop nor come to depend upon any belief in God — traditional or non-traditional – to stay sober. Their power is often external, such as the power of relationships. Or it can be internal, such as the deep, inner self that is "the self that is greater than who you seem to be on the surface." (p. 34)

Unlike the original AA literature, which attempts to convince the reader that a belief in God is necessary to maintain sobriety, this book is focused on exploring different perspectives on the Steps, in order for alcoholics to create their own path of recovery. Using the Steps as guides, the book helps them discover or rediscover what they think, feel and believe and connect this to their actions and their relations with other people in the world around them. Covington calls this experience "wholeness, or integrity."

The theme of integrating the inner and outer life runs throughout the book, because Covington believes that each of the Steps in some way touches on soul-searching and self-honesty and that:

> Ultimately, the underlying theme of the Steps is living a life that is consistent with your deepest values. The Steps are designed to help you discover what those values are – to look at your inner life —so that you can see how you may be acting contrary to your values and learn to honor them in the future–in your outer life. This is what recovery is about: integrating inner with outer and thereby creating integrity. *(p. 3)*

The book's length is 251 pages. There is a chapter devoted to each Step and there are several additional chapters entitled "A Step Before the Steps," "A Step After," "Self," "Relationship," "Sexuality," and "Spirituality."

Below is an interpretation from the book for each of the Steps:

91

Step 1 The first step in recovery is to look inside ourselves. Turning inward is the beginning of becoming more truthful with ourselves. Honesty is essential because addictions thrive on *dis*honesty: we have become accustomed to hiding from our true feelings and values. (p. 15)

Step 2 What can we believe in? Whom can we trust? The problem is that *life is more difficult and empty without someone or something to trust and believe in.* (p. 27)

Step 3 Of course, simple things aren't always easy. This Step says we turn our will over. When we cling to our will – our fierce determination that things should always go our way – we'll always be in conflict with something. Our willfulness keeps us pushing against, not flowing with life. (p. 51)

Step 4 When we carry intense guilt, we can hardly bear the thought of reviewing our past deeds. It may feel too painful to think about how we have hurt others and hurt ourselves. We may question the value of opening old wounds and remembering scenes we'd rather forget. It was a revelation to discover that Step Four wasn't just about agonizing about the past. Instead, it was about getting to know myself better. (p. 59)

Step 5 The Fifth Step offers healing. It shows us how to create a new kind of relationship with people. We make ourselves vulnerable and open, allowing ourselves to be seen for who we really are, maybe for the first time. (p. 93)

Step 6 In this Step we become willing to be open to change, willing to let go of habits or traits that cause our lives to be unbalanced. We become open to a deeper knowing and a clearer vision. (p. 95)

Step 7 But for all of our awareness, we may still not accept ourselves. Step Seven gives us the opportunity to move from self-awareness to self-acceptance. Acceptance is the key to change. Another paradox I have learned in recovery is that when *I accept myself just as I am*, I can change. (p. 120)

Step 8 Where is there ongoing bitterness, animosity, fear or hostility in our relationships? Whom do we resent or avoid? But as we continue to work this Step, we realize that "harm" has other meanings as well. We might want to consider relationships that feel unresolved – whether we believe we've harmed someone or not. Is there unfinished business to attend to? (p. 122)

Step 9 What does it mean to make amends to another person? It means taking responsibility for your part in a relationship. *Responsibility* refers to the ability to respond appropriately. When you do, you extend hope for something new to yourself and to another person. (p. 137)

Step 10 Now we make a daily commitment to continuing observation and reflection – recognizing when we're out of balance or hurting ourselves or others. Our ongoing awareness allows us to meet each day and each relationship with responsibility. (p. 152)

Step 11 We can choose whatever practice gives us a sense of inner peace. (p. 173)

Step 12 With recovery this can mean that we offer a straightforward explanation of the Twelve Steps, as well as our own personal experience – how we reworked, translated, revised, or otherwise molded the Steps until they were relevant to us. We all have more to offer than the party line and a by-the-book recitation of the Steps. We can share our story any way we like. (p. 188)

This book not only provides an outlet for the author's interpretation of the Steps, but each Step is also explored through the voices of other women in recovery, Women who have traveled "through and around" the Steps, having carefully examined the language and concepts, and discovered what fits or what doesn't for them. The women Covington interviewed for the book are not experts or voices of authority, but women who have created a personal interpretation of the Steps by listening to their own inner voices and the voices of other women in recovery.

The Varieties of Recovery Experience

> The roads to recovery are many."
>
> Bill W, 1944

Reviewed by Roger C.

At about 40 pages in length, *The Varieties of Recovery Experience* is an intriguing essay.

No-one should be misled by the brevity of the work, however. It is crammed with information, much of it the result of research in the field of alcoholism and addiction.

The authors distinguish between **pathways**, **styles** and **frameworks** of recovery.

They have a chapter on **the varieties of twelve-step experience**, followed by a chapter called, "**Still Other Varieties**."

They define **recovery** and examine its **scope** and **depth**. There is a section on the **durability** of recovery.

The authors of *The Varieties of Recovery Experience* distinguish between **solo**, **treatment-assisted** and **peer-assisted recovery**.

All of these distinctions are important to those of us who wish to have a greater understanding of addiction and recovery.

There is plenty of overlap in the various modes of recovery and addiction. To provide just one example, the authors point out that "(solo) recovery, treatment-assisted recovery and peer-assisted styles of recovery are not mutually exclusive. AA's 2004 membership survey reveals that 64% of AA members received some type of treatment or counselling prior to joining AA" And roughly the same percentage of members continues to receive treatment after joining the fellowship.

Three recovery "frameworks" are outlined in the essay: religious, spiritual and secular. These are different ways of understanding the path or means to achieving and maintaining sobriety or abstinence from drugs.

In **a purely religious framework**…

groups share a religious interpretation of the roots of addiction (e.g., as a sin of the flesh, idolatry or demonic possession), recovery founded on a total surrender to a religious deity, a religiously-based reconstruction of personal identity and values, and immersion in a faith based community.

The religious framework of recovery involves "confession, restitution, and forgiveness" as key to personal development along with the use of "prayer, reading, and witnessing (service to others) as daily rituals of recovery."

Members of AA will recognize a number of components of a religious recovery framework embedded in the 12 Steps.

This should not be surprising. The co-founders of AA (Bill W and Dr Bob) were both members of the Oxford Group, a protestant evangelical religious movement which was in its heyday in the 1930s.

The authors of *The Varieties of Recovery Experience* then go on to affirm that both religious and spiritual pathways "flow out of the human condition of wounded imperfection (what William James, 1902, referred to as 'torn-to-pieces-hood'), involve experiences of connection with resources within and beyond the self, and involve a core set of values (e.g., humility gratitude, and forgiveness)."

The spiritual approach is not attached to any particular dogma or creed but emerges from a personal sense of incompletness.

> Spirituality as a medium of recovery is rooted in the understanding that human beings: 1) are born with a vacuum inside themselves that craves to be filled with meaning, 2) can artificially and temporarily fulfill this need through the medium of drug intoxication, and that 3) more authentic and lasting frameworks of meaning can displace the craving for intoxication.

Those with a spiritual approach to recovery are comfortable with a 12 Step program of recovery, the Buddhist eightfold path or any other way forward, often in combination.

Whereas religious and spiritual frameworks of recovery involve going beyond and outside of oneself, **a secular path** to recovery involves an affirmation of the self and "the ability of each individual to rationally direct his or her own self-change processes."

Irrational beliefs about oneself and the world and ineffective coping skills are the roots of addiction, according to organizations such as SOS (the Secular Organization for Sobriety), founded by Jim Christopher in 1985.

The three frameworks of recovery have much in common but also differ in important ways, as well. All three paths involve (1) an essential "re-visioning" of self (2) a new understanding of one's place and role in the world, and (3) "a restructuring of life-stance (what is accepted as being of ultimate importance) and lifestyle." Interestingly enough, the authors report that these modes of recovery also share a three part story format as part of the re-visioning and restructuring process in which people share "in a general way what we used to be like, what happened, and what we are like now."

The authors affirm that of the three frameworks of recovery, AA is a spiritual path. In fact they write: "One of AA's innovations was its emancipation of spirituality from its explicitly religious roots."

There is, however, plenty of evidence to suggest that AA has not yet extricated itself from the clutches of its early Christian and faith-based origins. Indeed, it may take more than adding "as we understood Him" after the word "God" in the suggested 12 steps of recovery to achieve the much-touted emancipation of spirituality within the fellowship of AA.

Regardless of that, this is a wonderful and very scholarly essay.

The three frameworks of recovery discussed here form only a small part of its 40 or so pages (plus an extensive bibliography).

The authors have undertaken to explore "the growing varieties of pathways and styles through which people are resolving serious and persistent alcohol and other drug-related problems." The paper is a presentation in summary fashion all of the things we might want to know about alcoholism, addiction and recovery. It is remarkably successful in this effort.

And who are the authors?

None other than William White, author of many works on recovery including *Slaying the Dragon: The History of Addiction Treatment and Recovery in America* and Ernest Kurtz, author of *Not God: A History of Alcoholics Anonymous.*

Of Bill White and Ernie Kurtz it can confidently be said that "they know whereof they speak."

The Alternative 12 Steps: A Secular Guide to Recovery

Reviewed by Chris G.

In 1991, two women were successfully working their 12-Step programs… and they were atheists. They knew the program worked, and each had translated the Steps into secular terms for her own use. This book is their sharing of this secular translation.

And it is their gift to us.

The book is currently out of print. It was no doubt ahead of its time. There are now many secular groups forming, and the Internet is full of secular – non-religious – 12-Step activity.

It is time the book had a second release and thus this ebook version is proudly brought to you and published by AA Agnostica.

Simple in language and well organized, Martha and Arlys have captured the spirituality, depth and scope of the 12 Steps in a religiously-neutral way. The book is addiction-neutral as well; you don't have to be an alcoholic to find answers here. Tradition 5, for example, is translated into "Each group has one purpose: to be a support for recovering people." It's hard to get more inclusive than that.

This is my own experience on finding this book:

A few years ago when I first came to AA, I was a very sick drunk, and I only wanted some relief from the torture of drinking without end, unable to stop or even slow down. I was mentally, physically, morally and spiritually broke. The 12 Steps were about the first thing I met, and I was assured that if I learned what they meant, and what to do with them, I could stop drinking. That sounded good to me, and I eagerly applied myself to them, along with joining a group and getting a sponsor.

Like a miracle, it worked. Within a few weeks, the craving was gone most of the time. Within a year, I had "done" the 12 steps. I was recovering in mind and body. This progress continued for the next two years or so.

Then a strange thing happened. I began to get bored with the literature and bored in meetings. I got especially bored with the "god thing". The progress slowed down. As my mind cleared, my life-long agnosticism reasserted itself.

I realized that the easy faith enjoyed by many of my co-AAs was not going to cut it for me any longer. I had given it my best shot, but the Jesus road was not for me.

What to do? I sure was not going to give up, stop going to meetings, and maybe drink again. AA does fix drunks, first and foremost, never doubt that, but hitting the overwhelming local Christianity with my agnostic head was becoming a serious pain.

I began to explore the Internet for whatever might be going on with agnostic alcoholics. And of course it turns out that there is a very great deal going on. Many thousands of AAs are squarely in the same dilemma... and they are doing what AAs do best: sharing their experience, strength and hope with other alcoholics!

Through a long series of happy connections – my religious friends would probably use the word "miracle" – I was introduced to The Alternative 12 Steps: A Secular Guide to Recovery. And what a book it is. The title nowhere nearly does it justice. I started reading and stayed up nearly all night to finish it. It gave me the information and inspiration I needed to restart my program.

Take AA's Twelve Steps and Twelve Traditions, written by Bill W. in 1952, with it's (perfectly natural) heavy cultural background of Christianity. Now take 40 years of the experience of millions of people – sufferers and professionals alike – and distil what they have done with the original "12 & 12" down into 134 pages of concise, readable, understandable, practical actions. This is not just for AA. It is not just about being secular. This is the 12 Steps unleashed as an engine of recovery for almost anyone with an addiction of any kind.

Martha and Arlys scarcely address what we call "the God problem" at all, except in the introduction, as an impediment for many people who could otherwise do a 12-Step program. They don't have to, for what they do is find the root power of each step, and translate it into plain simple language of everyday life. Anybody can understand this. To use the steps, there is no need for any particular religiosity; nor is there any need for psycho-jargon. This is the 12 Steps for anyone.

When most of us come into AA, we feel that our craving is a problem that we have to solve. Many of us spend untold hours and angst "fighting the problem" or trying to "solve the problem". If we are lucky or maybe just work at it long enough, we realize that there is no problem at all to solve. We change and grow in certain ways, the craving disappears, and the "problem" simply evaporates. As Martha puts it in Step 1:

And this is when amazing things happen. When we stop trying to manage and control our problems, we mysteriously stop doing the things that are causing us the trouble.

In much the same way, the clash of religious tradition with non-religious sufferers – "the God problem" – need not be any problem at all if you think like Martha and Arlys. Addiction is a human condition. It eventually corrupts all our activity and behaviour. No matter how we come into addiction, we end up in a morass of confusion and hurt on every level. The 12 Steps, along with the support of our fellows, can guide our actions and thinking in such a way as to lead us out of this confusion. No religion is needed, but neither is it excluded. The 12 Steps, as presented here, are simply religion-neutral.

For example, in discussing Step 2:

> Step 2 tells us we can use spiritual resources beyond our own ordinary personal power to restore and heal ourselves… Lots of us confuse spirituality and religion. The words are often used interchangeably and we must realize that they shouldn't be, for they have different meanings. To call religion spiritual is true, but religion is only one source of spiritual power. There are many, many others.

One of the tools we need is spirituality. Yes, religion has it, but it is abundant elsewhere. Simply find it and use it. But how? What is spirituality? That is often a slippery word to define. The authors put it so well:

> The phrase "spiritual resources" can be interpreted in many ways. Does it have to mean something great and mystical? Probably not. Does it mean there are a certain number of clearly-defined sources of power that we can tap into? No. There are many sources of spiritual power, more than any of us will ever be aware of or be able to use.
>
> Spiritual power comes from whatever gives us peace, hope or strength and enhances our humanity.

In the Introduction, Martha and Arlys tell the stories of their 12-Step experience and introduce the purpose of the book. As Arlys says:

> This book is a map for anyone to use. But it is not a detail map or a topographical one. It is a map that only the person using it can understand – to others it may make no sense. It is to be followed within the context of each individual life. Each person's destinations will be unique, each person determines how far he or she will go

and how long it will take. The important thing is to decide to take the trip. It starts with the First Step.

In Chapter 1, "What Is Your Suffering," the story of Bill W. and Dr. Bob is used to introduce the 12-Step origins and concepts, and to make the point that the 12-Step program can be used by anyone, not just alcoholics. Chapter 2, "A Program For Living" gives an overview of the 12-Step program – what is it? How do we live it? What can we gain from it?

Chapters 3 through 13 examine the 12 Steps. Each one is broken down into easily digestible pieces, and many contain real-world examples from real individuals. This is the meat of the book.

Chapter 14 is devoted to "Groups: Shared Energy for Growth" – how they should function, why they are important, what to look for in a group that will meet your needs.

The 12 Traditions are covered in Chapter 14 as well. All are stated in religious – and addiction-neutral terms, the most remarkable being Tradition 2: "Group conscience is the group's authority. Decisions are arrived at by group conscience. Minority ideas get thoughtful attention. Leaders themselves have no authority; they are trusted servants."

"How To Work A Program," Chapter 15, is eminently practical advice on what you actually do in working a 12-Step program – what to focus on, the mind-set, how a group fits in, what to do every day. This is especially good guidance for anyone approaching a program for the first time, or for anyone who is trying but floundering a bit.

In the last chapter, "The Ongoing Journey," Arlys and Martha share their own experiences with where the program has taken them…up to the present…for both are continuing the journey…it has no end.

I hope I made it clear that I am very happy to have found this book, for the furtherance of my own personal program as an agnostic AA. Here is an anecdote that is worth telling: I am currently taking a sponsee through the steps. He is an AA, he has been through the revolving door a couple of times, he is very familiar with the "canonical" AA literature – and he is a reasonable devout and practising Catholic. I have begun using this book as an adjunct to the Big Book. He absolutely loves it. He is finding the plain-talk "what, why and how" tremendously enlightening – it is giving him a whole new start on his program, and does not interfere at all with his religious beliefs. The neutral and yet inclusive treatment of the Steps is amazing.

The one thing that grabbed me most when I first read this book was Step 7. Step 7 had been causing me a lot of concern – the big hand reaching down and plucking out my bad bits was an image I just couldn't handle. Martha and Arlys have an approach to Step 7 that I can really get a grip on. It becomes a human action step:

> We begin to change by actively letting go of our shortcomings, our actions and feelings that are liabilities. We cut our losses and start again. We begin by discarding old patterns of acting and old ways of thinking. We let go with slow, cautious and reluctant moves…

> Effort alone is progress, and we value our progress more than we value the perfection of the outcome. We learn not to judge our efforts in the short term because deep and lasting change for the long term takes a long time.

> Little by little, step by step, stage by stage, we will reach a goal. And when we look back, we can't really explain how we got there. So much depends on our willingness to "become entirely ready" and to work hard. So much depends on our willingness to be open to the spiritual energy that strengthens us. But for each of us it will happen, and we are grateful and we move forward.

> Work honestly, humbly and courageously to develop our assets and to release our personal shortcomings.

This is a process I can really work with.

The Big Book says in Appendix II, Spiritual Experience, "that the personality change sufficient to bring about recovery from alcoholism has manifested itself among us in many different forms." Martha and Arlys present many ways indeed to work on making this change happen, without reference to divine intervention. I hope that this review will encourage you to explore them, no matter what your experience into the 12 Steps has been to date.

If you choose to do that, you will have a hard time finding a better book than The Alternative 12 Steps: A Secular Guide to Recovery.

IV. Founders of We Agnostics in 1980 (Hollywood)

Megan D.

By Megan D.

The "God stuff" was difficult for me to swallow when I first achieved sobriety. As a working professional, my career meant everything to me but I was near to blowing it – big time. Fortunately, I decided none too soon, I'd be a son of a gun if I'd lose everything I'd worked for for years due to my alcoholism.

Having come from a chaotic family, I despised alcoholics, especially the women. Now, as a middle-aged woman myself, I was knee deep in self-loathing. So, as we do, I stumbled through the doors of AA with a load of resentments that was killing me.

The candlelight meeting I attended weekly was in the basement of a run-down church in Hollywood. I finally raised my hand and shared that I was an atheist and had paid enormous dues to be one. No one threw me out. Rather, they nodded their heads, and told me to keep coming back!

Despite being close to ending my own life, I despised their two-dimensional views. So I kept coming back – since there was no place left to go – above ground, that is!

After a time, a gentleman of about 60, with a woolen scarf and navy blue beret, approached me, "I noticed you weren't saying The Lord's Prayer." My response of "Yeah – what of it?" brought only laughter.

With over nine years of sobriety he claimed there were many like us working the program and fully enjoying the promises. I was amazed and for the first time breathed easier.

When I was six months sober, he presented me with an idea after visiting family in Texas where he'd attended meetings with some NASA scientists who'd resolved the God problem. "How would you like to help me start such a meeting in Los Angeles for AAs and newcomers who are having a tough time with God like you did?" I said, "You've got it!"

With childlike enthusiasm, we named our meeting "We Agnostics," after Chapter 4 in the Big Book.

The first meeting started in the summer of 1980 in West Hollywood.

Like Goldilocks, with porridge that was too cold, too hot, or just right, we were on a quest to discover a higher power that we could turn our worries over to. I soon realized I was on what I call a return to innocence.

We attracted brilliant sober and not sober members from many world denominations like Christian, Jew, Buddhist, atheist, agnostic, etc. The goal was to welcome newcomers; offer a safe setting to explore ideas. We assured them they could have a spiritual experience regardless of their beliefs. They could reap the rewards of AA – but only if they were willing to work for them.

To my great relief, I realized I had at least three higher powers. The universe – as solid as our earth in many cases, was the first. My highest self – my most evolved or selfless nature was the second. And of course the wisdom expressed at AA meetings – a power greater than myself.

Some painfully won lessons I've learned over the years are these:

> • A problem with the "God stuff" is not a viable excuse unless your NEED TO PICK UP A DRINK is greater than your NEED TO NOT PICK UP A DRINK.

> • Attend meetings often... and get a sponsor. They've had their own struggle.

> • Learn to really listen and focus on the similarities in members, not the differences. Our diversity is our strength.

> • Develop a spiritual connection with your own concept of a higher power. You'll find that there's a profound difference between religiosity and spirituality. Incidentally, many have returned to the traditions of our childhood, but taking only what works!

> • Prayer is great therapy. Charlie P. taught me that when in pain, try getting down on your knees like I've learned doing – with gratitude, reaching out to the universe or to your highest self or whatever. Nothing bad ever happens – only good comes from it!

> • Use the tool of translation. Remember G.O.D. as Good Orderly Direction if you like.

I don't know about you, but I never wanted a small piece of the pie of life. If I can't have the whole pie, I don't want any. In other words, I am willing to work towards being happy, joyous, and free – whatever that takes.

On January 19, 2011, Charlie celebrated his 97th year with 40 years of sobriety... and I am greatly honored to have celebrated my 70th year with 31 years of sobriety.

My life has changed considerably. To this day, I remain part atheist, humanist or Buddhist. Over the years I've learned to take each day as it comes. Admittedly, some are more challenging than others. But the bottom line is that most are happy, joyous, and free – because today the tools in my satchel are solid.

Epilogue

Eventually I started a second agnostics meeting in the San Fernando Valley, and I named it Wee Agnostics rather than We Agnostics. It was We Agnostics without the anger.

It was in a hospital with a detox ward. One day, a woman who was visiting a family member in that ward, came into our meeting without knowing that it was Wee Agnostics.

Towards the end of the meeting, she shared. She said that she was a nun and that she had just walked in cold. She said she rarely had gone to a more spiritual meeting. Instead of a "god" we had made "love" our higher power.

The next week, she led the meeting.

Over the years, I've had a priest take my hand, leading me from the podium to a silent and startled crowd saying that the atheists he's come in contact with in the program are among the most spiritual people he's known.

Father of We Agnostics Dies

By Shawn M.

I learned tonight that my AA sponsor, Charlie P, passed away in Austin, Texas at the age of 98.

Within recovery communities, one hears much about sponsors. Charlie was both a son of a gun and a saint. Also, the most spiritual man I have ever encountered. That is really saying something about a guy who claimed to be a raging atheist (more on that later).

Many years ago I was "meeting shopping" and in the Los Angeles AA Directory I noticed a meeting called "We Agnostics." There is a chapter in the AA Big Book titled "We Agnostics." In essence, the chapter emphasizes that all drunks come into AA as agnostics and godless but, over time, they rid themselves of that ridiculous concept and see the path towards a Higher Power (code speak for the more commonly used word – God). I thought this "We Agnostics" meeting was either one of two things, a Big Book thumpers meeting or – just maybe – something more interesting. It was indeed more interesting and was located on Barrington Avenue in a big old wood home which was part of the Unitarian Fellowship.

My first meeting there truly made me see the unique, complex components that make up the AA fellowship. This was a group of people that did not subscribe to any notion of canned theology or cultish adherence to anything besides this: "no matter what" one does not put alcohol anywhere near the lips or nostrils. Also, if craving or life itself made you feel like jumping out of your skin, you must pick up the phone and talk with another meeting member. We help each other "no matter what." That was the guiding principle of the LA We Agnostics AA group. Simple concept.

At the end of this meeting an old guy, obviously from NYC, asked me if I was a real alcoholic. I answered in the affirmative. He handed me a piece of paper that looked like one of the slips from a fortune cookie. This guy, Charlie, told me to call him sometime and we'd chat about the Higher Power stuff or anything else about being an alcoholic in the rooms of AA. By the way, the piece of fortune cookie paper he handed me simply said "Charlie" and had a seven digit phone number (he assumed, even then, everyone still lived in the 213 area code). Charlie had brought the AA We Agnostics format to California.

I still have that little slip of paper.

I called Charlie. It was a journey speaking with Charlie. After a month I asked Charlie to sponsor me and he laid out his ground rules. The criteria were, for me, stern and disciplined. This man was not into holding my hand.

He was not an easy sponsor. Doing the Steps with Charlie was hardly a warm, pleasant experience. Brutal in fact. Much better than almost any shrink I had ever encountered and overwhelmingly wise. That was my first Steps go around. Subsequent redoing of the Steps work proved simply enlightening with Charlie. It helped keep me sober then and still does now.

As the years passed, I watched Charlie perform countless acts of real kindness – without an audience. For example: I was at meeting when a deeply disturbed schizophrenic whose personal hygiene was lacking raised his hand and asked for a meal and a ride to a shelter. Charlie quietly took the man and led him out the door – and then into his car. Nobody noticed but me. Not a word was spoken about it. The personal hygiene deficient man kept coming around and the same routine continued for well over a year. Once he (the lacking-hygiene man) showed up clean shaven with clean clothes and looking nourished and healthy. Charlie's doing. This is but one small example. Charlie gave again and again – without looking for attention. To him, having acts of kindness witnessed or acknowledged somehow cheapened the act.

He was not merely about the 12th Step but adhering to a life of giving of oneself – always with unconditional love.

Charlie claimed to be a staunch atheist. His heritage was Jewish but unlike many atheistic Jews, Charlie did not observe the holidays or traditions. That would have been a treasonous act to Charlie. Yet, in later years, after endless hours discussing the definitions of God from the perspective of many belief systems and the nature of the universe from a philosophical stance, Charlie said to me that he had discovered a definition of "God" that he could tolerate. That power greater than himself was the "E" in the equation "$E=mc2$."

That worked for Charlie and I can embrace his logic.

Charlie's higher purpose and power was the act of loving and all the Energy (the "E" in "$E=mc2$" equation) contained throughout the universe (both known and unknown). Charlie gave unselfishly and saved countless lives. He did not care to keep score. He was a very devoted loving husband, father, grandfather and great-great-grandfather. Charlie was significant contributor.

He saved lives and reinstalled the ability to experience joy into many hearts. He was a holy man.

Charlie had a good run. A life worth living and I am forever grateful to have known this man.

In honor of Charlie, let's never forget the "no matter what" principle of the Los Angeles We Agnostics. My salute and love to Charlie P.

Charlie P, AA founder of "We Agnostics" in Los Angeles, California in 1978 and in Austin, Texas in 2001, passed away on February 27, 2012, after a year of failing health. He was 98 years old and had 41 years of sobriety in AA. Charlie remained active in the program, holding AA meetings at his bedside and receiving AA visitors up to the last week of his life. Two memorial services were held for him, one at the Northland AA Club in Austin, Texas and a second in Los Angeles, California.

He had many sponsees and affected the lives of many people in AA. Since and in response to Shawn's post, others have shared their knowledge of Charlie:

An elder statesman (by Richard N): As an "elder statesman" of the fellowship, he was never demanding, always accepting. He got all teary-eyed when I told him about my estranged daughter's phone call, after several years of not speaking to me, and then more years of my successful sobriety. She said, "I feel like I've got my Daddy back." As a loving father himself, he really identified with that. Charlie was a Jew and definitely an atheist, so I don't think the Vatican will canonize him any time soon. But in my loving memory he will always be Saint Charlie.

Candles and Charlie (by Sandra B.): I remember Charlie from my early days in sobriety and I knew he was an atheist. Started We Agnostics group and was one of the best AA members to ever have graced the earth. I call myself a Christian and I can't hold a candle to Charlie. RIP Charlie P.

He made a difference (by Bruce K.): My life is infinitely richer having known and loved Charlie P. He made a huge difference in my life, and the lives of countless others. He taught us the true meaning of living rigorously honest, consistently responsible, and unconditionally loving lives. And this very public atheist was truly one of the happiest and most spiritual people I've ever known. Those of us fortunate enough to have known him will carry little bits of Charlie's message and love with us, and we'll pass it on to others so that they also can also benefit from Charlie's experience, strength and hope. Thank you Charlie P.

He was legit (by kkash): Charlie. My friend. He lived the richest life of anyone I have ever known. He was brilliant, always cheerful, adored by his family, admired by his friends. Charlie shared his secret to living well often and it was this: "To live well, practice these principles – rigorous honesty, unconditional love, and consistent responsibility." He was legit.

His legacy continues to help (Nick H.): I met Charlie when he moved to Austin in 2000. He also handed me one of his pieces of paper with his name and phone number. During his last 12 years in Austin he became an icon (as it were) of the AA community in Austin and was loved by many all along the belief continuum. Through his influence the number of freethinkers meetings in Austin went from 0 to 6 per week. He has directly and indirectly helped and his legacy continues to help many people who would normally have walked away from a less tolerant AA.

V. Lord's Prayer

A Proposal to Eliminate the Lord's Prayer from AA Meetings

This is an excerpt of a document that was written on an Olympia manual typewriter and circulated by John L in New York City in 1976. There is nothing at all in this work that does not apply today, thirty-five years later.

By John L.

All too many AA meetings end with a group recitation of the "Lord's Prayer" (also known as the "Our Father"), a prayer peculiar to the Christian religion. This practice is wrong — contrary to the spirit of AA unity, and in obvious violation of the Third Tradition and the AA Preamble.

AA members can believe in anything they wish, including the fables of the Christian religion, but they have no right to exclude freethinkers from full membership in the AA fellowship. And we atheists and agnostics are not the only ones involved. There are also Jews, Moslems, Buddhists, Hindus, and many others who are recovering alcoholics.

The AA Preamble

The AA Preamble states: "*AA is not allied with any sect, denomination, politics, organization or institution.*" This is clear enough. If anyone claims that the habitual recitation of the so-called Lord's Prayer does not violate the AA Preamble, then he has the obligation to explain what the Preamble *secretly* means, as opposed to what it so clearly says.

The Third Tradition

The Third Tradition says: "The only requirement for AA membership is a desire to stop drinking." It does not say, "first-class membership for Christians, second-class membership for everyone else." It is true that no one is "forced" to say the "Lord's Prayer". The fact remains that someone who is not a Christian is forced into either dishonestly saying something he doesn't believe, or feeling left out as everyone else in the room participates in a Christian prayer ritual. This is unfair and unnecessary.

The Honesty Part of the Program

Many AA members are not Christians, and their sobriety compares favorably with that of the Christian religionists. Nevertheless, the pressure towards conformity is sufficiently great that most of these non-Christian members stand up during the "Lord's Prayer" (though many of them don't say anything, or just mumble, or keep their eyes open). They are afraid of "standing out," and probably — with reason — of being ostracized.

No one's sobriety is helped if he is forced to pretend to be something he's not, forced to say something he doesn't believe, and forced to do something he believes is wrong. AA should encourage honesty, not hypocrisy.

But Isn't It Traditional?

Reciting the "Lord's Prayer" after meetings is indeed a *habit*, and if it is a bad habit, then it ought to be broken. Every sober AA member has broken a dangerous and insidious habit, and it should not be too hard to stay away from the "Lord's Prayer," one meeting at a time.

What Makes AA Work?

Probably all sober alcoholics would agree that a requirement for sobriety is not picking up the first drink. Aside from that, alcoholics would give a variety of answers, for AA is an individual program.

I would say that for me, AA consists of the realization that I am powerless over alcohol; that total abstinence is required on a 24-hour basis; that alcoholics can provide practical help and moral support for each other; that life is worth living and things can get better; that honesty is the basis for lasting sobriety; and so on.

There is no evidence that religious belief is necessary for good sobriety. Thousands of alcoholics have stayed sober and helped others to sobriety without having the slightest belief in the supernatural, let alone the Christian version. In the Scandinavian countries, the steps have been reduced to seven, eliminating all references to "God", and AA seems to work just fine without "Him."

What Harm Does It Do?

The "Lord's Prayer" recitation is offensive to non-Christians. It makes it harder for us to feel comfortable in the AA fellowship and it undoubtedly prevents many non-Christian alcoholics from coming to AA in the first place. Who knows how many thousands of alcoholics never made AA because they were afraid it was a religious organization. And their fears will hardly be dispelled when they hear a Christian Prayer at their first meeting.

What If The Group Conscience Wants The Lord's Prayer?

If so, then the group should officially designate itself a Christian group, whose meetings would be terminated with a Christian prayer. It would be a special purpose group, and should be so listed in the meeting book. Just as there are special purpose groups for young people, or men, or women, or gay people, this would be a special group for Christians.

If a group is open to all who have a desire to stop drinking, then its meetings should not feature a sectarian religious practice that excludes those who are not Christian religionists.

Conclusion

The "Lord's Prayer" should no longer be recited at the end of AA meetings.

John L. (East Village) 1976.

John L. was born and raised in Nebraska. He attended Harvard College (AB 1963), majoring in Social Relations (Sociology, Anthropology and Psychology). In New York City he worked as a market research executive, writing on the side. He was in the antiwar movement since 1965 and the Gay Liberation movement since July 1969.

He founded Pagan Press in 1982 ("Pagan" denoting western Classical Antiquity). For a decade, beginning in 1985, John was a leading writer for the New York Native, which was then the foremost gay newspaper. He has twelve books to his credit. His writings have been widely translated.

John dates his alcoholism from his first bender in 1958 to his last drink in 1968. He considers himself a loyal, but by no means uncritical, member of AA.

John now lives in Dorchester, Massachusetts. He has an alcoholism section (paganpressbooks.com/jpl/ALK-FREE.HTM) on his website. His latest book, A Freethinker in Alcoholics Anonymous, is scheduled for publication in the next few months.

The Lord's Prayer and the Law

By Roger C.

North Americans appear to be getting used to life without the Lord's Prayer.

Many now accept that the recitation in public of a prayer associated with one particular religion is a form of discrimination against those who are not members of that religion or who are not members of any religion.

They accept that in a public environment there should be some effort made to respect the dignity and rights of all those present.

However, this does not apply to all Americans and Canadians. Some of our more religious members still resent the removal of religious observance in public places.

And in the rooms of AA, the Lord's Prayer is ever present, recited in many parts of North America at the end of meetings.

It begs the question, why do so many in AA still cling to the Lord's Prayer? Why have the changes seen in other important public forums not caught on in AA? How has AA somehow managed to remain anchored in a 1935 context, exempt from legal prohibitions against public prayer that have since been imposed on other organizations and institutions?

These questions are especially relevant when we look at how over the past fifty years various judicial bodies have reacted to the the public recitation of the Lord's Prayer.

The United States Supreme Court

Prayer in public schools in the United States has been prohibited since 1962 as a result of a Supreme Court decision.

The Court ruled on a case, (*Engel v. Vitale*) in which the parents of ten students filed an objection to a prayer that was said aloud each morning by students and teachers in public schools in New York. (Engel was one of the parents and Vitale was the president of the targeted school board.)

The prayer had been written by the State Board of Regents and so was known as the Regent's Prayer:

Almighty God, we acknowledge our dependence upon Thee, and we beg Thy blessings upon us, our parents, our teachers and our Country.

The parents argued that the use of this official prayer in the public schools was contrary to their own and their children's beliefs. Based upon the First Amendment of the American Constitution, the Court ruled that "it is no part of the business of government to compose official prayers for any group." Justice Hugo Black, delivering the opinion of the Court, went on to affirm that the State should not in any way "ordain or support" any religion "as one the greatest dangers to the freedom of the individual to worship in his own way lay in the Government's placing its official stamp of approval upon one particular kind of prayer." (*Engel v. Vitale*)

The Court was echoing Thomas Jefferson. The third President of the United States, and known for his religious tolerance, Jefferson had once written, "It does me no injury for my neighbor to say there are twenty gods or no God. It neither picks my pocket nor breaks my leg." (Notes on Virginia, 1782) But he will forever be remembered for his affirmation in 1802 of the need for "a wall of separation between Church and State."

This principle was clearly on the mind of Justice Hugo Black when he delivered the Supreme Court decision 160 years later that ended the use of prayer – including the Lord's Prayer – in public schools in the United States of America.

For the fifty years since then children in American schools have somehow survived without a daily dose of "Our Father."

The Ontario Court of Appeal

In Canada, children have been without the Lord's Prayer at the beginning or end of the school day for much less time.

It was only in 1982 that Canada adopted its own *Charter of Rights and Freedoms*. "Everyone has the right to the following fundamental freedoms," it begins and at the top of the list in the Charter is the "freedom of conscience and religion."

Six years later, in 1988, the Ontario Court of Appeal heard a case in which several parents, one of whom was Philip Zylberberg, objected to prayer at the beginning of the school day (*Zylberberg v. The Sudbury Board of Education*) on the grounds that it infringed their children's "freedom of conscience and religion," as guaranteed by the Charter.

113

Zylberberg was a Jewish man who, as a boy, had to stand outside in the school hallway during the Lord's Prayer. When he learned that his own children would have to stand in the hall just like he did, Zylberberg, a lawyer, decided to take legal action.

Every school in the Board's jurisdiction opened its day with the singing of "O Canada" and the reciting of the Lord's Prayer. The prayer was most often led by the classroom teacher or broadcast over the school's public address system. These practices were required by Section 28, Regulation 262 of the province's **Education Act**: "A public school shall be opened or closed each school day with religious exercises consisting of the reading of the Scriptures or other suitable readings and the repeating of the Lord's Prayer or other suitable prayers."

The Court of Appeal ruled that the "recitation of the Lord's Prayer, which is a Christian prayer... impose(s) Christian observances upon non-Christian pupils and religious observances on non-believers" and constituted a violation of the freedom of conscience and religion provisions in the Charter of Rights and Freedoms.

Zylberberg's children would no longer have to leave the room.

Interestingly, the respondents had not argued that the Lord's Prayer was not Christian but instead that no harm was done to those pupils who did not wish to participate in its recital. "The affidavits of two psychologists, filed by the Board, asserted that children from minority religions were not harmed by the policy... (They claimed) that religious exercises resulted in minority children 'confronting the fact of their difference from the majority.' This was said to be a normal and healthy part of growing up..."

Both matters were discussed in a letter written by AA co-founder Bill Wilson in 1959:

> There will always be those who seem to be offended by the introduction of any prayer whatever into an ordinary AA gathering. Also, it is sometimes complained that the Lord's Prayer is a Christian document. Nevertheless this Prayer is of such widespread use and recognition that the arguments of its Christian origin seems to be a little farfetched... Around here, the leader of the (AA) meeting usually asks those to join him in the Lord's Prayer who feel that they would care to do so. The worst that happens to the objectors is that they have to listen to it. This is doubtless a salutary exercise in tolerance at their stage of progress.

Any history student who suggested today that the Christian origin of the Lord's Prayer is "farfetched" would get an "F" for his or her contribution. Nevertheless, this dated idea is yet heard in the rooms of AA.

As for the notion that confronting one's differences with the praying majority is "a normal and healthy part of growing up" or "a salutary exercise in tolerance," the Ontario Court of Appeal found this suggestion "insensitive."

"The reality is that it imposes on religious minorities a compulsion to conform to the religious practices of the majority" the Court wrote in its decision. "(It) imposes a penalty on pupils from religious minorities... by stigmatizing them as non-conformists and setting them apart from their fellow students."

The need to seek exemption from saying the Lord's Prayer is in itself a form of religious discrimination and an "infringement of freedom of conscience and religion," the Court ruled.

Of course, some in AA may choose to ignore the American Supreme Court ruling or the decision by the Ontario Court of Appeals. AA is, after all, not a state institution.

However, the principles embedded in the American constitution and in the Canadian Charter of Rights are already beginning to have an impact on the now 77-year-old fellowship. If the history of the evolution of individual rights over the past few hundred years is any indication, this impact will inevitably become all the more powerful and significant in AA over the next several decades.

Between 1996 and 2007, for example, five High Courts in the United States ruled that neither the judicial system nor correctional facilities could force parolees, probationers or inmates to attend AA meetings. (*The Courts, AA and Religion*) The Courts ruled that a sufficient number of AA practices were "religious" and therefore coercing attendance at AA meetings would constitute a violation of the principle of the separation of church and state found in the First Amendment.

The High Court decisions were based in part on the presence of the Lord's Prayer at meetings:

> The "meetings were permeated with explicit religious content..." (*Kerr v. Farrey*, 1996)

> "Group prayer is common at the meetings attended by (the) petitioner. The meetings open with the 'Serenity Prayer,' essentially

115

non-denominational, and close with 'The Lord's Prayer', a Christian prayer." (*Arnold v. Tennessee Board of Paroles*, 1997)

The objection is to "any program that has explicit religious content. This includes, but is not limited to, the recitation of prayers at meetings, whether or not (someone in attendance) is required to participate in the prayer." (*Inouye v. Kemna*, 2007)

"All of the meetings ended with the Lord's Prayer, which is a specifically Christian prayer. In addition, those attending the meetings were strongly encouraged to pray." (*Griffin v. Coughlan*, 1996)

Not all probationers, inmates and parolees are opposed to attending AA or other 12-Step meetings. But these rulings – which are increasingly viewed as established law in the United States – make it more and more difficult over time for courts and prisons to force, facilitate or even encourage alcoholics to participate in AA.

It may be just this simple: the rules that define "religion" have become much clearer – and tighter – over the past three quarters of a century since the founding of AA. Calling the program "spiritual" but not "religious" doesn't cut it any longer.

For a fellowship that is committed to being there for all those who reach out for help, there should be some concern as these particular state/government sponsored doors to AA are slammed shut.

The Human Rights Tribunal of Ontario

There was quite the brouhaha the day Intergroup booted two agnostic groups off the official Toronto area AA meeting list.

At one point the representative for the soon-to-be-booted Beyond Belief group, Brian N, warned that excluding it from the meeting list and participation in regional AA meetings – on the basis of their lack of belief in a God – would be a violation of the *Ontario Human Rights Code* and that an official complaint could be launched with the *Human Rights Tribunal of Ontario*.

The hall at the Lansing United Church at Yonge and Sheppard erupted. "There was booing, hissing, shouts of 'bullshit' and other insightful comments," Brian, the duly chosen and recognized Intergroup representative of Beyond Belief, at the time, reported.

As far as many were concerned, this was strictly a matter of "group conscience" and the government had no place in the rooms of AA.

Brian's warning was based on the fact that the Ontario Human Rights Code prohibits discrimination based on religion (or "creed," as the Code puts it).

The provincial Code has actually been around longer than the federal Charter of Rights and Freedoms. It took effect in 1962, and was the first Human Rights Code of its kind in Canada.

Here is how the principle of freedom from discrimination on the basis of religion is articulated in the Code:

> Every person has the right to be free from discriminatory or harassing behaviour that is based on religion or which arises because the person who is the target of the behaviour does not share the same faith. This principle extends to situations where the person who is the target of such behaviour has no religious beliefs whatsoever, including atheists and agnostics who may, in these circumstances, benefit from the protection set out in the Code.

Nobody at Intergroup argued about why the two AA groups were expelled. It had everything to do with differences with regard to religious beliefs and practices.

Members of the agnostic groups had removed "God" from an agnostic version of the 12 Steps read at their meetings and published online on a page that was provided to them on the Intergroup website.

And of course, they did not say the Lord's Prayer at the close of their meetings.

In sum, the expulsion of the groups could reasonably be attributed to their non-acceptance of religious creed, to discrimination based upon religion.

Could a human rights complaint be filed, then, as Brian had warned?

Could an AA member argue, for example, that the recital of the Lord's Prayer at an AA meeting made him or her the target of discriminatory behaviour, in much the same way as its use in schools is considered an infringement of a pupil's freedom of conscience and religion under the Charter?

The Code covers specific areas such as jobs and services. As a "service provider," the fellowship of AA would no doubt fall under the jurisdiction of the Ontario Human Rights Code.

To benefit from "the protection set out in the Code" an AA member would have to lodge a formal complaint with the Human Rights Tribunal of Ontario.

In fiscal year 2011-2012 the Tribunal received a total of 2,740 new complaints. Out of all of these human rights complaints, 186 were filed on the basis of religious discrimination. Complaints are dealt with by the Tribunal through mediation. Where mediation fails, a hearing is held. As a result of such a hearing, an adjudicator may order a remedy to correct the discriminatory situation. As the Tribunal puts it: "A finding that a violation of the Code has occurred may lead to various orders, including monetary compensation, other forms of restitution to the applicant, and orders to take action to promote compliance with the Code."

The situation would no doubt be complicated by the lack of organization in AA. Moreover AA organizations are supposed to be strictly service organizations. (Tradition Nine: "AA, as such, ought never be organized; but we may create service boards or committees directly responsible to those they serve.") Nevertheless, the *Greater Toronto Area (GTA) Intergroup* has an executive committee, representatives from regional groups, regular monthly meetings, committees, an office and paid staff. Moreover, since it has sufficient authority to order that in the GTA "an AA group needs to adopt the 12 Steps, 12 Traditions and 12 Concepts of AA," as it ruled on June 26, 2012, it is certainly conceivable that Intergroup could be ordered by the Tribunal to take the necessary measures so that the Ontario Human Rights Code is respected within its jurisdiction.

There is one way that an AA group or service organization could avoid the kind of accommodations required by the Code. Under Section 18 of the Code it could identify itself as a "special interest organization."

Here, in full legalese, is what Section 18 says: "The rights under Part I to equal treatment with respect to services and facilities, with or without accommodation, are not infringed where membership or participation in a religious, philanthropic, educational, fraternal or social institution or organization that is primarily engaged in serving the interests of persons identified by a prohibited ground of discrimination is restricted to persons who are similarly identified."

In other words, if AA members wanted to identify themselves as a Christian organization and say the Lord's Prayer at the end of a meeting they would not have to accommodate those who come through the doors and don't like the Lord's Prayer.

But isn't that precisely what AA has been trying to avoid for the last 77 years?

What all of this means at the end of the day is that the bar for declaring that AA is "spiritual but not religious" is getting higher as society moves to demonstrably respect human rights via various Constitutions, Charters and Codes.

That society is moving in that direction should be celebrated by all.

Saying the Lord's Prayer in AA rooms "for all who suffer… regardless of their belief or lack of belief" may not be considered acceptable behaviour for much longer.

Self-Correction

A funny thing happened at the University of Windsor in Southwestern Ontario a few weeks ago.

For the first time in the university's history there was no prayer at its fall convocation ceremony. The graduation ceremony didn't "include an entreaty to God – nor any other religious reference," the *Windsor Star* reported.

The University of Windsor has been around for 155 years. It was founded by the Jesuits in 1857 and was initially named Assumption College. It accepted its first woman students in 1950. And it became the non-denominational University of Windsor through an Act of the Legislative Assembly of Ontario in 1962.

More than one hundred thousand students have graduated from the university since it was founded – and they have all done it with a Christian prayer.

The University's Office of *Human Rights, Equity and Accessibility* asserted that this was a "permanent" change and that it was done to promote "a more inclusive atmosphere" at the institution.

The move apparently was at least partly the result of a PhD student in clinical psychology. Shawna Scott, who is also the president of the Windsor-Essex County Atheist Society, wrote to the human rights office "about feeling 'extremely excluded and uncomfortable' when she was asked to stand in prayer for her undergraduate convocation in 2010."

Kaye Johnson, the university's Director of Human Rights, described the changes as timely and noted that if people only do what they have always done "we wouldn't have a lot of the advances that our society has made," the Star reported.

Then she said something that would remind at least a few AAers of something Bill Wilson once said. Johnson described the new secular format of the convocation ceremony as a way of "widening the circle."

In 1955 at AA's 20th Anniversary Convention, Bill expressed the belief that the agnostics and atheists in the early days of AA "had widened our gateway so that all who suffer might pass through, regardless of their belief or lack of belief."

History has not been kind to Bill's optimistic assessment.

More than half a century later, it is clear that much work remains to achieve that goal. More light must yet shine through the gateway so that all may feel at home in the rooms of Alcoholics Anonymous.

We know what needs to be done.

The Courts, AA and Religion

By Linda R.

Inside AA, one hears members frequently repeat the well-known phrase "AA is spiritual, not religious." AA takes pride in saying it's not religious. But what do outsiders, such as the court systems, think about AA's claim?

In the ten year period between 1996 and 2007, five high-level US courts — three federal circuit courts and two state supreme courts – did take a long and hard look at AA's claim. Each of these cases involved a person who was being forced to participate in AA meetings, either as a condition of their parole or probation, or while actually incarcerated. These cases reached the highest level of judiciary scrutiny — only one level below the US Supreme Court — because they involved the critical issue of separation of Church and State. This separation is a fundamental aspect of US law, known as the Establishment Clause, and is explicated in the first amendment to the US Constitution, which states "Congress shall make no law respecting an establishment of religion."

The parolees, probationers and inmates in each of these cases claimed that the State was using its power to force them to participate in a religious activity. They claimed that AA meetings were religious. Thus, their required attendance was a violation of the Establishment Clause, which requires governmental neutrality with respect to religion and a wall of separation between Church and State.

In Establishment Clause cases, the high-level courts use a three-part test to determine if the wall of separation has been violated. First, has the State acted? Second, does the action amount to coercion? And third, is the object of coercion religious rather than secular? The answer to the first part of the test was quickly answered: yes, these cases clearly showed action by the State, involving the governmental branches of probation, parole and imprisonment. The second test was likewise quickly answered: yes, the probationers, parolees and inmates were being coerced into AA attendance.

Next, the high-level courts addressed the third part of the test. They took a long look at the Big Book and its 200 references to God; a look at the Twelve Steps and their unmistakable references to God; the prayers in AA meetings; and based on a full examination of these, ruled that AA doctrines and practices must be viewed as religious. Because multiple high-level courts have ruled uniformly on this matter, these rulings now constitute "clearly established law" in the US. Here's what one of these courts, the New York Court of Appeals, in the case of *Griffin v. Coughlin*, had to say about the matter:

> A fair reading of the fundamental AA doctrinal writings discloses that their dominant theme is unequivocally religious.
>
> Indeed, the AA basic literature most reasonably would be characterized as reflecting the traditional elements common to most theistic religions. Thus, God is named or referred to in five of the 12 steps. "Working" the 12 steps includes confessing to God the "nature of our wrongs" (Step 5), appealing to God "to remove our shortcomings" (Step 7) and seeking "through prayer and meditation" to make "contact" with God and achieve "knowledge of His Will" (Step 11).
>
> While AA literature declares an openness and tolerance for each participant's personal vision of God "as we understood Him" (Steps 3 and 11), the writings demonstrably express an aspiration that each member of the movement will ultimately commit to a belief in the existence of a Supreme Being of independent higher reality than humankind.
>
> All of the meetings ended with the Lord's Prayer, which is a specifically Christian prayer. In addition, those attending the meetings were strongly encouraged to pray.
>
> The foregoing demonstrates beyond peradventure that doctrinally and as actually practiced in the 12-step methodology, adherence to the AA fellowship entails engagement in religious activity and religious proselytization. Followers are urged to accept the existence of God as a Supreme Being, Creator, Father of Light and Spirit of the Universe. In "working" the 12 steps, participants become actively involved in seeking such a God through prayer, confessing wrongs and asking for removal of shortcomings. These expressions and practices constitute, as a matter of law, religious exercise.
>
> Thus, while it is of course true that the primary objective of AA is to enable its adherents to achieve sobriety, its doctrine unmistakably urges that the path to staying sober and to becoming "happily and usefully whole," is by wholeheartedly embracing traditional theistic belief.

Arguments were presented to the high-level courts in an attempt to persuade them that the early AA texts had implicitly been superseded by later more secular doctrines. The courts were urged to discount the religious nature of the Big Book and 12 Steps, first written in 1939, and instead to rely exclusively on the 12 Traditions portion of the Twelve Steps and Twelve Traditions volume published in 1952. But the court rejected those arguments. It saw a dichotomy of roles between the 12 Steps on the one hand and the 12 Traditions on the other. The courts said the 12 Traditions were "designed not to supersede the reverent doctrines and practices of the AA literature which we have already quoted, but to address the essentially secular issues the AA movement confronted as it achieved public acceptance."

Because of the 12 Traditions, many groups in AA have grown comfortable thinking that their group is "not religious" particularly because the Traditions declare "against sectarian preference." As if "religion" is only practiced by particular sects that self-declare themselves as religious, such as Catholics, Presbyterians, Methodists, or Baptists. As if ending a meeting with the Lord's Prayer somehow doesn't count.

While AA may not call itself a "religion," these high court rulings clearly explain that when newcomers are told that in due course he or she should accept the existence of God as a requirement for continuous sobriety, and tell her or him to seek such a God through prayer, confessing wrongs to Him and asking Him for removal of shortcomings, and then expect the newcomer to recite the Lord's Prayer at the end of meetings, the fellowship is in fact practicing "religion."

Given that a major judicial system has branded the doctrines and practices of AA as religious, what does this mean for AA groups? Well, obviously one effect is that AA groups that use these doctrines and practices are now legally designated "religious." At least in the US. In response, an AA group can illogically put its head in the sand, and not look at the facts in front of it. An AA group can cling to its own definition of "religious." It can try to deny the long established and accepted definition of "religious" used in the world outside of AA, and used authoritatively by the US court system as the basis for designating AA doctrines and practices as "religious."

But denial just makes an AA group look confused (at best) or dishonest (at worst) to the rest of the world. When a group adheres to religious doctrines and practices, the group shouldn't expect the world to believe it when the group says it's "not religious." Repetition doesn't make it true, even though the saying is perpetuated and reinforced among the fellowship and with the newcomers.

Facts do not cease to exist because they are ignored.

– Aldous Huxley

When will good-hearted people stop denying the obvious? The rest of the world perceives AA's doctrines and practices as religious. And anyone who had that impression will now feel confident that he or she was right, after reading about the rulings of the US courts. Especially the still suffering alcoholic who avoids giving AA a try because of the perception – now reinforced by the US court system – that AA doctrines and practices are religious.

How does AA extricate itself from this conundrum? If the fellowship has any hope of being a non-religious fellowship for ALL suffering alcoholics with a desire to stop drinking, and being recognized as such by the Courts and by the public at large, it lies in strengthening its commitment to the 12 Traditions. The Traditions do not require AA groups to embrace religious doctrines and practices.

And there are some groups within AA — agnostic, atheist, freethinking — that are not religious in their thinking or practice.These groups don't recite prayers in their meetings nor do they suggest that a belief in God is required to maintain sobriety. If they use the 12 Steps, they use a secular version that has no reference to "God." Ironically, groups that do not adhere to AA's religious doctrines and practices are also the only groups that can truly – and legitimately, according to the US court system — claim to be "spiritual, not religious."

AA is at a crossroads. There are already many non-religious groups in AA and there are more of these groups being formed every day. Perhaps this reflects the skyrocketing numbers of non-religious people being reported by every population survey and poll across the world. AA already has Traditions designed to service this population. But the inherent discord between the 12 Traditions (non-religious) and the 12 Steps (religious) is a threat to AA. As a result, AA risks being further marginalized as a force of recovery for the still-suffering alcoholic, as an unexpected consequence of its own inner contradictions.

Separation of Church and AA

By Don S.

I stopped praying in meetings years ago, but held hands while others did. I recently stopped doing that, too. I now remain seated during the prayer. This adjustment brings up several issues which Americans have already dealt with in the courts.

When reading the Bible and leading prayer in US schools was outlawed in 1963, it was due to action brought by a Unitarian minister on behalf of his son. (The famous atheist, Madalyn Murray O'Hair, had a similar case pending and the two cases were combined on appeal to the Supreme Court.) The district court ruled in his favor, saying:

> The reading of the verses, even without comment, possesses a devotional and religious character and constitutes in effect a religious observance.

If a vote had been taken, prayer and Bible reading would certainly have been retained in the schools. Many Americans were outraged that a tiny minority, sometimes a single child, could keep them from expressing their faith. Billy Graham said:

> [I]n my opinion ... the Supreme Court ... is wrong. ... Eighty percent of the American people want Bible reading and prayer in the schools. Why should a majority be so severely penalized ...?

The US Congress drafted over 150 resolutions to overturn it, but it remains law. Today, many believers still feel like a persecuted majority. Some choose private schools for this reason. But the court reasoned that public schools must be kept neutral regarding religion since kids were required to attend.

But AA isn't like America; there's no Bill of Rights. Meetings are run by simple majority, referred to in Tradition Two as the 'group conscience' which is said to be the expression of a loving god. Each meeting is autonomous and can do whatever the majority wants. If you don't like a meeting, you can go to another one. This is the same approach businesses and churches take. Shopowners can display Hindu shrines or crucifixes. If you don't like it, you can go elsewhere. If you don't like the Lord's Prayer in a church service, you can go elsewhere.

125

So AA is more like a church or a business than the public schools. There is no minority protection and no expectation of religious neutrality. If you don't like a meeting, you can go elsewhere.

Do we want to say this to our fellow alcoholics? Is mixing religion and AA in line with our primary purpose? Or is it simply more comfortable for the majority?

My view is that separation of church and AA is best for the newcomer. It is the most inclusive stance we can take. This goes against 75 years of AA tradition, so we have to consider how important tradition is. Tradition is usually thought to embody distilled wisdom and provides a source of familiarity and comfort. When we think about prayer in AA meetings, we have a choice: we can show that mixing religion and AA is best for AA members, or give up some comfort in favor of being more inclusive.

Imagine travelling to Detroit and looking up a meeting in the local AA schedule. When you get there, it's plain that most members are Arab, apparently Muslim. (There is a large Muslim population in Detroit.) When they read How It Works, they say "Allah" in place of "God." When they end the meeting, they hold hands and say a Muslim prayer in Arabic. Are you comfortable? Do you return?

Here in Des Moines, there is one religiously-neutral meeting. It uses a script from an agnostic group in New York that is a paraphrase of How It Works omitting the supernaturalism. We share our experience that fellowship, personal inventory, restitution and social restoration have been central to our continued recovery. The vibe is this: whether gods exist or not, we have gotten and stayed sober without them. Believers are welcome, but might miss the prayers and the familiar cadence of How It Works. Our hope is that giving up some comfort and tradition will allow more people to get in the lifeboat. We have no way of knowing how many people have come to AA one time. Limiting religious talk is one area we can improve our inclusiveness. And it only takes a few months for new traditions to develop. In a short time, a new meeting format fits comfortably. There is more than one way to create the fellowship we crave.

There is good reason to think AA is not as welcoming as we would like. We are 95% white, 67% male and our membership is flat at 2.1 million members since 1993 (while the population has risen about 20%). We have no data on why some people never show up, or why some attend only once, never to return. Nonbelievers are more numerous than blacks and Jews combined (who are also underrepresented in AA). Do we continue as we are, hoping

126

that the lash of alcoholism will drive these people into our groups? Do we take our cue from The United States Supreme Court and keep religion and AA separate? Or do we simply start new groups that cater to our diversity?

With these thoughts in my mind, I attended my usual Saturday morning meeting today. It's New Year's Day, so there were several out of town visitors. I greeted one, Judy from Seward, Nebraska and sat down next to her. The chairman walked up and asked me to read How It Works. I said, No, thank you. He pressed me, and I told him I think the language is not very inclusive. Judy heard this exchange. At the end of the meeting, I remained seated while everyone else rose, held hands and said the Serenity Prayer. Judy told me that she attends 5 or 6 meetings each week in Seward. It's possible she'll tell her friends in that town of 6,000 about the guy in Des Moines who wouldn't read How It Works or join in prayer.

This is how change occurs. A few people show it is worthwhile, possible and not that big of a deal.

I don't know what AA will look like in 10 years, but I am working so that nonbelievers will feel welcome, or at least have a choice. Further, since separate is not equal, I have come out of the atheist closet in AA, to let others know they are not alone.

Tackling the Lord's Prayer at the Grassroots Level

By Linda R.

Is AA Just for Christians? is an article written by Barb C. for the October 2003 Grapevine. In the article she discusses the use of the Christian Lord's Prayer at the end of meetings. What she wrote then still holds true today. What I find troubling about the story she tells in her article is that she wasn't able to ask her AA group to take a group conscience vote to stop using the Lord's Prayer:

> One woman suggested that I bring the matter up for a group conscience vote. I'm afraid to do this because I think I know what the outcome will be, and it will make me angry, and resentment is a feeling I can't afford.

I wonder how many of us AA'ers don't even try to bring this matter up for a group conscience vote? Are there ways for us to help each other do this? This is an important issue because there will never be a mandate to prohibit the Lord's Prayer at a meeting.

First, any mandate to prohibit the Lord's Prayer violates the Fourth Tradition, which grants a group complete autonomy in its own affairs. In the Fourth Tradition, a very important principle is applied: "With respect to its own affairs, each AA group should be responsible to no other authority than its own conscience." – Bill W., "On the Fourth Tradition," Grapevine, March 1948.

Second, a mandate to prohibit the Lord's Prayer would be just as distasteful as a mandate to require the Lord's Prayer. Prohibiting or requiring anything in an AA meeting, except the desire to stop drinking, are the flip sides of the same coin and undermines the autonomy of all AA groups.

Third, who would issue the order to cease praying the Lord's Prayer at the end of a meeting? The General Service Office (GSO)? The Area Service Offices / Intergroups? I hope this kind of power is never given to those offices. Could these offices then order AA groups to recite a Jewish prayer or a Hindu prayer or a Moslem prayer?

Instead, the solution to this issue needs to be at the grass-roots level, not through a dictatorial mandate. Those members of AA who object to the Lord's

Prayer should talk to their group members about this. They should explain the reasons it is objectionable and offer an alternative.

There are plenty of alternatives to praying. For instance, some meetings open with a moment of silence and close with the Responsibility Pledge:

> I am responsible. When anyone, anywhere, reaches out for help, I want AA always to be there. And for that, I am responsible.

Some groups may be so religious that they will resist this type of change. One alternative for religious groups would be to switch to the non-denominational Serenity Prayer. For non-Christians, this prayer is typically not alienating, unlike the Lord's Prayer. And for those who do not believe in God, the religious phrase "God grant me" at the beginning of the prayer can be replaced with one of their choosing, such as:

> May I find
> Serenity to accept the things I cannot change
> Courage to change the things I can, and
> Wisdom to know the difference.

Here are some suggestions to increase the likelihood of getting a positive vote at a group business meeting:

> 1. Gently let members know that this matter will be considered at a group business meeting. Do not discuss it at a regular meeting.
>
> 2. Present alternatives to the group. For instance, suggest that the meeting could close with the Responsibility Pledge.
>
> 3. If the group is highly religious, make sure the matter being voted on is to switch to using the Serenity Prayer, instead of the Lord's Prayer. People might be more inclined to vote yes if they feel they are voting a prayer preference, rather than voting against a prayer.
>
> 4. Provide any written materials, such as a copy of Barb C.'s Grapevine article, to the group to read prior to the business meeting, so that members have a chance to carefully review them before they vote.
>
> 5. Make sure the group knows that they are not violating any AA "rules". Explain the Fourth Tradition and how it is traditional for each group to decide these matters for themselves. The AA fellowship does not impose or require specific prayers.

6. Try to determine if there are others in the group who would support the vote, and ask them to make sure they attend the business meeting where the vote will be taken, so that they can vote yes.

It's difficult to tell if a grass-roots effort like this will be effective. But if no effort is made, nothing will change. There may be a few groups that vote to keep using the Lord's Prayer instead of the Serenity Prayer. If so, so be it.

That is "Live and Let Live" in action.

Undeniably, being pro-active about addressing this issue with their groups may be very uncomfortable for some AA members. However, if AA'ers begin to take action, it is more likely than not that at least over time, AA will become a more inclusive fellowship.

Our Father Who Art Not in Public Schools

By Bob K.

The Professional Golfers' Association of America (to its own embarrassment) had a "Caucasians Only" membership policy until 1962.

Viewing a recent miniseries about the Kennedys reminded me that it took the United States National Guard to overcome the objections of the Governor in getting James Meredith (a black student) admitted to the "all-white" University of Mississippi in 1962.

Were we to trot out letters from 1959, written by the presidents of the PGA and the University itemizing the justifications for these exclusionary policies, they would be no more than historical curiosities. The idea of 1959 letters having "enforcement" power over 2011 social policies, regardless of the "authority" of their writers, is an unsupportable concept.

In fairness, the context of the times must be considered. Smart people, fifty years earlier still, wrote treatises explaining why women should not concern themselves with "men's business" like voting.

Thus, when in the debate over the Lord's Prayer in AA, Bill Wilson's 1959 letter addressing the subject is advanced, our respect and gratitude to our founder exhorts us to ignore fifty-two years of dramatic changes in our North American societies. Bill's 1959 position that potential objectors included only newcomer atheists and agnostics was certainly closer to truth in 1959 than in our modern era of vastly broader parameters of spirituality and religious faiths. To be non-denominational in the nineteen fifties was to respect equally Baptists, Presbyterians, Lutherans, Methodists and all other Christian Protestants plus possibly Roman Catholics and Mormons.

Today huge numbers of God-loving Americans, Canadians, and of course, AA members do not follow or belong to these more conventional religious groups. Within my small to medium sized home group, we have a Zen Buddhist, three Hindus, a Jew, and a majority who have no (current) religious affiliation and categorize themselves as "spiritual". The meaning of non-denominational has been expanded.

The appropriateness of Lord's Prayer use in AA really hinges on the answer to a single question: "Is the prayer predominantly Christian, or is it generic?" Bill, as he must, addresses this issue and makes a very cogent argument in the context of nineteen-fifties America: "...it is sometimes complained that the Lord's Prayer is a Christian document. Nevertheless this Prayer is of such widespread use and recognition that the arguments of its Christian origin seems to be a little farfetched."

"Widespread use" absolutely was truer fifty-two years ago.

We recited it in football huddles, cub scout jamborees, political rallies, and in our state-sponsored public schools. A Supreme Court decision of 1963 led eventually to the removal of the Lord's Prayer from public schools on the grounds that it is NOT generic. Rarely has an issue been more debated – the ultimate determination being that the Lord's Prayer and other Christian teachings and readings contravened the public schools need to be public and totally non-denominational.

In AA we take pride in being "not allied with any particular faith, sect or denomination..."

Using the Lord's Prayer in our meetings is in contradiction to our own stated policy of non-alliance. The "widespread use" defence is without validity in today's world.

The use of the Lord's Prayer is now quite restricted to churches, Christian events and AA.

When I was an elementary school student at the time of Bill's letter, on meeting a new kid the common first question was, "Do you go to Catholic school or Protestant school?" In 1959, there was very little 'political incorrectness' in such a question. Ninety-nine percent of students were Protestant; eighty percent went to Church on Sundays. It was a different time. In 1959, the Christianity of the Lord's Prayer was a debatable point.

Possibly Emmet Fox (of Sermon on the Mount fame) erred in calling the prayer "the most important of Christian documents." Billy Graham and others have called the Lord's Prayer "a concise summation of Christian doctrine." Famous Christians tell us that it is a Christian prayer. And the Supreme Court has demolished the "generic" argument. Too denominational for public schools, it must be too denominational for us as well.

In 2003, the Grapevine published a wonderful article, "Is AA Just for Christians?" by Barb C., a Jewish woman from Gainesville, Fla. She very eloquently states her frustration at being told she could choose her "own conception of God" and then, at the end of every meeting, being confronted with someone else's.

132

I hope she is still around.

Alcoholics Anonymous is so inclusive in so many ways, but not in this. The use of the Lord's Prayer in AA meetings inadvertently (at best) sanctions the Christian religion with which it is associated, and bestows upon it some level of "officialdom."

Arguments of tradition could be made in favour of sustaining the racial prejudice in the examples at the start of this article. Tradition should not trump principles.

Bill's letter also offers a version of the commonly used "disclaimer defence:" "However, around here, the leader of the meeting usually asks those to join him in the Lord's Prayer who feel that they would care to do so. The worst that happens to the objectors is that they have to listen to it. This is doubtless a salutary exercise in tolerance at their stage of progress."

A bit insensitive in an organization with the slogan "You are no longer alone."

Again the courts provide helpful information. Justice Clarke writes in rendering the district court ruling – "The fact that some pupils, or theoretically all pupils might be excused from attendance at the exercises does not mitigate the obligatory nature of the ceremony."

The Lord's Prayer is not religiously neutral and is no longer in "widespread use" outside of Christian gatherings. The worst offence in its use is that we contradict our own stated resolve to be non-denominational. It's time to move forward to a more spiritually neutral tomorrow.

Prayer at Meetings: A Word View

By The Cyber Sot

One of the many paradoxes of AA is that while we are not a religious organization, nor are we affiliated with one, we sure take our meeting prayers seriously. If you don't believe me, suggest that your home group change the prayers used at meetings.

Prayer at meetings, specifically the Lord's Prayer, is a long-running "hot" topic that crops up on a regular basis at AA meetings around the world. To many AAs, the 12 Steps may be, as the Big Book puts it, merely "suggested as a program of recovery," but the Lord's Prayer is mandatory.

Here's what sober AAs – Christians, Jews, Muslims, Buddhists, Hindus, Shintoists, Mormons, American Indians, atheists and pagans – have to say about it from around the world, from Ireland to India and Australia to New Zealand. Here too are some thoughts about closing meetings with the Responsibility Declaration, a practice that is growing. The Declaration, or Pledge, we will see later, focuses on what AA is all about.

Surveying AA is like counting grains of sand during a hurricane. Instead, this is an e-mail sampling of responses to some fairly simple questions: What prayers do you use at your meetings? Why? They were sent to AAs and groups around the world.

Nowhere in the Big Book does it say "how" to hold a meeting. Instead we have what some people say is "tradition." Well, we have 12 Traditions, and the prayers we use at a meeting are not in any of them.

There are numerous arguments for keeping the Lord's Prayer, dating back to the fact that our founders were Christians and that we are, in some respects, a stepchild of the Oxford Movement. But Bill and Dr. Bob pulled Alcoholics Anonymous out of the Oxford Movement because it was more concerned with converting people to Christianity than getting them sober. It was also a Protestant movement closed to non-Christians, and even Catholics.

If you want to hear more of the arguments, bring it up at your home group. Doug C, reports that in New Zealand, "they usually start and finish with the Serenity Prayer and that's it. No other prayers are used that I'm aware of. That's probably because in New Zealand in my experience most AAs stress

'God of their own understanding,' so other prayers might be regarded as inappropriate. But that's just my experience."

Andy K in India says "There are numerous views about what should and should not be read at the meeting. However, one thing we all agree upon (something rare in AA) at meetings in Calcutta is the Serenity Prayer. To the best of my knowledge all the meetings in West Bengal use the Serenity Prayer at the beginning and at the end of the meeting." Krishna I, of Bangalore, India, says that the Serenity Prayer has been translated into eight other Indian languages, and is used throughout the predominantly Hindu and Buddhist country.

American Indian meetings normally use the *Prayer to the Great Spirit*.

Myles W. says most groups in Toronto, Canada, begin with the Serenity Prayer and end with the Lord's Prayer, but "some start with the Serenity Prayer and end with the Responsibility Pledge," also called the Responsibility Declaration.

Use of the declaration is growing

Jay S., a sober Jew in Connecticut, says that "The meetings I've been to in Jerusalem open and close with the Serenity Prayer. Here in Connecticut, about one third of the meetings I go to use the Serenity Prayer, the rest the Our Father. If they use the Our Father, **I just say a silent prayer while holding hands**."

Maxine U., a sober Jew in New York, echoes the sentiments of P.J., a sober Muslim in Jakarta, Indonesia, when she says: "In some ways the Lord's Prayer is a political statement. My biggest objection to it is the fact that it is irrevocably attached to a particular religion and AA is supposed to be completely neutral when it comes to religion." Maxine goes on to say that she would feel the same way "if a Jewish prayer was adopted."

Another sober Muslim, in Prague, in the Czech Republic, writes that his group opens and closes with the Serenity Prayer, "and there is no controversy."

"My Personal [repeat PERSONAL] opinion is that no Christian prayers ever have any place at an AA meeting. The Lord's Prayer is a Christian prayer and a religious prayer. I have nothing against Christians or Christianity. My parents and my sister are Christians and wonderful people. But I wouldn't feel comfortable facing Mecca and kneeling and pressing my head to the floor at the end of an AA meeting either. That is Islam, not AA. If I want to do religion, I do it on my own time. AA meetings are AA time, and the Serenity Prayer does the job quite well."

Elena, a former Californian now living in Athens,Greece, says, "We use the Serenity Prayer as well as the Lord's Prayer. We have an English speaking meeting as well as Greek speaking meeting. Ninety percent of Greeks (like myself) are Greek Orthodox and firmly believe in God and in prayers in and outside of AA."

Jack H., in Cork City, Ireland, says "I haven't ever come across any problems with regards to the prayers, but then again Irelandis 100% a Christian country (Catholic and Protestant)." But in that same bath of e-mails, came this reply from non-Christian Bob. B., in Northern Ireland. He says that at one meeting he attends, different members are sometimes asked to lead the Lord's Prayer. "While I will respect their group conscience, as a non-Christian, **I will not join in** with the words of this prayer, and if asked to lead, then I would have to decline and run the risk of offending many. "Religion, I believe should not be practiced in AA as it is another cause, and certainly in Northern Ireland it has always caused controversy."

Mireille U., in Belgium, Erik B, in Norway, and Poul in Denmark say the Serenity Prayer is the prayer of choice. Sometimes the Promises are also read from the Big Book. It's the same in Rome, says Stephen S., who adds, "Once in a while, if a visitor from the U.S.decides unilaterally to use the Lord's Prayer, we do that. But it is not our choice at all. Strange for the home of the Pope, eh?"

Arthur in Australia writes: "Commonly in Australia, the Serenity Prayer is used to close a meeting, either holding hands or not. The Lord's Prayer is used by some groups but these are relatively rare in my experience. "I personally don't participate in these rituals which are not in keeping **with my spiritual practice**, and while I get odd looks from some people, I haven't been thrown out yet, and after a while most come to respect my right **to abstain** from what, for me, would be hypocrisy.

"At times, not participating makes me feel, passingly, a little alienated from the group which is the usual argument used by those against the use of prayers. Today, however, I am a recovered alcoholic and my reason for being at meetings is to spread the message of my E. S. & H. (Experience, Strength and Hope) to the alcoholic who still suffers and if in some ways I don't agree with rituals the group chooses to engage in that is of minor importance."

David, in Darwin, Australia, says, "We only say the Serenity Prayer and those who do not believe in a God replace that word with one of their choosing. No other religions are mentioned, and no other religious prayers are spoken. We do however pray for people in the fellowship."

Joel P, in Tokyo, writes that in the English-language meetings in Japan, "We open with the Serenity Prayer and close with the Lord's Prayer. We had an Orthodox Jew here awhile and closed with the Serenity Prayer while he was here. He was an inspiration to the group with solid sobriety. His request to change the prayer was a unifying act as we all prayed together."

As far as Japanese language meetings are concerned, Yukie writes: "Most Japanese AA Meetings in Kanto (including Tokyo) area close with a Serenity Prayer sitting at their seat, not standing hand in hand. But some groups don't say any prayer at all, to say nothing of Lord's Prayer. In some area such as Kyushu, almost of the groups in the area don't. At one group I visited in Tokyo, they omitted "God" from the first line of the Serenity Prayer."

Carolyn B, of Minneapolis, writes that many area meetings "still use the Serenity Prayer to open and the Our Father to close," and some use the Responsibility Declaration. "There is one group which opens with the Third Step Prayer (on their knees!) and closes with the Responsibility Statement." Her home group opens and closes with the Serenity Prayer. "We had a few members who were not Christian and who expressed discomfort with the Our Father as a closing. So we decided that since there are so many prayers available in Alcoholics Anonymous which are unifying, it ill behooved us to cling to one which was divisive, and we voted to stop using the Our Father."

John P, in Texas, says they use the Lord's Prayer because it is traditional, "dating to the earliest meetings in Akron and Cleveland. I have never heard it challenged as a practice in Texas, though, as would be expected, the question is sometimes raised on the Left Coast (California)." Claims that use of the Lord's Prayer has never been challenged are quite common, even though, as we have seen, it continues to be challenged around the world, not just in California.

Jeanne G., a sober pagan in the Los Angeles area, says her home group, Pagans in Recovery, closes their meetings with their own prayer:

> Closing prayer, the Circle Chant: "I am a circle, I am healing you. You are a circle, you are healing me. Unite us, be as one. Unite us, be as one.

These responses, and those I don't have room to quote, show that there is room for variety in AA, but not according to all AAs. I once heard a member declare that he "knows" that if we don't address God by His "correct name," He will not listen to our prayers.

Many pro-Lord's Prayer arguments remind me of my days as a reporter in the '60s, covering the Civil Rights Movements. I would regularly interview white men and women who just didn't understand why "uppity" blacks were so upset, and wished that they wouldn't "rock the boat" by demanding their rights. I heard the same sorts of arguments when I covered the feminist movement, but then they came from men – both white and black.

Telling non-Christians they "shouldn't be upset" by the Lord's Prayer, or that they should "learn to live with it because it's part of the program" shows a certain amount of thoughtlessness, intolerance, self-righteousness and even arrogance.

If you really want the program Bill and Bob started, all members must be like them: white, male, married, never-divorced Christians with specific college degrees – either pharmacists and doctors, like Dr. Bob, or stockbrokers with law degrees, like Bill W. – who were born in Vermont and first belonged to the Oxford Movement.

The foreword to the 1939 first edition of the Big Book says: "The only requirement for membership is an honest desire to stop drinking. We are not allied with any particular faith, sect or denomination, nor do we oppose anyone. We simply wish to be helpful to those who are afflicted."

Prayers you say in private, or at your Church, are between you and your Higher Power. What you say at an AA meeting affects the entire group. Insulting people with a prayer they do not believe in, or making them feel apart from instead of part of is not "helpful." It violates the spirit of the 12th Step: "Having had a spiritual awakening as the result of these steps, we tried to carry this message to alcoholics, and to practice these principles in all our affairs."

The message is recovery, not Christian prayer. And the message I want to leave my meeting with is the one spelled out in the **Responsibility Declaration**: "I am responsible. When anyone, anywhere, reaches out for help, I want AA always to be there. And for that, I am responsible."

VI. Many Paths to Recovery

My 10 Favourite Recovery Websites

By John M.

I'll begin by confessing that AA Agnostica is my favourite recovery website and I'll say no more given that you are currently reading this blog and you will have your own opinions about where it is placed among your favourites.

So, in no particular order here is my list of my 10 preferred sites.

1. I begin with *The Fix* (thefix.com) for no other reason than it is produced daily and serves very much like a morning newspaper. *The Fix* offers up to date news about recovery (or the search for it) for pretty much everything that is called "addiction" these days, whether it is in the form of alcohol/drugs or food and gambling, or sex and sugar. Some of the best writers are featured making for a varied and diverse set of opinions regarding what constitutes addiction and recovery, with some very original, highly articulate commentary. *The Fix* does not "hold back" on engaging in issues that may be deemed controversial. One finds issues raised that are often only whispered about among friends in the rooms of traditional groups like 12 Step meetings.

2. *Guinevere Gets Sober* (guineveregetssober.com) is a personal blog site by the pseudonymous "Guinevere" who occasionally writes under her real name for *The Fix*. Guinevere has stepped back a bit from writing entries daily to a more occasioned and selective posting timeframe. She is a very good writer who comes from a background of multiple addictions in her family but she highlights her struggles with prescription drugs as to what awakened her to a life of sobriety. As well as commentary on the "recovery movement," and everyday sobriety, her website includes interviews, book reviews, and reports on current issues of interest. Her blog elicits quite a bit of response from her readership. I used to look forward to her almost daily posts but, as mentioned, she is more cautious with her time but the site has easy to access thematic headings from which to search earlier material that is still timely, relevant and inspirational.

3. *Barefoot's World* (barefootsworld.net): A few years ago I discovered Bob Pearson's (GSO senior advisor) 1986 General Service Conference prescient warning about the danger of AA's growing rigidity, here at this website created by the legendary Barefoot Bob Hardison (1933-2009; sobriety date, Feb. 28th, 1974). On entering the site, you will find scads of material on American history, the defense of liberty, and the promotion of tolerance – fascinating in and of itself – but scroll down to Barefoot's *Recovery Pages* and enjoy the ride – especially fun are his "cowboy-isms." A truly remarkable free spirit, he embraces all forms of spirituality and, if you continue scrolling down, you will find his *Native American Pages*. He follows one commandment in life: "Harm no one, then do what thou wilt." And his philosophy of life includes: "Live simply. Love generously. Care deeply. Speak kindly. Do the next indicated right thing." There is more varied AA material at this site than you can shake a stick at!

4. *Rebellion Dogs* (rebelliondogspublishing.com) acknowledges with the Big Book that "rebellion dogs our every step." I'll throw out any pretension that I view this site objectively since its author, Joe C., is simply one of my favourite people around the rooms. Joe is a regular contributor to AA Agnostica and has written for *The Fix, Renew Magazine* and *In the Rooms*. You will also know him as the author of *Beyond Belief: Agnostic Musings of 12 Step Life*. Joe's new book speaks for itself and *Rebellion Dogs* offers readers very timely articles (and some music!) on the state of recovery in the 21 Century. And Joe is not beyond interviewing a few interesting folks in the field of recovery. Some very important links to other free thinker sites is included.

5. The *Buddhist Recovery Network* (buddhistrecovery.org) is an extraordinary resource for those who want to explore spirituality and recovery in non-"western" ways. And you don't have to be Buddhist either! Ever respectful of all ways people choose the road to recovery, this site emphasizes, as one would expect, compassion, mindfulness, and meditation as ways of overcoming addiction to mind/body altering substances as well as offering guides to living in an increasingly fast paced and an often mind-numbing modern society. The recommended books to read, the book reviews, downloads to articles and links to other spiritual and "liberating" ways is here, in one location, simply one of the best sites to explore, either as a neophyte or as one already into Buddhist precepts, alternative methods for sobriety and staying sober.

6. *William White Papers* (williamwhitepapers.com): Arguably the foremost North American scholar and researcher of recovery movements, William White and his friend, Ernest Kurtz, have long been staunch supporters of AA and Twelve Step recovery without undermining other, very valid methods and philosophies that address the modern addiction malaise. White's website includes some of his best published scholarly work, interviews with other

140

renowned researchers, as well as book reviews. In general, it is a comprehensive resource for the history of both addiction and recovery ever since people starting taking an interest. One will find here just about every subject or every angle one would want to learn more about. The material on this website is written in well researched and well documented ways without being too scholarly obtuse.

7. *Hazelden* (hazelden.org), of course, publishes more of the most popular literature dedicated to addiction and recovery than any other single publishing house. Besides publishing much "conference approved" AA literature, one will also find in the "Book Store" section of the site much that is not tied to AA or even Twelve Step programs. Recent books published by Hazelden include Marya Hornbacher's, *Waiting: A Nonbeliever's Higher Power* and Ernest Kurtz's classic, *Not God: A History of Alcoholics Anonymous* among many others. As well as offering actual treatment opportunities, the website directs readers to its monthly news letter, Graduate Studies in addiction counseling, and a listing for a wide assortment of weekend seminars and retreats.

8. *Stanton Peele Addiction Website* (peele.net): Love him or hate him (I'm somewhere in between), at least you will know the arguments 0f those who are not fond of AA and 12 Step programs. A psychologist, Peele is clear that he believes the disease model of addiction is not only an inadequate representation of what lies behind addiction but, as well, the model causes far more harm than good. Other disagreements with AA: spirituality in AA, for Peele, is merely a euphemism for religion; harm reduction as opposed to abstinence is the better way for most people to go; and most alcoholics/addicts recover on their own with either no recovery counseling or with short term, cognitively based programs. Peele writes for *The Huffington Post, Psychology Today*, and is often an invited guest on the major American TV networks.

I include Stanton Peele's website in that knowing all the arguments, both pro and con, regarding the 12 Step model can only serve to make all of us better informed about our own recovery.

9. *Hindsfoot Foundation* (hindsfoot.org): A plethora of documents here dedicated mostly to the history of *Alcoholics Anonymous*. There are plenty of recently written essays as well but they are firmly grounded in "traditional" ways of experiencing recovery from alcoholism. Whether one is fully committed to the AA model as it was developed by the early pioneers of the program or whether one is seeking to contemporize AA into the 21 Century, this site will provide you with lots of material for your research.

10. *Addictions Unplugged* (addictionsunplugged.com) focuses on our growing awareness of the realities of food addiction. Just because you are a recovering alcoholic does not mean you are not obese; and just because you are not obese does not mean you are not a food addict. Even if you are neither, this site is a great way to start understanding the suffering of our fellow addicts in food. It has been said that every alcoholic should spend time with those with other addictions not only so we can help out where we are able but, perhaps as well, learn something more about our own alcoholism. This site is maintained by Dr. Vera Tarman, the well respected physician for the Renascent Treatment Centre in Toronto (where I did my treatment for alcoholism and am a proud alumnus). Great articles and a number of very fine videos and audio resources are easily accessed here. There is much to learn about this growing (sic!) epidemic – the direct and indirect health care costs to our society as well as the special nature of suffering by the food addict of which many of us, alcoholics, drug addicts or "normies" are simply oblivious.

So, these are my 10 favourite recovery websites!

John M. got sober in June 2007 at the age of 54 and acknowledges he was fully aware that he was an alcoholic in his early 30's. He confesses to being a slow learner. His wife affectionately calls him the dumb mutt. He also indicates without a touch of melodrama that these are the best years of his life. He is living proof that you can teach an old dog new tricks.

Culture and Addiction

By Allen Berger

In this article I want to discuss how our culture sets us up for becoming an addict. Before I do it's important to realize we are all in a trance. We are hypnotized by our culture. This is not necessarily a bad thing, it just is the way things are. It happens in every culture, It has to.

Culture is transmitted through the family. Parents teach their children a world view. This world view is like a filter, it defines what is real and what isn't, it proscribes what is appropriate behavior and what isn't, it dictates how we should be and what we should feel. It defines what is and what isn't. It creates a socially constructed reality. The way this world view is taught in any particular family is unique because it is also influenced by the dynamics that shaped our parent's in their childhood.

The first world view we must discuss is that our culture is excessively focused on "having." This focus emerges from capitalism. Capitalism needs consumers. We are all indoctrinated in the absurd idea that more is better so we will want to buy a new car, new clothes, the latest mobile phone or tablet. In fact Erich Fromm observed that we internalize this attitude. We measure our self-worth by the quality and quantity of the material things we possess like money, homes, cars, and adult toys. I'm sure you heard that quote, "He who finishes with the most toys wins." This attitude can be summarized as "I am more, the more I have." We end up believing that our self-worth is determined by what we have, rather than on who we are. We have lost sight of the importance of character.

This obsession with "having" influences how we relate to self and others. We end up treating ourselves and others as objects. We become obsessed with how marketable we are. Women are typically viewed as sex objects and relate to themselves in this manner too. While men are usually viewed as success objects and also relate to themselves in this way too. A big problem is our society is that what makes a man successful on his job makes it nearly impossible for him to have a warm and loving intimate personal relationship. Any woman who treats herself as a sex object cannot be intimate with someone because she is overly concerned about her looks. This is part of the insanity. Our self-worth becomes other validated. We become dependent on our environment to make us feel good about ourselves. We never learn to validate ourselves.

143

This insanity also creates another problem. We become obsessed with more. More is better, isn't it? This is the nonsense we learn in our culture. And this is one of the ways our culture sets us up for addiction. I remember the moment I realized that we are all taught that more is better. It was one of those moments of clarity when I realized that this is at the heart of addiction. Addiction is the experience of believing that more is better. If one beer makes me feel good than more will make me feel better. If partying one night is great than partying every night is better. Unfortunately this nonsense applies to nearly everything in our lives. We are rarely satisfied with what we have or who we are.

We are obsessed with becoming something we are not. True self-esteem is rare, we just don't feel good enough as we are. Our idealized image of who we should be is corrupted by our world view. We are driven to be perfect. To fit into our idealized image of who we should be. It becomes all about more, more and more and more. We spend millions of dollars on the latest exercise equipment so we can become more attractive and have a better body. (Unfortunately most of it is gathering dust underneath our beds, closets or garages.) We pursue schemes to get rich so we can have more money which in some magical way will make us feel more secure. Women spend billions of dollars on plastic surgery to have the "perfect body." Men are also visiting the plastic surgeon more than ever before. Men become workaholics because they are devoted having a successful career to have a better life. It's all about having, not being. We turn into humans, doing and performing, rather than humans, being (sic). What a tragedy!

Another nonsense that is promoted in our culture is that life should be easy and gratification instantaneous. We become obsessed with seeking to find the easier, softer way, and then hope for instantaneous results. We have lost the ability to wait, to have patience. Well life isn't easy and most worthwhile things don't come easily. But nobody tells us that. Instead we are bombarded with messages that tell us to take a magical pill and your headache will immediately disappear. There is no need to figure out a better way to handle your stress. If you are depressed take an antidepressant it will make you feel better. No need to figure out what you are doing that makes you depressed. We buy weight loss medication from the infomercial on TV that promises to help us lose weight while we sleep, so there is no need to spend hours in the gym. It's easy.

When we turn to drugs they really work. I mean really work, instantaneously we feel better. We are sexier, more fun, more comfortable, more relaxed, more spontaneous. We are free from fears and concerns. We are free from

144

the false-self that develops to fit into this insane culture. I had a friend who stated that he didn't know if he was born an alcoholic but the moment he took his first drink he knew that an alcoholic was born. It worked. It was easy. It set him free from all of this nonsense.

We are set up to become addicted. We become addicted to drugs including alcohol, to sex, to gambling, to compulsive overeating or restricting. We become addicted to spending money, buying new clothes, finding a better boyfriend or girlfriend, wife or husband. We become addicted to more.

I may sound paranoid but there is a cultural conspiracy that undermines the development of our true, spiritual self. We are encouraged to abandon our true-self and become an idealized self riddled with our culture's proscription of who we should be. We sell out but deep down inside we know something is wrong.

Our dissatisfaction with this nonsense – is good news. Maybe this is what we really mean when we say we have a "dis-ease." We are dissatisfied with who we are and how we are living our life. Don't run from this pain. It means that something is "right" about you. Jung described us as having a "spiritual thirst." It is our spiritual self or our real-self that is reaching out to us, to be actualized. It is like an alarm clock that will continue to ring until we wake up. So it's what is right about us that doesn't allow us to completely abandon ourselves to all of this nonsense.

Recovery helps us find our lost, true-self. It helps us reconnect with who we really are. Recovery is about "being," not "having." It's an incredible journey that begins with shattering our false-self. This opens the door to discovering our true spirit. Every spiritual discipline is concerned with "being" not "having." That's why the 12 Steps work so well in helping those who suffer from all different types of addictions. They facilitate a spiritual experience based on a pedestal of hopelessness as Bill Wilson noted.

In recovery we experience a 180 degree shift in our attitude and perceptions, this is a remarkable personal transformation. Recovery is paradoxical, which means that it is beyond belief. We shift from an obsession with "having more" to a focus on "being," and living a life guided by spiritual principles. We become concerned with developing character and integrity. This breaks the trance and cures our cultural sickness. We, like Alice in Wonderland, come to realize that what is, isn't, and what isn't, is. What an amazing journey.

Allen Berger, Ph.D. is an international expert in the science of recovery and a popular recovery author for Hazelden. He is the author of 12 Stupid Things that Mess Up Recovery, 12 Smart Things to do When the Booze and Drugs are Gone, *and* 12 Hidden Rewards of Making Amends. *His interpretation of the 12 Steps is included in* The Little Book: A Collection of Alternative 12 Steps. *You can learn more about Dr. Berger and his work at his website* (abphd.com)

LifeRing

By Mahala Kephart, LifeRing Board of Directors

A Clever, Reassuring Device

> It seems to me that the Higher Power notion can work if you absolutely don't think about it. It's a clever, bright, reassuring device. Just shut your eyes tight, believe it, and don't ask questions. Once you lift the cover and peek at the wiring, you see that the batteries that make the Higher Power light up are in your own head. The Higher Power is nothing and does nothing unless you make it so: it is your own sober desire that supplies its energy.

> Once you understand that you are the mechanism that makes it work, you can no longer believe in the notion of the Higher Power. But then, you no longer need it: you have found the sober power within yourself.

> Martin Nicolaus, LifeRing founder

> LifeRing Press, 2003

Choosing Secular Sobriety

A secular approach to recovery allows individuals freedom of choice in following whatever religious or spiritual paths they wish to explore. Because LifeRing does not promote religious concepts in published materials, and because we avoid religious practices of any sort in our meeting formats, LifeRing provides a safe environment for individuals of any and every spiritual belief system, including, importantly, non-belief.

In the early stages of recovery, it seems especially critical to us that individuals be encouraged to conserve mental energy and focus that energy on making abstinence and sobriety the priority in all aspects of their lives. In the words of one counselor, "Early recovery is hard work enough. When we ask people to also take on the issues of spirituality, oftentimes it's just too much for them."

Medical science now offers a wide choice of treatment modalities for most health conditions, combined with an increasing focus on individualized medicine. Doesn't it stand to reason that treatment for chemical dependency

147

would be likely more effective it, too, were able to offer an array of treatment approaches tailored to meet individual needs and circumstances?

If given the choice, only a small fraction of the American public would choose a faith-based treatment protocol to combat a life-threatening medical condition. At LifeRing, we wonder why addiction treatment should be viewed any differently.

When sobriety is described to the addicted individual in a simple negative construction of "the subtraction of alcohol or drugs from your life" often expressed in ways that carry sinful overtones, the addicted individual, in turn, sees the prospect of sobriety and long-term recovery as nothing but a scary, gaping void.

Which is of course ironic, because it is substance addiction that creates the void as it systematically shackles the human spirit, poisons every bodily system, tortures the emotions, and impoverishes the intellect. It is when alcohol or other mind-altering, addictive drugs are taken out of the equation that what emerges is usually a wonderful, miraculous, precious, and capable human being.

Being the Protagonist of Your Own Recovery

In LifeRing, the recovering person — that miraculous, precious, capable human being — is considered the protagonist of their own recovery. We define abstinence from alcohol and drugs as a practical, doable project and encourage each individual to take this project into their own hands, and with hard work and perseverance, rebuild their life.

Most people begin their recovery journey following a long, painful struggle between their sober and addicted selves. That internal struggle, a series of battles, really, rages on unabated until the sober side acquires a decisive superiority of force and begins winning those battles and, eventually, the war.

Most people also begin their recovery journey somewhat lucky to still be alive. They may have achieved and accomplished many things while in the throes of active addiction, but for many, simply staying alive and being able to begin a recovery journey at all is an achievement of extraordinary magnitude.

In LifeRing, we believe individuals can and must learn to stop ingesting addictive substances before worrying what to call themselves or wrestling with their religious or spiritual beliefs. In LifeRing we are united by the practice of a behavior — abstinence. That we lived long enough to begin the recovery journey at all should probably be accorded more awe and respect than is our societal norm.

To us, the idea of starting out one's recovery journey by focusing on shortcomings, deficiencies, and lost opportunities seems counterproductive. In LifeRing, we encourage individuals to focus, instead, on cutting their losses, focusing on their assets, and moving forward with their lives. Yes, there may be some messes to clean up, and individuals in recovery may have to make up for lost time, but in that, are we so different from most of humanity? What is different about those of us in recovery is that our internal addictive substance control units are burned out and gone.

Apart from that, we're pretty much like the ordinary human being. And all human beings need connection. In LifeRing, we encourage conversational engagement, and forging focused, sober, purposeful connections with others. In such an environment, the sober self — with all its potentialities — can surface in a stable, resilient manner.

Conversation Breeds Connection

We believe conversation drives connection. A typical LifeRing meeting might look like a group of friends — relaxed, sober, spontaneous, secure — sitting around a table, or in a circle of some sort, talking about the current concerns in their lives. We encourage individuals to ask questions if something is unclear, or respond to the questions of others if they feel they have something to contribute.

LifeRing participants report greater engagement in this type of meeting than in meetings that do not allow for respectful give-and-take between participants. They report that tool-sharing and collective work fortifies their analytical and intellectual selves, and the supportive conversational atmosphere supplies emotional sustenance. This, they have reported over and over, is a combination that facilitates their all-around growth and competence in sobriety.

The underlying assumption of the LifeRing meeting format is that recovery is a work in progress, and that participation in the group is both a privilege and a mark of self-respect. We provide encouragement and support for each individual to build a personal recovery program that works for them. The Recovery by Choice Workbook, published by LifeRing Press, lays out a series of secular sobriety tools and checklists in the context of nine work areas, or domains. The workbook is used individually and by some LifeRing groups, in both structured and unstructured formats — allowing individuals and working groups to focus on areas of immediate concern and to save others for completion, or reflection, later. Some individuals who participate in LifeRing also choose to participate in other sobriety support groups, including traditional twelve-step groups, because such involvement offers them additional tools and connections that strengthen their sober selves.

Individuals who have become addicted to chemical substances are often said to be a special case, or class, of people, powerless to manage their lives. In LifeRing, we believe the addicted person is not powerless to learn and maintain abstinence. The addicted individual may have to struggle, but so long as they keep addictive substances out of their body, that individual can, and will, prevail.

Addiction research has consistently demonstrated that no treatment modality brings lasting improvement unless it mobilizes an individuals's own natural, inherent recovery resources. In LifeRing, every individual is encouraged to select and assemble a personal set of sobriety tools appropriate to their particular needs at any point in time; to choose freely from among the ideas and reflections of others; and to discard tools that didn't prove to work for them, or tools they no longer need.

So it is that in LifeRing, each participant can say, "No one else has a program precisely like this one. It works for me because I built it myself; I know it intimately; I own it and I operate it; I made it; it is mine." With those feelings come investment, commitment, motivation, and hard work.

The LifeRing approach isn't — and will never be — for everyone. But once sober — abstinent — we believe we can stop merely surviving and begin to live again, shaking off our inner addict's plan for our life and forging a new path. In LifeRing, we believe we can do more than just get through the day. We can seize it.

Carpe diem! Sobrietas Contra Spiritus.

LifeRing is an abstinence-based, worldwide network of individuals seeking to live in recovery from addiction to alcohol or to other, non-medically indicated drugs. In LifeRing, we offer each other peer-to-peer support in ways that encourage personal growth, continued learning, and personal empowerment. Our approach is based on developing, refining, and sharing our own personal strategies for continued abstinence and crafting a rewarding life in recovery.

Founded in the San Francisco Bay Area more than a decade ago, LifeRing has grown to include more than 150 face-to-face meetings, and supports several vibrant on-line communities with participants from, quite literally, around the world. LifeRing is a 501(c)(3) organization, governed by a nine-member board of directors, all of whom are practicing sobrietists. LifeRing holds an annual meeting and conference in May of each year in which board member elections and policy decisions are acted upon democratically, with each meeting and on-line venue represented by an individual elected to vote on its behalf. *How Was Your Week?*, *The Recovery by Choice Workbook* and *Empowering Your Sober Self*, authored by Martin Nicolaus, may be purchased through the LifeRing website (lifering.org). The LifeRing Service Center is located in Oakland, California.

Mahala is a musician by training. Her career was spent in university fundraising and fundraising management. She is now in active recovery from addiction to alcohol, and credits her involvement with LifeRing for giving her recovery serious traction. She will tell you, without hesitation, that regaining the voice and actions of her sober self has been the hardest work she has ever done. But also the most rewarding. A member of the board of directors of LifeRing, she lives with her husband in Salt Lake City, Utah, where she is an active member of the local recovery community.

Faces and Voices of Recovery

By Patricia Taylor

Faces & Voices of Recovery is the national American voice of the organized addiction recovery community.

With over 30,000 members, we work to improve the lives of the millions of Americans affected by alcohol and other drugs. We believe that our nation's response to the crisis of addiction should be based on sound public health science and the grassroots engagement and involvement of the recovery community – men and women in recovery, their families, friends and allies.

Long-term recovery is a reality for over 23 million Americans: living proof that people can and do recover.

Founded in 2001 at a Call to Action forum held in St. Paul, Minnesota, Faces & Voices of Recovery encourages people in recovery and our allies to be active in the growing recovery movement so that individuals and their families receive respectful, nondiscriminatory care and support on the same basis as people with other health conditions. The "faces and voices of recovery" from all walks of life serve powerfully to educate the public, policy makers and the media about the reality of addiction recovery, creating widespread public understanding of the many pathways to recovery.

We are all about taking action to end the discrimination and stigma facing people in recovery from addiction.

We released the first-ever survey of people in recovery from addiction to alcohol and other drugs, the Life in Recovery Survey. The survey documents the heavy costs of addiction to the individual and the nation and for the first time, measures and quantifies the effects of recovery over time.

Not surprising to the recovery community, but virtually unknown to our friends, neighbors and policymakers, the dramatic improvements associated with recovery affect all areas of life. For those in recovery, for example, there is a ten-fold decrease in involvement with the criminal justice system and the use of emergency room departments at hospitals and a fifty per cent increase in participation in family activities compared with active addiction.

And life keeps getting better as recovery progresses. Yet, discriminatory practices in housing, employment, health insurance coverage and elsewhere remain tremendous barriers to recovery.

152

Over 23 million Americans aren't getting the help they need to recover. As Life in Recovery documents, investing in recovery makes sense. When people get the help and support that they need, they are employed, pay bills and taxes, vote, volunteer in our communities and take care of our health and families.

To secure public and private policies to help individuals and families get the help they need to recover and reverse policies that discriminate against people in or seeking recovery, the recovery community is getting organized and speaking out.

As recovery historian Bill White puts it:

> Many of us have carried a message of hope on a one-to-one basis; this new recovery movement calls upon us to carry that message of hope to whole communities and the whole culture. It is time we stepped forward to shape this history with our stories, our time and our talents.

For too long those most affected by alcohol and other drug problems have been absent from the public policy debate.

Faces & Voices of Recovery's Board of Directors developed a statement of the principle that all Americans have a right to recover from addiction to alcohol and other drugs, the Recovery Bill of Rights.

In 2011, Faces & Voices launched the Association of Recovery Community Organizations (ARCO) to unite and support the growing network of local, regional and statewide recovery community organizations. ARCO links recovery community organizations and their leaders with local and national allies, and provides training and technical assistance to groups.

The Recovery Community Organization Toolkit is chock full of detailed information on starting a recovery community organization.

Recovery community centers are one of the innovative services that have been developed by ARCO members offering a public and visible space for recovery to flourish in the community: Recovery on Main Street. They serve as a "community organizing engine," providing opportunities for civic engagement, leadership development, and advocacy.

Recovery community centers are taking off all across the country. There should be one in every community, just like there's a seniors' center in every community.

As we've developed our advocacy agenda, we realized that many people didn't have the language to talk about addiction recovery in a way that the public and policy makers could hear our message and understand the reality of recovery. We found a way to describe and talk about recovery so that people who are NOT part of the recovery community understand what we mean when we use the word "recovery."

Our Stories Have Power is a way to clearly and passionately convey the living reality of long-term recovery from addiction and talk about recovery... not addiction. And as recovery advocates, we're telling our stories with a purpose – to help our friends and neighbors understand that there's more to recovery than not using alcohol or other drugs, and that part of recovery is creating a better life.

Faces & Voices has organized other successful trainings and campaigns.

As part of the *National Recovery Month*, observed every September, Faces & Voices developed *Rally4Recovery!* to bring together individuals and organizations for an annual national day of advocacy and recognition.

In 2012, over 100,000 people participated in walks, town hall meetings and rallies all across the nation, demonstrating publicly the reality of recovery and calling on public officials to support recovery.

With the release of the inspiring documentary film *The Anonymous People*, Faces & Voices of Recovery and our partners have collaborated to launch a new campaign to engage and mobilize the newly emerging constituency as we work to transform public attitudes and policies.

With the enactment of national health reform, recognition of innovative peer recovery support services, state and national policy makers' attention to recovery, health and wellness and a maturing network of recovery community organizations, we are at a very exciting time to bring the message of recovery to the nation and build recovery-oriented communities.

Faces & Voices of Recovery is a call to action to build communities of recovery and accord dignity to people seeking or in recovery from addiction, recognizing that there are many pathways to recovery.

Whether behind the scenes or on the front line, every recovery voice is needed. Join us!

A Buddhist's Views on AA

By Taiyu

In Buddhism there is a myth about a hell-realm populated by beings whose appetites exceed their capacity for satisfaction. Their stomachs are huge but their throats are tiny. No matter how much they try to eat, their hunger remains. In ancient India, they are called hungry ghosts. We call them alcoholics and drug addicts.

In the United States prior to the 1940s, efforts to help addicts and alcoholics relied primarily on prison, hospitals, sanatoriums, and evangelical religion. Outcomes were terrible. Locking up or converting hungry ghosts at best kept the sufferer sober in the most basic sense but ultimately did nothing to resolve the deeper issues that make drinking or using clearly appear as a very good idea. External force and appeals to higher truths rarely reach the psychic depth necessary to support real change.

Alcoholics Anonymous in the late 1930s changed everything. Through it, recovery became a meaningful possibility. Within a few short decades, AA and its progeny (Narcotics Anonymous, Overeaters Anonymous, and so on) grew to be the hallmark and solution of choice for anyone struggling with addiction. Since then, AA has continued to serve as the primary avenue for recovery in America. It exists in most communities, its literature is published in all major and many minor languages world wide, and the fellowship has helped literally millions of addicts and alcoholics return to sober productive lives.

Even the medical community, with its emphasis on primary treatment, recognizes this. Nearly all hospital-based and free-standing programs throughout the US follow a 12-Step model of recovery. Indeed, the standard modality for helping hungry ghosts everywhere involves a few days to a week or so of medically supervised detoxification, a longer period of intensive immersion in the principles of AA, and an aftercare model that funnels graduates towards the fellowship.

This is so if for no other reason than because AA members understand first hand the real work of recovery doesn't involve getting sober, it involves staying sober. For most of us, the effort to sustain recovery quickly assumes an order of magnitude that dwarfs any life endeavor previously or subsequently undertaken. Indeed, quality sobriety entails a kind of commitment that is simply incomprehensible to anyone who hasn't actually done it. And with the success of AA's recovering community, there finally appeared an ongoing community whose singular commitment and capability was and is to support, educate, and enable addicts to get and remain sober through life's ups and downs.

Alcoholics Anonymous is a wonderful thing. It embraces the scope of ongoing change people in recovery must undertake. It provides an easy functioning and accessible kinship system. Its program is comprehensible and accessible to nearly anyone. And its willingness to welcome newcomers is close to perfect. The collective wisdom of the fellowship serves as a goldmine of truths that resonate deeply within the hearts and minds of recovering people everywhere. And the loving commitment it fosters for suffering addicts may very well exemplify the purest kind of compassion in action the world has ever seen.

But AA isn't perfect. Its language and underlying principles, to varying degrees, are outdated and sometimes petrified, its message seems at times far too simplistic, and its insistence that recovery requires a commitment to an external higher power (implicitly and often explicitly "God") increasingly fails to resonate even with theistic members. The AA tradition favoring mentorship of newcomers by more seasoned members sometimes fosters cult-like tendencies, and ultimately, for better or worse it's very easy for recovering persons to simply substitute an AA addiction for their initial drug of choice. And while no one ever died from participation in the fellowship, without the deeper inward effort recovery requires, the allure of resuming active addiction frequently becomes overwhelming.

After all, if merely subscribing to a new outward identity were sufficient, AA wouldn't be necessary in the first place.

To recover is to escape the realm of hungry ghosts. And we who have addiction find ourselves in this realm not because our throats are in fact too small nor our natural appetites too large, but because we're utterly and beyond all doubt convinced we're doomed without some external substance. Our lives are the experience of profound insufficiency. The belief we simply cannot survive without some sort of relief colors reality in such a hue that without more we are literally blind to everything else.

This delusion regarding the necessity of addiction is, for us, so deeply entrenched in our identity that it thoroughly covers and colors every last bit of our waking and sleeping moments.

156

Even in sobriety, we continue to obsess and wallow in the collective belief we're broken people with few redeeming capabilities. We litter our talk with discussions of core character defects, addictive tendencies, and fundamental flaws. We actively run from life's commitments and opportunities. And we habitually insist without more the doom we evade through ongoing recovery lurks just beyond our conscious reach. This nearly universal experience flows not from anything we did during the years of active addiction. It precedes those times and serves as the cognitive basis for why we used in the first place, and continued long after its limitations became apparent.

These perceptual truths don't just disappear when we swear off our substances of choice; indeed they intensify after sobriety. People who are new to all this sometimes experience a bit of a honeymoon during which they find satisfaction in being sober, attending more fully to the details of their lives, making amends, and participating in the fellowship of recovery. Almost invariably, however, that experience ends. In its place comes increasing sensitivity and emotional pain, a myriad of discouraging thoughts, beliefs, and perceptions, and a sense of meaninglessness and lack of purpose that easily becomes overpowering.

AA's diagnosis and prescription, at heart, grapples with all this rather nicely. We're invited to accept whole heartedly that a life of continued active addiction dooms us, that there is a way out which leads to a meaningful and fulfilling destiny, and that we can and should embrace with a deep sense of hope, faith, and commitment the idea that this better way is indeed accessible to each of us.

At once, we're then invited to turn our attention inward and begin to fearlessly examine our thoughts, feelings, beliefs, and history. We're asked to review and accept the past, to identify our mistakes, and to try and clarify the patterns and habits that fueled our behavior. We're encouraged to directly or symbolically clean house and make amends, and we're advised to adopt a far more honest and transparent approach to daily life.

Finally, we're urged to internalize and continue this reflective process on a routine ongoing basis, and to turn our attention to helping others with the same problem come into and remain in recovery.

These ideas aren't controversial. Viewed from a distance the foolhardiness of active addiction should be obvious. Clearly there exist innumerable ways to navigate life more effectively. Just as surely lives based on honesty, integrity, openness, and decency prove more beneficial than the insanity we once

157

embraced. These are AA's values. No one – addict or not – who embraces such ideas ever willingly discards them.

So the difficulty the program struggles with isn't in its basic prescription. The trouble instead resides in the way that message is often presented. AA's founders inherited a primitive religious view of addiction they accepted as basic reality. Seen through this prism, addiction became primarily a spiritual sickness whose symptoms involved character defects, moral insufficiency, and lack of faith. They viewed belief in God as an absolute necessity. They thought the path to a recovered life flows from cognitive and behavioral change in favor of new, more honest, and wholesome ideas. All this can be learned through meetings, sponsorship, the Big Book, and prayer. In the end, so this vision teaches, recovering alcoholics have the opportunity to graduate not from addiction itself, but into the fellowship of the spirit, a place where – but for routine maintenance – recovery is largely complete, and where thereafter the primary task is service and mentorship to less evolved members.

Some of these mistakes are mitigated by the efforts of the larger fellowship, the actual experience of recovery by the founders themselves, and the structural openness AA emphasizes. But the program nevertheless routinely risks becoming quasi-religious, institutionalized, and bent upon its own survival at the expense of actually helping people recover.

In a sense, AA has acquired an ego and now finds itself in the difficult struggle to sustain relevance in a Universe that no longer fully subscribes to its world view. Whatever the founders meant by "character defects," "moral inventories," and "spiritual sickness," we now view these ideas with justified suspicion. We often experience meetings less as an opportunity for sharing experience, strength, and hope, and more as evangelizing and cheerleading. We sense a tendency to elevate the literature to sacred-text status that makes even the most benign constructive criticism unacceptable. We endorse a de facto leadership defined by years of sobriety and charisma that allows some individuals a great and improper ability to define the meaning of recovery. And all this, to varying degrees exists at the expense of the founders' original goal: to zealously and by any effective means help addicts recover from the horrors of addiction.

What were envisioned as the collective living truths learned through one addict joining with another have tended to evolve towards a dogmatic insistence that recovery requires rigorous attendance at meetings, full acceptance of hyper-active sponsorship, early securing and defining of a higher power, and then turning individual autonomy (often mediated by the

158

sponsor's intercession) over to that entity. Failure to sufficiently undertake this behavior leads to judgment and criticism. To resist such efforts is to be in denial, to allow our addiction to speak for us, or to be unwilling to accept real recovery. Those who don't fully subscribe to the orthodox view face ostracism and exclusion. And in the end, when this process gets loud enough, people who might have recovered simply don't.

Nonetheless, it's hard to imagine what recovery might consist of were it not for the fellowship and program of Alcoholics Anonymous.

To be released from the shackles of active addiction is to escape the realm of hungry ghosts. There's no particular one-size-fits-all "right" way to do it. We're all, in this sense, pilgrims on an unknown journey to the new world. If the vision of recovery just criticized here does in fact work for particular addicts, they'd be fools not to rely upon it. That being said, for those of us who find great value in the fellowship of AA and its core program, yet struggle with its less helpful tendencies, this is a reminder:

Recovery is a broad avenue of increasing choices, opportunities, and solutions. AA is a community of explicit equality. The Big Book is but one of an entire library of texts. And no single member, group, or larger recovering community has the capability or authority to define what anyone's continued sobriety requires.

Abstractly, the work of recovery involves an initial deep and abiding commitment, based almost wholly on personal faith alone, to significant fundamental change. Usually at first we simply commit to attendance at AA meetings and promise not to drink or use in the interim. Later, and again based largely on hope and faith, we're asked to do much much more. That is to say, right away and always we do whatever we can simply not to drink or use. But it takes time – a lifetime – to turn and attend to those aspects of the ego self whose needs required drinking and using in order to survive. Without this larger effort, simply going to meetings and not drinking usually ultimately fails. So does memorizing the Big Book, performing service work, talking to our sponsors every day, talking to sponsees every day, and trying to discern what our ego's notion of God would have us do in perplexing situations.

Recovery is the grandest of endeavors. It calls on those who enter the path to turn and face their demons in ways people who don't have addiction simply cannot fully understand. There is a sensitivity in alcoholics and drug addicts that, before sobriety, we manage only through the numbing authority of chemical substances and addictive behavior. Removing our drug means removing the best solution to meaninglessness, sadness, anxiety, and massive suffering we addicts ever encountered. There's something about hungry ghosts that makes life loud and unhappy with or without the substance, so much so that drinking and using past the point of addiction and well on towards death itself seems at times like a very very good idea.

And so, ultimately, the work of sobriety is the task of finding meaning, purpose, joy, and satisfaction in life without the searing anesthesia of active addiction. How that happens is as unique to each person as snowflakes on a winter night. While some in AA argue there's only one true path, the real truth is no one recovers the same way as anyone else.

There are however, certain principles in recovery that carry a tremendous amount of force for nearly everyone. The sense of doom, hope, and commitment outlined previously are centerpieces to most people's ongoing efforts. Likewise, the program's middle steps, having to do with fearless and loving introspection, end up being the ongoing primary requirement of continued success in long-term recovery. And as we resolve our issues and meaningfully reconnect into the world as it is, the last requirement of AA – helping others who come after us – becomes a wonderful method of reinforcing our own life journey while also assisting our brothers and sisters to find and remain on their path when times get hard.

Buddhism teaches that life has suffering that comes not from outside us but instead from what's within. By letting go these internal struggles we overcome pain and find fulfillment. This isn't (or shouldn't be) at odds with anything anyone encounters in recovery nor in AA. Indeed, those of us with addiction have no trouble understanding from the very beginning the nature of suffering. Time and work usually leads to the second truth, that the genesis of pain lies within us and in our responses to experience. And, although AA teaches that it's God who lifts our delusions, the texts also provide a conceptually concise method of manifesting that change which is God-neutral and completely consistent with what the Buddha taught.

And so, only in ultimately trivial and easily overcome ways does Buddhism not fit squarely within the same process as 12-Step programs in general. Indeed, the spiritual solution of AA is the same solution any serious meditation practice uncovers, and if we come to understand all the talk about character defects in 12-Step programming is really talk about ego-self and delusion, even this aspect of recovery becomes uncontroversial. After all, the Buddha himself probably holds the copyright on the idea we need to see, accept, and let go any aspects of ego that lead to suffering.

160

AA redeems itself whenever members speak from the heart about experience, strength, and hope. Buddhism too, as well as all religions, all psychologies, and all personal disciplines and practices are saved in the ongoing effort to honestly discern truth and wisdom. It is a fluid process, not a static thing. Words, ideas, concepts, and proclaimed truths ultimately don't reach the Universe because they always come after the fact, after the experience, after the awakening. And whether we're active or recovering addicts, whether we're awakened or deluded, and even if we're the proverbial and illusory well adjusted perfectly normal individual with no issues or concerns whatsoever – none of this ultimately changes the far deeper truth which is simply that we are all seekers on the path to wisdom, redemption, and peace.

All Paths to Recovery are Cause for Celebration

By John M.

This past February at AA Agnostica, I wrote about my ten favourite recovery websites. The *William White Papers* was included among them not only for the wide range of material one can access there but also because I believe William White to be one of the most gifted and knowledgeable practitioners in the field of recovery research as well as one who is also able to speak from first hand experience about addiction.

White is Director of the Research Division of the Chestnut Health Center established in 1986 employing about 90 people engaged in a "science based understanding" of addiction and recovery. What happens in recovery over the long term is the center's particular research mandate and is not solely for what happens to those in recovery over the first thirty days to six months. The science of addiction is continuing to be produced and collected to better evaluate many issues that were previously known only anecdotally (though sometimes falsely or at least ambiguously). More than 600 scientific studies/papers are used by White and his colleagues.

At his website you will find over 400 scholarly (but highly readable) articles by him including interviews with some of the most well known research professionals and advocates in the field of addiction and recovery. You will also find a stunning array of addiction bibliographical material as well as very useful chronologies listing the histories of such societies like AA, NA, Smart Recovery, the Addiction Recovery Advocacy Movement (dating back to the 18th Century), and more. You will find book reviews by White on some of the most relevant texts to appear over the past few years. There is much to explore at this site!

What I want to draw your attention to, however, is White's three-part video of his 2009 Recovery Oriented Systems of Care (ROSC) Symposium. The total viewing time is about 4 1/2 hours but with it's three-part format, and between 15-23 segments in each of the three parts, separated into easily navigated portions, you can simply set your own timeframe for relaxing and taking it all in without wasting time later searching for where you were in the video from your last viewing.

White is an engaging speaker who confesses that in this presentation he will sound at times like a country preacher and he does so as a recovery

162

advocate and as a person himself in long term recovery; at other times, he says he will sound like a stuffy researcher, flashing graphs and numbers at us; and finally, he shares that he will give voice to the experience of a number of pioneering groups that are helping to transform behavioural health care in a number of American cities today.

The common theme reiterated by White on numerous occasions throughout the symposium is a paraphrase of Bill Wilson's often forgotten acknowledgement that there are many paths to recovery and ALL are cause for celebration. He will argue that we have to give up the single pathway recovery model and adopt a multiple pathway model conducive to the needs of each individual while, at the same time, taking into account multiple patterns of addiction and multiple sub-cultures. This includes a "menu" of all sorts of recovery philosophies and support services and sometimes combining and sequencing them as they apply to the unique needs of individuals within a particular environment.

There is such a vast range of material covered by White here that I cannot adequately do justice to it by providing a synopsis so I hope only to tweak your interest by highlighting a tiny sample of salient points that caught my attention.

1. Science is discovering that alcoholics/addicts fall into two distinctive categories: transient and chronic. Transient recoverers "mature out," or "naturally recover," or are said to undergo "spontaneous remission" after around a 24 month period of alcohol and/or drug abuse. The data indicates that after five years most are healed or are healthy in ways we commonly use to define personal well-being. The chronic sufferers, or those who are said to manifest "chronicity" through longer periods of time, need the standard intervention we have come to know as treatment and recovery "programs."

2. The data indicates that four to five years is the time it takes to statistically predict a sustainable and stable point of recovery for alcoholics and heroin addicts. Eighty-five per cent of alcoholics who attain four or five years of continuous sobriety stay sober after this point whereas 75% of heroin addicts will not relapse. Researchers, White points out, do not know why there is a ten per cent difference between the recovery rates of alcoholics and heroin addicts. No studies have been undertaken to track cocaine, marijuana or narcotic/prescription drug addicts over the long term. The science is simply not yet there for these latter types.

3. Science shows that you cannot predict the success of recovery from an alcoholic's/drug addict's initial contact with and/or motivation for entering treatment facilities or peer support programs. Rather, motivation is an outcome, not a pre-condition, of the criteria for successful treatment and support. How many of us have met enthusiastic, highly motivated newcomers who we thought would definitely "make it" only to find that the initial motivation could not be sustained by that individual within the program or the group he or she was associated with. (White has lots more to offer on this subject!)

4. A qualification, however, must be raised for the previous observation. In his many years as a street worker, treatment centre worker (and Director) and as a researcher, White has often speculated (given AA's disinterest in rigorously gathering data on the progress of its members) that AA has perhaps been far more successful than membership lists, numbering slightly over two million, suggest. Just because a newcomer arrives at a group, stays around for a period of time, and then is no longer seen again, does not mean that when that person no longer attends they have "failed" and have "gone out" again. Some of AA's hidden success may lie in the fact that AA provides readily available meetings and often serves as a catalyst for getting the newcomer's attention for the very thing that needs his or her attention and they subsequently follow a different path to recovery - and do, in fact, recover. All paths to recovery, White reiterates, are cause for celebration.

5. When clients in treatment find themselves recycled four to five times (or more) and are told that they have entered the "best" treatment facility, is it the client who fails or is it the "system?" Are these clients actually being given a realistic chance at recovery or have they merely been "set up" to fail?

6. The recovery model should mirror the medical model if we are serious about designating alcohol and drug abuse as part of a "disease model." In reality, we either do so half-heartedly or do not really believe that addiction is a disease. If we were serious or if we begin to correlate scientifically the data coming out of recent research with the data that has been present for some time now in the treatment and care of cancer, diabetes, or heart disease patients, then addiction treatment falls short. It cannot therefore just be tweaked to improve it but must undergo a radical paradigm shift and be redesigned.

We know with alcoholics and heroin addicts that four to five years is a key indicator of success and we know that cancer patients, for example, have five years of follow-up care and tracking from their medical practitioners. The medical community knows that five years for cancer remission is the time-period for essential post-treatment monitoring but given that the statistics tell us that the five year period is essential to the well-being of alcohol and heroin recoverers, why don't we in fact follow the medical model? Instead we leave it to recoverers themselves, to their families and friends (and to peer groups, like AA) to get them to the five year "safety mark" without any medical and, in most cases, long term, treatment centre post-recovery monitoring.

7. The current addiction treatment and recovery model is politically and medically unsustainable. It mirrors the following analogy used by Native American Don Coyhis of the Wellbriety movement. Coyhis compares current treatment models to digging up a dying tree which is rooted in bad soil, replanting the tree in good soil, watching it grow and thrive and then digging it up and replanting it back in the bad soil. What do we expect will happen! The current treatment model is like this. We take the alcoholic/addict and place them into a treatment centre, and even the small percentage that want to be there and who thrive in that treatment environment, we return them to their previous lives and communities and expect them to thrive as if we expected the rejuvenated tree to remain healthy when returned to bad soil.

8. We have to start talking in terms of "recovery capital." It is a threefold engagement by the recoverer drawing on: one, strengths from within himself or herself; two, an engaged group of family and friends; and three, a recovery-friendly community within which the recoverer interacts on a daily basis. Unless this threefold multiple support network exists we will continue to see the recovery data reflect perpetual cycles of relapse in and out of treatment centres as well as low percentages of recoverers making it past the five year stability point for long term recovery.

Recovering doctors, for instance, statistically have the best recovery rates because they have access to the most "recovery capital." (And no, we are not solely talking about money here, though wealth certainly factors into all kinds of individual, family, and community-engagement opportunities.)

On a personal note, I am not abundantly wealthy, though I am comfortable, and as I reflect on my past six years of recovery in light of what White says about "recovery capital," I am less mystified as to why my "miraculous" recovery occurred. I had certain core strengths, in spite of my alcoholism; I had a loving and supportive wife, sisters, in-laws, non-alcoholic friends as well as new-found friends in the rooms of Alcoholics Anonymous. My bosses at work; my fellow employees; a job I love to go to each day; and a wonderful psychiatrist to work with on my fourth and fifth Step - all the above point to White's notion of "recovery capital" as a legitimate and profound concept.

With this concept in mind and looking back on the early days of my sobriety, I now have to ask myself: how would it have been possible for me NOT to get sober? You can call it "grace." I certainly recognize the graciousness of all those who helped and supported me and I am exceedingly grateful to them. But I will call it "recovery capital."

9. Faith based, spiritually based, and secular based models are all legitimate pathways to recovery and all are cause for celebration. Taking just one example, Project Match's eight-year study beginning in 1989 comparing Cognitive Behaviour Therapy, Motivational Interviewing and 12 Step based programs consistently showed that there was statistically pretty much the same success rate of recovery among the three.

10. Among various ways to categorize certain typologies, one way is to look at three types of responses to the uses and abuses of alcohol and drugs: abstinence based, moderation based, and medication-assisted based recoveries and these as legitimate options, White insists, should no longer divide us into antagonistic camps.

White confesses that early in his career as an addictions worker and as one fully committed to a 12 Step model, he attended a lecture by Dr. Ed Senay (later to become a friend) who had talked about the importance of methadone-assisted recovery for a great number of addicts. White was appalled that this learned man could argue for anything that didn't get to the root of the sufferer's problems, and methadone, White felt, only addressed the symptoms among other physiological problems. With arms flailing, looking a bit like a lunatic, White proceeded at the end of the lecture to tell the man how very wrong he was. Dr. Senay stood patiently, arms folded, and when White had finished speaking Senay responded: "Young man, your passion is in inverse relation to your knowledge."

White laughs at himself now but he asks how many of us have taken our well intentioned and passionate belief in our own model and tried to impose it on those who might not be helped by it, or at other times when we have failed to support other methods that at least deserved a fair hearing.

11. Advocacy with Anonymity: "By our silence we have let others define us!" White believes it is time to deal with one of the great barriers to recovery that exists in the form of social stigma and shame. To rid society of the stigma and shame that many people in recovery still feel even after many years of being clean and sober requires the kind of social movement which has parallels with the civil rights, women's, and gay rights movements of earlier decades.

As an historian of all recovery movements, White understands that for the fellowship of the recovery community of AA, the Traditions seem to prevent loyal members from participating publicly in gatherings and marches designed to show the face of recovering addicts and alcoholics as happy and responsible citizens just like everyone else. But White points out that no AA Tradition needs to be violated by its members since people gather and march as part of the larger movement of "persons in recovery" (New Recovery Advocacy Movement) and no one identifies as particular participants in any such organizations like AA or NA or WFS or any other autonomous entity.

Individuals who are comfortable with their sobriety and who are in a position where stigma and discrimination have little or no social and employment repercussions (not everyone is in such a position) are needed to advocate on behalf of addicted people of all sorts in their communities at large and to the politicians who can propose and enact beneficial social policy.

12. A note of concern by White: If we continue to sell, highlight and promote the treatment model as it currently exists in most forms, we could be in danger of what White calls the "perfect storm" of the recovery movement's possible demise. Here is his final slide in his three-part presentation:

> Overselling what the Acute Care model can achieve to policy makers and the public risks a backlash and the revocation of addiction treatment's probational status as a cultural institution that can threaten the very existence of this addiction field.

> ROSC and RM (Recovery Management) represent not a refinement of modern addiction treatment but a fundamental redesign of such treatment.

As resources are needed for a full commitment to this necessary recovery management remodeling (i.e., ROSC and RM), given the times we live in, White sees the "perfect storm" playing itself out in something like the following:

> We could have a "virtual avalanche" of celebrities moving in and out of rehab to escape the responsibilities of their latest indiscretions in ways that can totally discredit the reputation and integrity of addiction treatment. Coupled with this we could have a financial crisis of unprecedented proportion that would force State and Federal politicians to make a decision whether to fund roads, schools, or addiction treatment.

13. White admits that some of the scientific research often verifies many past practices of which any old time AA'ers with grade five educations could have told us. Still, science must either confirm or dispel what is sometimes indistinguishable between wisdom and fact, ideology and myth.

14. New ground, White tells us, is being explored every day. But the science of addiction and recovery is still really just scratching the surface of what needs to be positively and adequately known and this means mobilizing and coordinating social and political awareness which is just gaining momentum in breaking through the stigmatization and the ignorance of the past. White is excited about the future yet as an historian – and he talks about the demise of a flourishing recovery movement in early 20th Century America – he is quite realistic as to what can happen to any movement which fails to seize the appropriate moment at the appropriate time and place.

If science is only scratching the surface of addiction and recovery research thus far, this introduction to William White's video has also only done just that. In fact, the best reason for why I highly recommend taking some time out to watch the video is the following: if White had purposely set out in these 4 1/2 hours to address every question or issue you have ever heard raised about addiction, 12 Step models, AA, and other recovery, medical, and scientific modules, he would pretty much have succeeded in his intent.

It is clear from the format of his presentation that he did not set out to do so. But, so knowledgeable is he within the contours of his presentation, and so quick to respond off the top of his head in detail to questions from his audience of recovery professionals, you can only be amazed at the breadth of his research and his ability to apply this research to the most pressing issues facing the addiction and recovery community today (as well as addressing those politicians who must realistically and adequately begin to put the addiction epidemic at the top of their social policy agendas).

White accomplishes all this by calling for a veritable "fourth step" of current treatment models to see where existing strengths ought to be preserved but also where the models themselves are inadequate or are "working" at cross-purposes or are downright self-defeating.

I hope you will take some time to share in the experience of this simply magisterial presentation. Enjoy!

VII. Early History

AA Started in Riots

By Roger C.

What would become AA was born and bred within the Oxford Group, an explicitly Christian religious movement.

The early (pre-AA) get-togethers were of "alcoholic squads" within and a part of the Oxford Group. This was true both in New York City (where at least the squad met at Bill Wilson's home) and in Akron, Ohio, where the alcoholics "did not meet separately from the Oxford Group." (*Wikipedia*) The gatherings were explicitly religious ones, and included Bible readings and prayers, with the participants often on their knees, in supplication to our Lord Jesus Christ for a reprieve from alcoholism.

Bill and the New Yorkers broke with the Oxford Group in 1937 or, as his wife Lois put it, "they were kicked out" for focussing too much on alcoholism and not enough on Christ. In Akron, however, the gatherings of the alcoholic squad remained within the Oxford Group and focussed on the principle: "Trust God, clean house and help others."

Until "AA started in riots."

————

The first AA meeting – the first meeting called "Alcoholics Anonymous" – was held in Cleveland on May 11, 1939, one month after the Big Book had been published.

To put it mildly, "the first AA meeting in the world was not uneventful." (How It Worked, p. 142)

The previous night, the Clevelanders, who up until then met as part of the alcoholic squad every week in Akron, announced at the Akron gathering that they had decided to start their own meeting in Cleveland and make a complete break with the Oxford Group.

"You can't do this," Dr. Bob shouted.

"The meeting almost turned into a riot as the Cleveland Group got up as a whole and walked out." (How It Worked, p. 140)

The next evening was much more disturbing.

> According to Clarence, the entire group from Akron showed up the next night and tried to "discourage" the Cleveland meeting from happening. Discourage was a very mild term, according to Clarence; and he used it sarcastically. He said:
>
> "The whole group descended upon us and tried to break up our meeting. One guy was gonna whip me. I want you to know that this was all done in pure Christian love... AA started in riots. It rose in riots."
>
> Clarence was often quoted as saying, "If you don't stand for something, you're liable to fall for anything." (How It Worked, p. 142)

Thus began the very first "AA" meeting. It was completely free of the Oxford Group. "It was a meeting of Alcoholics Anonymous. It was a meeting held by, and for alcoholics and their families only." (How It Worked, Mitchell K., p. 141)

And it began in riots.

———

A few months ago, AA Agnostica provided a form on the home page of the website for those who want to be part of organizing an agnostic AA meeting in their own communities.

The response has been remarkable with hundreds and hundreds having completed the forms. In spite of the fact that there are hundreds and hundreds of cities and towns in hundreds and hundreds of states, provinces, counties and territories throughout the world, a number of agnostic AA meetings have already been started with more coming down the pike in the next weeks and months.

170

Here is a sampling of some of the quotes from people who have completed the form:

"I have only been sober for 70 days, but I have been stuck on Step Two for about 50 days. I am confident that I am healthier and happier sober, but I simply do not believe in God or a Higher Power." (Vandra)

"I have over 25 years of sobriety – having for the first 15 had a strong faith and belief in a 'power greater than myself' that I called god. For the past 10 years, it doesn't make sense to me anymore and the god talk I hear at meetings keeps me away." (Susan)

"I do not want to pray at meetings." (Julia)

"I find it offensive to say the Lord's Prayer. I would say that I am agnostic with a heavy leaning to atheism. The fact of the matter is that a traditional AA meeting is thoroughly Christian religious based and there is never going to be a way around that." (Greg)

"I can't stay sober without AA, but the god thing is a pain in the ass. It's getting really hard to keep my mouth shut in meetings, but I don't want to knock how someone else stays sober. I feel AA has really helped me stay sober, but god has nothing to do with it." (Dave)

"I have been sober in AA for 17 years and have been agnostic for the last 15 of those years... For the most part I have been able to get by and keep my mouth shut on the 'God topic.' However for the fear of conformity I have twisted my non-theist views to appear to be theist in a lot of circumstances... But more and more I started feeling very untrue both to myself and others. I see more and more newcomers come in and get shoved out by the God talk." (Jake)

"I have gone to AA meetings off and on for many years but the G O D thing was a large deterrent to continued attendance... I am an atheist and I cannot see that as ever changing although I have firmly believed in the need for spirituality in my life. I have been afraid to bring up my beliefs in the meetings for fear of being ostracized." (Greg)

"There is a small group of sober AA members who are atheist or non-religious who wish to help other atheist/agnostic people benefit from the steps and fellowship. We have seen the 'God talk' drive a lot of newcomers straight out of the rooms." (Lynn)

Back in the day, Clarence Snyder didn't lead the break with the Oxford Group and the Akron gatherings because of a large number of non-believers in

Cleveland. It was more because of Catholic alcoholics who were threatened with excommunication because of their participation in a Protestant organization, the Oxford Group.

Today, the differences in AA are centred around non-belief. An exponentially increasing number of people can't abide meetings that end with the Lord's Prayer.

Nor is that entirely new in our fellowship. While in Akron the guiding principle of the alcoholic squad was "Trust God, clean house and help others" that didn't work in New York. There, the principle was a much simpler "Don't drink and go to meetings."

Even today "our more religious members" argue that the New York approach is not really AA.

The riots merely continue within Alcoholics Anonymous.

———

The first ever meeting in AA explicitly for nonbelievers was held on January 7, 1975, in the city of Chicago. And thus was born Quad A: Alcoholics Anonymous for Atheists and Agnostics (AAAA).

And similar meetings sprung up in other parts of the United States... In California... In New York City...

However, in *A History of Agnostic Groups in AA* we learn that two-thirds of all agnostic AA group listed with the General Service Office have held their very first meetings after the millennium.

Times change.

In the twenty-first century, a faith in God, personal salvation and a life after death is sinking faster than a metaphoric Titanic.

AA was always meant to be an umbrella organization for all with a desire for a reprieve from the affliction of alcoholism.

And so when the Clevelanders started the first-ever meeting of Alcoholics Anonymous and broke away from the alcoholic squad anchored in the Oxford Group in order to make room for Catholics that was the right thing to do.

And so when we start new meetings and break away from the religiosity of the Christian Church in order to make room for atheists and agnostics that is the right thing to do.

You do what you have to do. As Clarence Snyder so correctly put it: "If you don't stand for something, you're liable to fall for anything."

We are merely part of Alcoholics Anonymous moving from alcoholic squads of the Oxford Group in the 1930s to the new millennium.

Ever onwards and upwards.

Will some object?

Guaranteed. The *White Paper*, written in 2010, describes meetings for agnostics and atheists as "dangerous deviations" and call for "a course of action for eliminating them and returning our Fellowship to the pure spiritual oasis that has nourished suffering alcoholics for 75 years."

Groups will be tossed from Intergroups and others will not be listed.

No surprise. Change doesn't come easy for any of us. And, while we would by far prefer unity and harmony, that is not our call. We're not the ones threatening others with "elimination," which was the stated goal of the Greater Toronto Area Intergroup when it booted two agnostic groups out of AA two and half years ago. Didn't work.

As Clarence reminds us from his experience over seventy years ago with the first AA meeting: "One guy was gonna whip me. I want you to know that this was all done in pure Christian love... AA started in riots. It rose in riots."

AA started in riots. If need be it will continue to rise in riots. But, if it is to fulfill the visionary mission of its founders, it must now move forward and find a way to be relevant to all suffering alcoholics in the twenty-first century.

AA in the 1930s: God As We Understood Him

By Bob K.

The wheels were set in motion for what would eventually become Alcoholics Anonymous at Bill Wilson's kitchen table in November of 1934. Bill's old school chum and sometime drinking buddy, Ebby Thacher, came to visit and he arrived in a shocking condition. He was sober!

> The door opened and he stood there, fresh-skinned and glowing. There was something about his eyes. He was inexplicably different. What had happened? I pushed a drink across the table. He refused it. Disappointed but curious, I wondered what had got into the fellow. He wasn't himself. "Come, what's all this about?" I queried. He looked straight at me. Simply, but smilingly, he said, "I've got religion." (BB p. 9)

Over the years, there has been some misunderstanding regarding Bill Wilson's pre-conversion "belief status." The author of the We Agnostics chapter in the Big Book was neither atheist nor agnostic. "I had always believed in a Power greater than myself.... I was not an atheist." (BB p.10) Essentially parentless, and strongly under the influence of a liberal maternal grandfather, Wilson confessed some admiration for Christ, but disdain for the hypocrisy of his followers and the mandates of the Preachers. As were so very many others, Wilson was further jaded by the horrors of the "Great War," and "honestly doubted whether, on balance, the religions of mankind had done any good.... (T)he power of god in human affairs was negligible, the Brotherhood of Man a grim jest." (BB p. 11)

William Griffith Wilson, and Grandfather Gardner Fayette Griffith were deists. Our friends at Wikipedia help us here: "According to deists, the creator does not intervene in human affairs or suspend the natural laws of the universe. Deists typically reject supernatural events such as prophecy and miracles, tending instead to assert that a god (or "the Supreme Architect") does not alter the universe by intervening in it." This was undeniably a fairly radical position among the Christian super-majority of the era, but neither was it agnosticism nor atheism.

The desperation of an advanced state of alcoholism propelled Wilson to consider abandoning "the vestiges of my old prejudice... (reconsidering) that there might be a God personal to me...." (BB p. 12) After some resistance,

174

and some further drinking, a second visit from Ebby, still more drinking, and the passage of a couple of weeks Bill Wilson (only half-drunk) ventured to the very Christian Calvary Mission and made a public "testimony" of his newfound faith in a rescuing God. Buoyed by a renewed optimism that the solution to his drinking problem was at hand, he headed to Towns Hospital for his fourth and final de-tox AFTER a few more days of serious drinking.

At Towns, as per the procedures of the time, Bill was drugged with barbiturates and belladonna. He awoke in a state of severe depression, but a visit from Ebby renewed his resolve to attempt the "God cure." After all, he had nothing to lose. Now, students of AA history may well know that Bill's paternal grandfather, a prodigious drinker, was moved by the words of an itinerant preacher at a revival meeting to "surrender liquor." Many times, young Bill heard of grandpa's "spiritual experience" involving the ever-present white light and the refreshing coolness of a mountain breeze. Cynics will find Bill's hospital "experience" remarkably similar to Grandpa Willie's!

William James has cited "deflation at depth" as a pre-requisite for "spiritual experience." Even without the assistance of Monty Hall, our founder could clearly see death and alcoholic insanity behind doors number one and two. The choice of door number three required only the swallowing of some intellectual pride, and the conversion from belief in an uninvolved Creator, to One who would help in his time of need.

Many see, in instances such as these, the awesome power of the supernatural. Others detect the tremendous power of the fear of death or disability. The case for the "fear theory" is made by wealthy, and otherwise clear-thinking people, who plunk down tens, or hundreds of thousands for bogus cancer cures, or at cryogenic clinics. A recollection of Psychology 101 brings to mind the surprising effectiveness of the "placebo effect." The incredible power of the mind can produce some amazing results. Mothers who, to save an endangered child, lift great and weighty objects – angelic assistance or adrenaline rush?

So on went Bill to a new and sober life and a motivating missionary zeal for helping others. Although his somewhat preachy proselytizing produced no lasting conversions, he was managing to keep himself sober. A tip from Dr. Silkworth to ease up on the salvation story and "white light experience," and instead to open with powerful truths of the progressive and fatal nature of the disease, led to a new approach with Dr. Bob Smith. The good Akron doctor was well along the "God-path," but achieving no relief from his dissipation. He did react favourably to the "one alcoholic talking to another" tactic, and the living example of another such as he. This was the start of Alcoholics

175

Anonymous (as yet unnamed). These were the godliest of the Christian glory days. New converts in Akron, like Bill D., Ernie G. the first, and Phil S. delighted in their new-found recovery with resistance to neither God nor Jesus Christ. The "alcoholic squad" of the Oxford Group's Christian fellowship was enjoying some success. Of course, a number of others, Eddie R., "Victor" and "Lil" famous for AA's first thirteenth step, and many others sought the "God-cure," but no "miracle" was forthcoming.

Back in New York, Fitz M., a minister's son resentful against God, dropped his resentments, returned to the fold, and got sober – a grateful prodigal son. Then, the whole religious "kumbaya" singing unit was thrown for a loop by the arrival of Hank P., who though happy to be sober, attributed this "blessing" to the power of the fellowship. Although in his story, The Unbeliever, desperation drives him to attempt prayer, it is widely known that he continued in his disbelief and lobbied for a book EXCLUDING God entirely. Spiritual solidarity had lasted a mere four months. The chapter We Agnostics tells us that although many started as atheists or agnostics, these failing philosophies were quickly and easily abandoned once their "lack of power" was understood. This is not at all true. The New York Group detached completely from the Oxfords in 1937. Many wanted a more secular path, and others a non-sectarian path. Ohio AA was very Christian, but New York was quite eclectic.

January, 1938, brought Jim Burwell, atheistic, aggressive and argumentative. Those sympathetic to his lack of belief did not rally round Jimmy's cause as the "Don't Tell" attitude was producing results. Those believing in the power of the group, wisely do not aggressively attack the group. Many undoubtedly did some ungodly praying that Jim would get drunk, and after seven months, he did. He returned and was far less argumentative. However, it is not true that he abandoned his disbelief. Months later, when the book was written, it did NOT include his story. Still sober in 1955, his story was added to the book. He states quite clearly that, for many years, his higher power was the group itself.

Jim's biography "Sober for Thirty Years" makes it quite clear that he never developed any belief in a supernatural god. And aAccording to Clarence Snyder: "Jimmy remained steadfast throughout his life and 'preached' his particular [non-God] brand of AA wherever he went."

For the man credited with the phrase "God, as we understood Him," in extreme situations such as his own, this could be stretched to "even if we understood Him to NOT be God." In 1991, when it was sensed that I had a resistance to the religious aspects of AA, the more liberal members invited me to use God as "G" "O" "D" – Good Orderly Direction, or Group Of Drunks. This I found to be very awkward, but serviceable. I took consolation in the study of AA history which clearly illustrates that the spiritual homogeneity touted in our book NEVER existed past September or October of 1935. "To show other alcoholics precisely how we recovered" is a gross oversimplification. Of course, it was expected that over time I would develop a higher Higher Power. It hasn't happened yet.

It is somewhat irksome that the success of cases such as mine are used to militate AGAINST any change in the wording of the steps, or the book. Of course, the same fine folks in a different conversation, will tell you with great assurance that those who recover on "human power" were never "real alcoholics" in the first place.

In the AA of the new millenium, there are several ongoing, and vocal movements of "Big Book Fundamentalism." It is no overstatement that the book is worshipped, and all ideas not contained within the covers of the book (most particularly the first 164, 103, or 88 pages) are summarily dismissed! The common thread: GOD, GOD, and MORE GOD. Tolerance for higher powers other than God are on the decline. Newcomers resistant to God are told to return to drinking. Sober non-believers were NEVER "real" alcoholics. The number of "God" references in the book is continually cited (albeit the number fluctuates quite a bit). Appendix II, Spiritual Experience, with its talk of "psychic change" is seen as diluting the message. The rather significant "Back to Basics" movement would love a return to Oxford Group Christian principles. Sharing of experience is being replaced by the unapologetic preaching of absolutes.

All of the above is based on the misguided notion that the venerated "First 100" followed precisely the formula described in the book. This is ridiculously untrue and akin to claiming that Dalton McGinty was unanimously elected in the past provincial election.

It all kind of reminds me of a very exciting day at the Keep It Simple Group, in 1992. A rather defiant "Richard the Atheist" was vociferously expressing some "non-conforming" views when one of the more orthodox disciples was propelled by Christian love to leap across the table, with fists flying, in an evangelical effort to bring about in Richard the requisite "religious experience." Didn't work – the obstinacy of some being beyond all imagining!

Washingtonian Forbears of Alcoholics Anonymous

By John L.

For several weeks now I've been engrossed with the Washingtonian Temperance Society, or Washingtonian Movement, which was founded and thrived a century before Alcoholics Anonymous came into being. The Washingtonians not only had many of the best features of Alcoholics Anonymous, but, I'll argue, were even better in some ways. In their brief heyday, from 1840 to about 1845, the Washingtonians succeeded in sobering up tens or even hundreds of thousands of drunkards or inebriates (the word "alcoholic" had not yet been coined), who had previously been regarded as hopeless and incorrigible. Then, after less than a decade, the movement declined, for reasons I'll try to explain.

Founding of Alcoholics Anonymous

My interest in the Washingtonians was renewed when, at a Crossroads meeting in Boston, I won the raffle for "any book on the table". I chose *Alcoholics Anonymous Comes of Age: a brief history of AA* Reading this history, I began to doubt that AA ever had a single moment of founding, or that only Bill Wilson (Bill W.) and Dr. Robert Smith (Dr. Bob) deserve to be considered co-founders — although they considered themselves to be, and AA went along with them. Bear in mind that Ebby Thatcher brought the message of sobriety to Bill W., and someone else before that sobered up Ebby, and well before Bill W. got sober or met Dr. Bob, Henrietta Seiberling in Akron, Ohio had organized an alcoholics squad within the Oxford Group — and the best ideas and principles of AA really do go back to the Washingtonians. All of these things, and other events and people unknown, led eventually to Alcoholics Anonymous.

Nowhere in *Alcoholics Anonymous Comes of Age* is it explained why Bill & Bob, and they alone, should be considered co-founders of AA. Beginning on p. vii is a chronology, "Landmarks in AA History", which includes this item: "1935, June 10 — Dr. Bob has his last drink. Alcoholics Anonymous founded". But this is absurd. Why should the alleged event of AA's founding be Dr. Bob's last drink? In this appalling episode, Bill gives Bob a beer so that his hands won't shake too badly as he performs surgery! Bill is conveniently vague as to why or whether the surgery was an absolute emergency, or Dr. Bob had to be the one to do it. It should be obvious that someone with shaking hands, recovering from an alcoholic binge, has no business

178

performing surgery — but even many years later, Bill (advocate of the "searching and fearless moral inventory") still didn't see anything morally wrong with what he and Bob did.

Clarence Snyder angered Bill & Bob by asserting that he was the real founder of AA, or at least as much a co-founder as they were. His case is strong. Clarence, along with Dr. Bob, was a recovering alcoholic within the Oxford Group, a religious movement with fascist tendencies. All of their meetings contained non-alcoholic Oxford Groupers as well as alcoholics, and were concerned more with piety than with sobriety. Clarence explained to Bob that Catholic alcoholics in Cleveland, where he lived, were prevented by their religious leaders from attending meetings of the Oxford Group. Bob said: "We can't do anything about it." Clarence replied, "Yes, we can." He intended:

> To start a group without all this rigmarole that's offensive to other people. We have a book now, the Steps, the absolutes. Anyone can live by that program. We can start our own meetings. (from Dr. Bob...)

Bob was adamantly opposed to this, but Clarence was undaunted:

> I made the announcement at the Oxford Group that this was the last time the Cleveland bunch was down as a contingent — that we were starting a group in Cleveland that would only be open to alcoholics and their families. Also that we were taking the name from the book 'Alcoholics Anonymous'.

> The roof came off the house. "Clarence, you can't do this!" someone said.

> It's done. ... (ibid.)

Organized by Clarence Snyder, the first meeting of Alcoholics Anonymous was held in Cleveland, Ohio on 11 May 1939. The Akron Oxford Group sent a goon squad to break up the meeting; Clarence was physically assaulted, but the Clevelanders stood their ground. The significance of this event goes well beyond the use of "Alcoholics Anonymous" as the name for the group. It was the first time since the Washingtonian movement that alcoholics themselves, independent from religionists, organized to help other alcoholics achieve and maintain sobriety. Clarence was not an atheist or agnostic, but he favored tolerance for those of all faiths or none. He especially promoted Fellowship: "Not too much stress on spiritual business at meetings.... Plenty of fellowship all the time." The Cleveland meetings, open only to alcoholics and their families, were a big step towards AA's current alcoholics-only membership policy and its single purpose: to carry the message of sobriety to the alcoholic who still suffers.

The Akron group, still within the Oxford Group, was moribund. In New York, Bill W. — rejected by the Oxford Groupers as too uncouth — had only a handful of alcoholics around him. But the Alcoholics Anonymous meetings in Cleveland grew by leaps and bounds, and served as a model for the rest of the country.

In support of Clarence Snyder's claim, a list of the first 226 members of Alcoholics Anonymous in Akron, Ohio, prepared in the early 1940s, lists three men as co-founders: Bill Wilson, Dr. Bob Smith, and Clarence Snyder.

The Washingtonians

In sharp contrast to the AA imbroglio, we know exactly when, where, and by whom the Washington Total Abstinence Society was founded, and what its mandate was. Several men in Baltimore, who considered themselves "tipplers" rather than "drunkards", attended a temperance lecture, intending to scoff and then report on the meeting for the amusement of their friends in Chase's Tavern. Instead, the evangelist made such a deep impression on them that they decided to quit drinking together and to form a society to cure intemperance — to rehabilitate drunkards and inebriates. On 5 April 1840 these "six poor drunkards met in a grog shop in that city, took the pledge to reform, and organized a society, to which they gave the name Washingtonian." (from *Washingtonian Pocket Companion*)

The six founders were David Anderson (blacksmith), Archibald Campbell (silversmith), John F. Hoss (carpenter), James McCurley (coachmaker), William K. Mitchell (tailor), and George Steers (wheelwright). (from Crowley)

The older temperance movement, led by the clergy, had regarded the drunkard with disdain, as damned and incorrigible; they expected him to die, thus reinforcing their prohibitionist narrative: alcohol leads inevitably to death. Washingtonianism, in sharp contrast:

> makes *special* efforts to snatch the poor inebriate from his destructive habits — aims to *cure* as well as *prevent* intemperance. It considers the drunkard as a man — our brother — capable of being touched by kindness, of appreciating our love, and benefiting by our labors. We therefore, stoop down to him in his fallen condition and kindly raise him up, and whisper hope and encouragement into his ear, and aid him to *aid himself* back again

to health, peace, usefulness, respectability and prosperity. (From the *Washingtonian Pocket Companion*)

And this they did with spectacular success. Within a mere five years, hundreds of Washingtonian groups were formed, in every major city in the country. By 1842, there were 23 Washingtonian Societies in New York City alone, with a claimed membership of 16,000. Many tens of thousands of hopeless inebriates found new lives in sobriety.

The similarities with the best practices and principles of AA are striking: above all, alcoholics helping each other in practical ways and through the sharing of "experience, strength and hope". The Washingtonians developed the tripartite temperance story — which in AA is called a "qualification": how one's life had been destroyed by drinking, what happened, and what one's life is like in sobriety. Like AA, the Washingtonians held weekly meetings. Like AA, they believed in total abstinence.

The Washingtonians anticipated many of AA's Traditions. They believed in the autonomy of groups (AA Tradition Four), in avoiding divisiveness (AA Tradition One), and avoiding controversy on outside issues (AA Tradition Ten).

The Washingtonian approach was essentially secular: human beings, reformed drunkards, helped the drunkard to help himself. William K. Mitchell, the first president, was leery of the clerical leadership of the older temperance movement, and he rejected the premise that religious conversion was necessary for sobriety. In this respect, Washingtonianism was superior to Alcoholics Anonymous, which is vitiated by Bill W's insistence that a "spiritual awakening" and belief in a "Higher Power" (aka "God") are necessary for sobriety, and by the embarrassing religious claptrap found throughout the *Big Book* and the *12 & 12*.

This is not to say that the Washingtonians were anti-religious; their meetings often featured the singing of hymns — although the hymns were not cloyingly religious. My favorite, included in the *Washingtonian Pocket Companion*, is the "Song of 'the Six' of Baltimore":

> Hurrah! hurray! we've burst the chain:
> O God! how long it bound us!
> We run! we leap! O God, again
> Thy light, thy air surround us.
> From midnight's dungeon-depths brought out,
> We hail hope's rising star;
> Ho, comrades, give the stirring shout,

Hurrah! hurrah! Hurrah!

[Five more stanzas follow.]

And I like to imagine the reformed inebriates really belting out the "hurrah!" lines.

Nonetheless, some Washingtonians were hostile to the clergy, and with good reason. In *Narrative of Charles T. Woodman, A Reformed Inebriate* (1843), Woodman bitterly recalls that "in my hours of degradation, no friendly hand in the old temperance times ever gave me encouragement to rise and live; but many were not only indifferent to my situation, but actually, in more ways than one, were my oppressors." (quoted in Crowley) When Woodman took the Pledge of abstinence, and began a new life in sobriety, one clergyman, who ought to have offered him support and hope, instead went around the community, telling people that Woodman would soon be back to drinking. Woodman confronted him:

"I told him plainly that it was such religious bigots as he that had kept the drunkard confined to his cups for years, and that I considered him more in the way of the cause than ten open opposers; and in fact such men are complete icebergs around any reform, chilling the atmosphere wherever they approach." (Crowley)

Some of the clergy were hostile to the Washingtonians, who seemed to be trespassing on their turf. Good causes were supposed to be led by themselves, the men of the cloth, not by mere laymen. The Washingtonian approach totally ignored sin; it espoused the heretical notion that drunkards could be reformed without religious conversion; it undercut the prohibitionist narrative, that alcohol leads inevitably to death; and it bypassed the sacred cause of Prohibition. The hostility of some clergy is undoubtedly among the multiple causes that led to the demise of Washingtonianism as a movement.

By the end of the 1840s, Washingtonianism had died out as a movement, although some groups lasted for many more decades (the Washingtonian Home in Boston lasted until the middle of the 20th century). However, it was hardly a failure. One may hope and assume that most of the many tens of thousands of reformed drunkards, with the support of friends and family, maintained their sobriety. One may reasonably imagine that on the local level, reformed drunkards continued to carry the message of sobriety to other drunkards. And the Washingtonian ideas lived on, even if underground.

Numerous factors have been suggested as leading to the demise of Washingtonianism. In my opinion there were two main causes: the failure to restrict membership to alcoholics, and the failure to maintain a single purpose: rescuing drunkards. Let's examine these two, closely related causes:

Membership. Unlike AA, whose membership is open only to alcoholics, the Washingtonian Societies were open to everyone. As the Washingtonian cause became explosively popular, it seemed that everyone wanted to get into the act. Walt Whitman describes a meeting at Grand Street's Temperance Hall in March 1842, where there were not only speakers, but musical entertainment as well, including "a choir, composed mainly of ladies" and a glee club composed of "fine looking young firemen". The vast presence of non-alcoholics tended to dilute the movement and to draw it away from its original goal; in addition, it allowed the clergy and others to co-opt and subvert the movement for their own purposes.

Single purpose. The survival of AA owes much to having a single purpose: to carry the message of sobriety to the alcoholic who still suffers. The Washingtonians also started out with a clear mandate: to "snatch the poor inebriate from his destructive habits", but their original purpose got lost as non-alcoholic members promoted their own causes: prohibition, abolition, etc. These extraneous causes introduced dissension, and destroyed the unity that was necessary for the movement's survival.

Conclusions

One conclusion I draw from the compared experiences of the Washingtonians and AA, is that religiosity is detrimental to the task of sobering up alcoholics. The Washingtonians took off like a rocket when they approached drunkards with human kindness and understanding — without the condemnation and moralistic preaching of the old, clergy-led temperance movement. Likewise, when AA came into being in Cleveland, it got off the ground when it burst the shackles of the religious Oxford Group and began to emphasize Fellowship. Before this, Bill W. in New York City had been preaching at alcoholics with a religious message, and in a year he didn't succeed in sobering up a single one.

Another conclusion is that AA's survival depends on safeguarding its Traditions, and especially its single purpose and alcoholics-only membership. I have encountered AA members who think the Program is so wonderful that it should be open to everybody, and should embrace all good causes. As well demonstrated by the Washingtonian experience, this would mean the death of AA.

In some groups we go around the room identifying ourselves. I will say, "I'm John, and I'm an alcoholic." Then the next person will say, "I'm Elmer, and I'm an addict." I have talked to some of these people, and determined that they are not, nor consider themselves to be, alcoholics, but they think that AA is also for them. When I ask if they have attended meetings of Narcotics Anonymous, some have said yes, but they didn't like the people as much.

Here in Boston, there are very few closed meetings (for alcoholics only), with the result that many of those in attendance have only a vague idea what AA is about. Some of the more godly members really do believe that "working the steps" in order to achieve "spirituality" is more important than staying away from the first drink. We should not take AA's survival for granted, but must vigilantly safeguard its Traditions and its best features.

References/ Further Reading:

Anonymous, *Alcoholics Anonymous Comes of Age*, Alcoholics Anonymous World Services, Inc., NY 1957.

Anonymous, *Dr. Bob and the Good Oldtimers: A biography, with recollections of early AA in the Midwest*, Alcoholics Anonymous World Services, Inc., NY 1980.

Leonard U. Blumberg with William L. Pittman, *Beware The First Drink: The Washington Temperance Movement and Alcoholics Anonymous*, Glen Abbey Books, Seattle, Washington, 1991.

John W. Crowley, *Drunkard's Progress: Narratives of Addiction, Despair, and Recovery*, The Johns Hopkins University Press, Baltimore and London, 1999.

Walt Whitman, *Franklin Evans or The Inebriate: A Tale of the Times*, edited by Christopher Castiglia and Glenn Hendler, Duke University Press, 2007.

Jim Burwell

By Linda R.

Jim Burwell's contribution to Alcoholics Anonymous is truly significant and second only to that of AA's two co-founders, Bill Wilson and Dr. Robert Smith. Jim is credited with adoption of AA's Third Tradition – "The only requirement for membership is a desire to stop drinking" - as reported by Bill in Twelve Steps and Twelve Traditions (pp. 143-145).

In addition, it was primarily Jim, along with Hank Parkhurst, who convinced Bill to change the 12 Steps to be more inclusive for those who did not believe in "God." Bill writes about the contentious battles over the use of the word God in the 12 Steps and the Big Book during the time they were written. Bill says that in New York the AA's split into three factions, which Bill labeled "conservative", "liberal" and "radical."

The conservatives thought that "the book ought to be Christian in the doctrinal sense of the word and that it should say so." This faction was led by Fitz Mayo, an Episcopal minister's son from Maryland and the third man to recover at Town's hospital, after Hank Parkhurst and Bill himself.

The second faction, the liberals, had no real objection to using the word "God" in the book. The liberals pointed out that most members already believed in a deity. The liberals mainly wanted the book's Christian religious content to be toned down.

And the third faction was the radical faction, consisting of the agnostics and atheists, led by Jim Burwell and Hank Parkhurst. They wanted "God" removed from the book.

> But the atheists and agnostics, our radical left wing, were still to make a tremendously important contribution. Led by my friend Henry and obstinately backed by Jim B., a recently arrived sales man, this contingent proceeded to have its innings. At first they wanted the word "God" deleted from the book entirely. Henry had come to believe in some sort of "universal power," but Jimmy still flabbergasted us by denouncing God at our meetings. Some members had been so angered that they wanted to throw him out of the group. (*Alcoholics Anonymous Comes of Age*, p. 163)

What Jim, Hank and the other agnostics/atheists wanted was a psychological book to attract the alcoholic into AA, and once the alcoholic was in, the alcoholic could take God or leave Him alone as they wished. Bill reports that to the rest of the group, this was a "shocking" proposal. And the battle raged on for almost a year, until just before 400 copies of the completed manuscript were to be sent into circulation. Bill writes about his own role in insisting that the word "God" be used:

> We were still arguing about the Twelve Steps. All this time I had refused to budge on these steps. I would not change a word of the original draft, in which, you will remember, I had consistently used the word "God," and in one place the expression "on our knees" was used. Praying to God on one's knees was still a big affront to Henry. He argued, he begged. He threatened. He quoted Jimmy to back him up. (*Alcoholics Anonymous Comes of Age,* pp. 166-67)

Finally, at the last minute, Bill partially relented and a compromise was reached. The compromise resulted in four extremely important changes to the 12 Steps:

> 1. Substituting the phrase "a Power greater than ourselves" for "God" in Step Two
> 2. Modifying the word "God" to the phrase "God as we understood Him" in Steps Three and Eleven
> 3. Eliminating the expression "on our knees" from Step Seven
> 4. Adding the sentence "Here are the steps we took which are suggested as a Program of Recovery" as a lead-in to all the steps, so that they became only suggestions.

After agreeing to these changes in the 12 Steps, Bill acknowledges the contribution of Jim, Hank and the other agnostics / atheists in the group:

> Such were the final concessions to those of little or no faith; this was the great contribution of our atheists and agnostics. They had widened our gateway so that all who suffer might pass through, regardless of their belief or *lack of belief.* (*Alcoholics Anonymous Comes of Age,* p. 167)

Jim joined the fledgling New York AA group in January 1938. His sobriety date was June 1938 and he remained sober for 36 years, until his passing in September 1974. His story, "*The Vicious Cycle,*" was published in the Big Book's 2nd through 4th editions. He wrote the first history of AA called The Evolution of Alcoholics Anonymous, which sketched AA's beginning years from 1935 to 1940. He played a key role in the publication of the 1940 Saturday Evening Post article written by Jack Alexander. Working with Fitz Mayo, Jim started the first AA groups in Philadelphia, Washington and

Baltimore. After moving permanently to San Diego, he was instrumental in the growth of AA there.

There are some who say that Jim later "mellowed" in his atheism, but according to Cleveland AA founder Clarence Snyder: "Jimmy remained steadfast, throughout his life and 'preached' his particular [non-God] brand of AA wherever he went." (How it Worked: The Story of Clarence H. Snyder and the Early Days of Alcoholics Anonymous in Cleveland, Ohio, p. 107)

Jim himself, thirty years sober, wrote an article for the May 1968 Grapevine, and in it he writes: "Gradually, I came to believe that God and Good were synonymous and were found in all of us." Jim's words have an eerie similarity to the humanist slogans in recent ad campaigns, such as: "Why Believe in a God? Just be Good for Goodness' Sake" or "Humanism is the idea that you can be good without believing in God" or "Good, Without God." Funny thing, because in a sense, humanism begins where atheism ends. Unlike atheism, humanism is primarily concerned with ethics, not with the debate concerning the existence of God. Perhaps Jim evolved into a secular humanist? Perhaps like Jim, non-believers and believers can find common ground between good and God.

At any rate, what is known is that Jim remained an atheist for his entire life, regardless of the evolution of his ethical life philosophy toward goodness. He never developed a belief in a supernatural God.

The controversy over his atheism seems to stem from Jim's one and only slip, six months after he joined AA. Prior to his slip, Jim aggressively attacked any belief in God. After his slip, Jim came back with a different attitude. He realized that he needed the group to stay sober. And the group was against him because he openly attacked their beliefs. So Jim "mellowed." Jim says that "his closed mind opened a little." Did this mean he started to believe in a supernatural God? No. He realized that for the group to let him back in, it would be wise for him to stop aggressively challenging the beliefs of others in the group. And when his "closed mind opened a bit," he was finally able to recognize that for some of the others in his group, their belief did help keep them sober. Apparently, what was not useful to him was useful to them. As Jim says, "Who am I to say?"

Did Jim's changed attitude to be more tolerant of believers stop him from arguing against the use of the word "God" in the new book. No. It was in the period immediately following his slip, June 1938 through April 1939, when Jim argued unrelentingly and most vehemently against the use of the word "God" in the 12 Steps and the Big Book.

Jim's experience will be familiar to most agnostics, atheists and freethinkers in AA. When interacting with the believers in his group, Jim found that it was important to respect their beliefs and stop his "constant haranguing" against "God," which he had done when he first joined the group. Belief in "God" is an extremely important component of sobriety for many. And arguing against the religious beliefs of others can become dysfunctional on many levels, for as Jim said about the believers in his group: "Who am I to say?"

On the other hand, it is frustrating to agnostics, atheists and freethinkers to be subjected to the proselytizing of the believers in the rooms. Would that believers would respect the lack of belief of others. Unfortunately, while believers no longer hold prayer meetings on what to do with the non-believers, as they did in Jim's case (see Jim's article below), they do push the idea that belief in God is an essential component of sobriety. If only more AAs realized that from the beginning, there was a lot of controversy over the idea that belief in God was essential to sobriety. There were some, such as Bill and Dr. Bob, who truly thought belief in God was essential. But there were others, such as Jim and Hank, who did not think that belief was essential to sobriety. Jim and Hank argued that the alcoholic should be able to "take God or leave Him alone as he wished." For Jim, as he says in his article, it was the group that kept him sober, not "God." After his slip, Jim was humbled with the realization that he could not stay sober alone. He admitted that he needed the group.

It is remarkable that individuals like Jim and Hank were able to accomplish so much in those early years, given the religious and social climate of that period. They paved the way for what is happening now, seventy-four years later, with a growing population of agnostics, atheists and freethinkers who are asserting their rightful place in the fellowship.

Marty Mann and the Early Women of AA

By Bob K.

A tremendous change has taken place over the past few generations in the way alcoholics are viewed in our society. Although it is undeniable that some level of unawareness and misunderstanding remains, substantial improvements have been effected since the 1930s. We have cause to be grateful.

The once virtually universal stigma that besieged alcoholic men was exponentially greater for women. "Nice women" didn't drink to excess. This made it extremely difficult to admit to a drinking problem in the first place. As our pioneers battled not only for their own sobriety, but for some level of "respectability," their reluctance to associate themselves with "beggars, tramps, asylum inmates, prisoners, queers (sic), plain crackpots, and fallen women," (12 & 12, p. 140), can be looked on with some degree of sympathy.

Of course, many men failed to get sober, but were able to come and go without fanfare. The women drunks seemed more disruptive. Explosions took place over "out-of-bounds" romance and the arrival of alcoholic women at the early gatherings. According to Bill Wilson, "Whole groups got into uproars, and a number of people got drunk. We trembled for AA's reputation and for its survival." (Dr. Bob & the GO, p. 241)

It did not help that AA's earliest efforts to rehabilitate women did not go well. When Caroline, ex-wife of Hank Parkhurst, called her sister Dorothy, the wife of Cleveland AA member Clarence Snyder, to tell her that she was bringing a woman to Akron from Chicago for "the cure," Dorothy was nervous about telling Dr. Bob. From Dr. Bob and the Good Oldtimers we know that her trepidation was warranted: "Dr. Bob threw up his hands and said, 'We have NEVER had a woman and will NOT work on a woman.' But by that time, Caroline was on her way with Sylvia K." (p. 180)

Sylvia K.

Sylvia arrived in the late summer of 1939, and the men of AA were immediately tripping over themselves in their efforts to talk to her. By all accounts, the drunken divorcee and heiress from Chicago was stunningly beautiful, and in an era when America was still feeling the effects of the Great Depression, Sylvia was getting alimony of $700 per month. A comparison to

Dr. William Silkworth's rather paltry salary of forty dollars a week as a psychiatrist at Towns Hospital puts proportion to the enormity of this stipend.

All too soon after her arrival in Akron, Sylvia began tripping over herself. Clearly, the "little white pills" that she was taking were NOT "saccharin" as she was claiming. A nurse was flown down from Chicago to take care of her.

> After talking to Bob, Sylvia decided to live in Akron. This caused great consternation, since her presence threatened to disrupt the whole group. But someone told her it would mean a great deal more if she could go back and help in Chicago. This appealed to Sylvia, so the members put her and her nurse on the train. Sylvia headed for the dining car and got drunk. (Dr. Bob & the GO, p. 181)

This tale has a happy ending as she sobered up when she got back to Chicago. Sylvia's personal story "The Keys of the Kingdom" appears in the 2nd, 3rd, and 4th editions of our book. Sylvia K. was the first woman to achieve long term sobriety in AA, although that distinction is often erroneously conferred on Bill Wilson's close friend, Marty Mann.

"Lil"

Dr. Bob's concerns about women in AA pre-date Sylvia's 1939 arrival. The first woman, ever, to seek help from the folks who were not yet, but would one day be, AA is identified in Dr. Bob and the Good Oldtimers only as "Lil."

> There was a man we'll call "Victor," a former mayor of Akron, and a lady we'll call "Lil," who was the first woman to seek help. Together, Victor and the lady known as Lil started out to write the "thirteenth step" long before the first twelve were even thought of. What is more, they say it began in Dr. Bob's office – on his examination table – while he was at the City Club engaged in his sacrosanct Monday night bridge game. In any case, Victor decided it was time for him to go home – but Lil was loaded. (p. 97)

Lil wouldn't leave so Victor called Ernie G., (AA #4), for assistance. Lil grabbed some pills from Dr. Bob's medicine chest and was trying to gobble them while the two men chased her around the examination table in what must have appeared like a scene from "Benny Hill," or "The Keystone Cops."

> Ernie recalled, "Then she made a dive for the window. I caught her halfway out. She was strong as a horse and used some profanity I have never heard before or since. I got her quieted, and Doc came. We took her out to Ardmore Avenue (the Smith home) and put her in a room in the basement. She stayed there two or three days, and then her people took her home. Of course, they were never too

190

kind about it and thought we didn't handle her right." (Dr. Bob & the GO, p. 98)

This tale also has a happy ending, as well as a message of open-mindedness. According to Sue Windows (Dr. Bob's daughter), "Lil" straightened out after a few years – but NOT through the AA program – got married, and had kids. AA isn't the answer for everyone. "They say that Dr. Bob was leery of anything to do with women alcoholics for a long time thereafter, although he still tried to help as best he could with any who came along." (p. 98)

Florence R.

Some consideration that was being given to the name "One Hundred Men," as the title of what would become the Big Book, was squashed by the presence of Florence Rankin, whose story "A Femine Victory" appeared in the Big Book's First Edition. At the time Florence had been sober for a little more than a year. Florence's hard-drinking ex-husband, who knew Bill Wilson from Wall Street, brought Lois to talk with her. This was in March of 1937. She reports having great difficulty in seeing herself as an "alcoholic," but after some slips she got sober in early 1938.

Again, this is another tale of AA's early women that does not end well. Florence moved to Washington D.C. where she tried to assist Fitz Mayo ("Our Southern Friend") in getting AA off the ground in and around the nation's capital. One of the prospects drew her romantic interest and they married. The bridegroom was unable to stay sober and after a time, Florence got drunk as well and disappeared. When Fitz finally located her, it was at the morgue – she had committed suicide.

Jane Sturdevant

> Women who joined the Akron group in the earliest days had adequate, if not impressive social credentials. Jane was married to the vice-president of a large steel company, and Sylvia was an attractive heiress. (Silkworth.net)

Dr. Bob's February, 1938 list of 'successes' showed Jane S., 12 months. Jane was making the 35 mile trip from Cleveland from early 1937. Described as "colorful and vivacious, with a fine sense of humor, Jane was the first woman to "have attained any length of sobriety – meaning a few months." (Dr. Bob & the GO, p. 122) That she has no story in the First Edition is evidence that she relapsed, AND by the time of Sylvia's arrival in September, 1939, she remained only as a bad memory for Dr. Bob, prompting the

191

previously-cited "we have never had a woman, we will not work with a woman" remark.

Dr. LeClair Bissell

Bissell was an M.D., an addiction researcher with an "inside knowledge" of the malady, and the co-author of the 1987 book, *Ethics for Addiction Professionals*. Joining AA in 1953, at the age of twenty-five, she stayed sober until her death in 2008. William L. White, who interviewed Dr. Bissell in 1997 described her as "an unabashed atheist, a vocal lesbian, and a visible woman in addiction recovery before such openness was in vogue." Dr. Bissell's specific relevance to this essay is that she was personally acquainted with Mrs. Marty Mann, and was able to relay to us Mann's own experience of AA in 1939:

> Marty shared with me that when she went to her first AA meeting at Bill and Lois' home in Brooklyn, the men were very afraid. The experience of some of the earlier women was that the men were very threatened by them, and didn't want them in the group. That is what happened with Marty Mann... It was Lois Wilson who made her welcome, and pretty much insisted the men behave themselves. (White, William, *Reflections of an addiction treatment pioneer: An Interview with LeClair Bissell, MD (1928-2008)*, conducted January 22, 1997)

Marty Mann

Born in 1905, Margaret "Marty" Mann grew up in Chicago, where her wealthy family provided her with every advantage including the finest boarding schools and finishing school in Europe. In her Big Book story "Women Suffer Too" we are told "My family had money – I had never known denial of any material desire." An attractive and popular debutante, Marty's circle was a young, privileged and fast-moving crowd. It was the "roaring twenties," after all.

Following her own "debut" in 1927, at the age of twenty-one, Marty eloped with a handsome New Orleans "party boy" from a socially prominent family. Both bride and groom were considerably "high on alcohol" at the time. The young husband's dubious "claim to fame" was being his town's "worst drunk." In her words, "My husband was an alcoholic, and since I had only contempt for those without my own amazing capacity, the outcome was inevitable. My divorce coincided with my father's bankruptcy, and I went to work (1928), casting off all allegiances and responsibilities to anyone other than myself." (Women Suffer Too)

Described by those who knew her as "favored with beauty, brains, charisma, phenomenal energy, and a powerful will," she merged these with strong social connections to forge a successful career in Public Relations. "I had my own business, successful enough for me to indulge most of my desires." She even "went abroad to live." That her life of success, hedonism, and fulfilled desires left her "increasingly miserable," is reminiscent of Oscar Wilde's insightful dictum – "There are only two tragedies in life: one is not getting what one wants, and the other is getting it." The fun and frolic of the late 20s had become something altogether different ten years later.

> Hangovers began to assume monstrous proportions, and the morning drink became an urgent necessity. 'Blanks' became more frequent... With a creeping insidiousness, drink had become more important than anything else. It no longer gave me pleasure—it merely dulled the pain—but I had to have it.

A return to America and her "drinking grew worse." The one-time debutante, then PR whiz kid, found herself on the charity ward of first Bellvue Hospital and then the Blythewood Sanitarium in Greenwich, Connecticut.

Mann's psychiatrist, Harry Tiebout had been given a manuscript of the book Alcoholics Anonymous which he gave her to read.

> The first chapters were a revelation to me. I wasn't the only person in the world who felt and behaved like this! I wasn't mad or vicious —I was a sick person. I was suffering from an actual disease that had a name and symptoms like diabetes or cancer or TB—and a disease was respectable, not a moral stigma. (Women Suffer Too)

Spreading the message expressed in the previous quotation would eventually take Marty Mann far beyond the rooms of AA.

Meeting Bill Wilson

In spite of not being happy with "the number of capital 'G' words" present in the manuscript, in April 11 of 1939, Marty was driven by Popsie M. to the Clinton St. meeting of Alcoholics Anonymous. The occasion must have been somewhat somber as the government-imposed moratorium on foreclosures had been recently lifted, and the Wilsons were about to lose their home. At the gathering of "this group of freaks or bums who had done this thing" a surprising thing happened: "I went trembling into a house in Brooklyn filled with strangers... and I found I had come home at last, to my own kind."

In spite of this auspicious debut, and a somewhat secular "awakening" about the need to let go of anger, Ms. Mann did not go deaf to the siren call of

193

fermented beverages. Several relapses preceded her achieving a long term sobriety well into 1940 – possibly just one more illustration of the insidious nature of the malady.

The Yale Plan for Alcohol Studies

When Dr. E.M. Jellinek, America's premier researcher into alcoholism, joined Dr. Howard Haggard (medicine) and Dr. Sheldon D. Bacon (sociology) to form "The Yale Plan for Alcohol Studies," they had a problem. In order that they not be viewed as "Ivory Tower" types with only a superficial, academic knowledge of "real" alcoholism, they needed a "real" alcoholic, "Exhibit A." Of course, this issue was not unrelated to fund-raising. Marty Mann joined these men in their noble cause of bringing change to public attitudes toward the disease and its sufferers. She felt the calling to work in the field of alcoholic education, and in particular she desired to help women alcoholics who were cursed with a "double stigma."

> The National Committee for Education on Alcoholism, Inc., the organization Marty founded, opened its offices on October 2, 1944. N.C.E.A. – eventually to become the National Council on Alcoholism – received an enthusiastic endorsement from the Grapevine, itself only four months old. It also received the support of many prominent (and some not so prominent) people, whose names, including those of Bill Wilson and Dr. Bob Smith, appeared on the committee's letterhead... The AA co-founders' names on the letterhead gave the impression that the two groups were connected. To confuse matters further, Marty, as she spoke across the country on behalf of her new organization, was breaking her own anonymity. (Pass it On, p. 320)

Ultimately, Wilson and Smith withdrew from N.C.E.A. and became persuaded that total non-affiliation was the only answer, as they had inadvertently associated AA with the plea for public funds by Mann's organization, a solicitation that went out at some point to AA members. Additionally, Marty agreed to discontinue publicly identifying herself as an AA member. Anonymity issues aside, the N.C.E.A., with Mrs. Mann as spokesperson and 'Exhibit A,' was quite successful in communicating the three tenets of its core message:

> 1. Alcoholism is a disease, and the alcoholic is a sick person;
> 2. The alcoholic can be helped, and is worth helping;
> 3. Alcoholism is a public heath problem, and therefore a public responsibility.

These ideas are so universally accepted today, that it can be difficult to imagine that they were both revolutionary and counter-intuitive at the time.

In the 1950s, famous journalist and newscaster (he was HUGE, young people), Edward R. Murrow included Marty Mann on his list of the ten "Greatest Living Americans." (Murrow is brilliantly portrayed by Canadian David Strathairn in the 2005 film "Good Night and Good Luck," directed by George Clooney and nominated for several Academy Awards.)

Mann's breach of her own anonymity "for the sake and good of others" clearly had mostly positive outcomes. It is hard to know the causes leading to her relapse at twenty years sober. Perhaps the aggrandizement of ego that is at the core of AA's fears for members who "go public" was a factor. AA also warns of the dangers of being a "secret keeper," and Mann was an "in-the-closet" lesbian for decades. Her close friends knew the truth, but she shielded this additional "stigma" from the public to the point of retaining and using the title "Mrs." her entire life, in spite of returning to the use of her maiden name. Her volatile love affair with "the Countess" may have also been a factor – all matters of speculation.

People have also speculated that later in her life she had been drinking at times when she was representing herself as sober. Regardless, she is an iconic character in the history of AA, and at a far broader level in the worldwide treatment and understanding of alcoholism. Mrs. Marty Mann died in 1980 shortly after suffering a stroke. She was seventy-five years old.

There are few things that have changed more since these earliest days than the position of women within the fellowship of AA. From this less than auspicious debut and a mere token presence in 1939, women now comprise fully thirty-five percent of our society. Young women, arriving new to AA in the twenty-first century, may well be surprised and even displeased with the male-dominant language of the Big Book, but it is a reflection of a different era, fully three generations in the past. Much is owed to these intrepid female pioneers, for blazing the trail for the women of today.

Responsibility Is Our Theme

By Roger C.

Bill W spoke at the General Service Conference held in New York City in April, 1965. The Conference theme was "Responsibility To Those We Serve."

AA was thirty years old. Bill was 70 years old. It was a period of reflection for him. "We old-timers are a vanishing breed," he said of the early members of AA. "The greater part of us have gone out into the sunset of this world."

He expressed the hope that the disappearing early AAers had left the members of the day a heritage sufficient to their needs, one which could be "enlarged and enriched."

Bill was preparing for the 30th Anniversary International Convention to be held later that year in July in Toronto. Much of the spirit of the Conference would also prevail at the Convention, where the theme would be, simply, "Responsibility," and Bill would repeat much of this speech.

Bill looked back over the years; he did a bit of an inventory of AA's history, "the better to reveal the areas in which we can improve ourselves."

"Without much doubt, a million alcoholics have approached AA during the last thirty years," he said. Estimating that "350,000 of us are now recovered from our malady" through the fellowship of AA, he continued, "So we can very soberly ask ourselves what became of the 600,000 who did not stay."

No doubt some alcoholics "cannot be reached because they are not hurt enough, others because they are hurt too much. Many sufferers have mental and emotional complications that seem to foreclose their chances," Bill acknowledged.

But what about all the others?

"How much and how often did we fail them?" he asked. "Our very first concern should be with those sufferers that we are still unable to reach."

He had some sense of the failings of the fellowship he had helped launch and which he still clearly revered. One of the themes for his talk was one he had broached before: a growing rigidity in AA.

He referred directly to a contingent within the fellowship which, often unwittingly, made it difficult for an increasingly large number of people to feel comfortable in the rooms of AA. "It is a historical fact," he said, "that practically all groupings of men and women tend to become dogmatic. Their beliefs and practices harden and sometimes freeze. This is a natural and almost inevitable process."

He discussed some of the ways that this rigidity could harm the fellowship.

"In no circumstances should we feel that Alcoholics Anonymous is the know-all and do-all of alcoholism," Bill said, referring to the work of other organizations in the United States and Canada engaged in research, alcohol education and rehabilitation.

"Research has already come up with significant and helpful findings. And research will do far more."

"Those engaged in education are carrying the message that alcoholism is an illness, that something can be done about it."

Bill then talked about the growth of rehabilitation facilities in North America and the number of alcoholics treated by these agencies. "True, their approach is often different from our own," he said.

"But what does that matter," he asked, "when the greater part of them are or could be entirely willing to cooperate with AA?"

"Too often, I believe, we have deprecated and even derided these projects of our friends."

"So we should very seriously ask ourselves how many alcoholics have gone on drinking simply because we have failed to cooperate in good spirit with all these other agencies whether they be good, bad or indifferent. Assuredly no alcoholic should go mad or die simply because he did not come straight to AA in the first place."

Bill was of the view that hardened or frozen beliefs and practices were dangerous in AA. "Simply because we have convictions that work very well for us, it becomes quite easy to assume that we have all of the truth."

"Whenever this brand of arrogance develops," he warned, "we are sure to become aggressive. We demand agreement with us. We play God."

"This isn't good dogma. This is very bad dogma. It could be especially destructive for us of AA to indulge in this sort of thing."

Bill defended the right of all AAers to have their own beliefs and to be able to freely express them.

197

"All people must necessarily rally to the call of their own particular convictions and we of AA are no exception." Moreover," he continued, "all people should have the right to voice their convictions."

Bill then returned to the subject of those who had come into AA but not stayed. "Newcomers are approaching us at the rate of tens of thousands yearly. They represent almost every belief and attitude imaginable."

"We have atheists and agnostics," he said. "We have people of nearly every race, culture and religion."

And then Bill got to the heart of his message of responsibility.

> In AA we are supposed to be bound together in the kinship of a universal suffering. Therefore the full liberty to practice any creed or principle or therapy should be a first consideration. Hence let us not pressure anyone with individual or even collective views. Let us instead accord to each other the respect that is due to every human being as he tries to make his way towards the light. Let us always try to be inclusive rather than exclusive. Let us remember that each alcoholic among us is a member of AA, so long as he or she so declares.

Towards the end of his address, Bill commented on how difficult it has been for AA to grow at important moments in its history. "Our fears and reluctances and rebellions have been extreme each time we have been faced with great turning points in this society," he said.

"Let us never fear needed change," he concluded. "Once a need becomes clearly apparent in an individual, a Group, or in AA as a whole, it has long since been found out that we cannot afford to sit still and look the other way."

The theme of AA's 30th Anniversary International Convention held later that year was "Responsibility" and those present adopted the Responsibility Declaration. After Bill's speech on July 3, 1965 at Maple Leaf Gardens in Toronto, more than 10,000 delegates, trustees and AA representatives from 21 countries joined hands and, recited the new AA declaration with one voice: "I am responsible. When anyone, anywhere, reaches out for help, I want the hand of AA always to be there. And for that I am responsible." Inspired by this unconditioned affirmation of inclusivity, agnostic AA groups invariably end their meetings with this declaration.

VIII. An AA Pamphlet For Agnostics and Atheists

The General Service Conference Stumbles

By Roger C.

At the 1965 General Service Conference held in New York, Bill Wilson had a very clear message for the area delegates, trustees, directors and General Service Office staff in attendance: "Our very first concern should be with those sufferers that we are still unable to reach."

He spoke of the hundreds of thousands of people who had approached AA over the course of its thirty year history but had not stayed. "We have atheists and agnostics," he said. "We have people of nearly every race, culture and religion."

"How much and how often have we failed them?" he asked.

The General Service Conference held its latest annual meeting in the last week of April in New York.

And, sadly, it managed to stumble, if not fail outright, in an important way, yet again.

———

A recent article by Thomas B., *First AA Meetings*, had to be changed at the very last minute.

The ending, as Thomas had written it, was very positive and hopeful:

> A key recommendation of the AA trustees' Committee on Literature calls for stories from atheists and agnostics who are sober to be included in AA literature about spirituality. Whereas on the local group level there may sometimes be bias against non-believers, wiser hearts and heads prevail at the level of the General Conference Board.

Apparently the hearts and heads at the AA General Service Conference may not be quite as wise as Thomas thought.

The Conference – consisting of 92 delegates from AA areas in the United States and Canada, trustees, AA World Service and Grapevine directors and staff from the General Service Office and the Grapevine in New York – met between April 21 and 27 in New York.

This is of course the body that decides which literature is "Conference-approved."

Those present considered a pamphlet called "AA – Spiritual not Religious." It contains several stories by agnostics who have achieved long term recovery in AA without any religious belief whatsoever, without a belief in God.

But you're not going to be seeing it on literature tables at AA meetings anytime soon.

The pamphlet was rejected.

It wasn't put quite that bluntly; these resolutions never are. The Conference recommended that the "draft pamphlet, 'AA – Spiritual not Religious,' be recommitted to the trustees' Literature Committee for additional discussion and brought back to the 2014 Conference Committee on Literature."

———

It might have been a relatively minor stumble except for one thing: it wasn't the first time that the General Service Conference failed in this way. The denial at the Conference level of AA that agnostics and atheists can and do achieve long term sobriety in AA and the refusal to publish stories of agnostics who have done just that has been going on for quite a number of years.

Almost forty years, in fact.

The trustees' Literature Committee first considered a pamphlet with the stories of recovered non-believers, athiests and agnostics in AA in 1976. It formed a subcommittee which began preparing the document and made several recommendations as to why it was necessary, including the following:

> • The number of non-believers in the program, or who need the AA program but are discouraged by its theism, may be more substantial than is probably realized.

> • The chapter "To the Agnostic" in the Big Book is fine as a start but more material is needed to assure non-believers that they are not merely deviants, but full, participating members in the AA Fellowship without qualification.

• This pamphlet will probably also help the God believer in AA to understand his/her own spiritual values better, as well as to develop tolerance and understanding of many newcomers to AA.

• This pamphlet would affirm in clear and concise fashion that "the only requirement for membership in AA is a desire to stop drinking" and that our founders and the group conscience of the fellowship does not and has never considered an alcoholic's spiritual beliefs as necessarily relevant to the achievement of healthy and happy sobriety.

The full trustees' Literature Committee read the subcommittee's report and decided not to go forward with the project and thus not to ask the 1977 Conference to consider a pamphlet for and about agnostics and atheists in AA.

But the issue eventually made its way to the Conference.

A little more than a decade later, in April 1989, the General Service Conference (via its own Literature Committee) first considered – and rejected outright – a pamphlet about and for non-believers. It did not believe that there was "a sufficient need" for such a pamphlet "at this time."

That has since then been the pattern followed by the General Service Conference.

The issue has come up with some regularity and the Conference has consistently and repeatedly found a way to reject the publication of "a pamphlet directed to the concerns of the non-believer (athiest and/or agnostic) alcoholic," as it was put in 1995 by Paul S., who later became the Chair of the Conference Literature Committee, by either not making any recommendation at all or by recommending that the matter be referred to a future Conference.

In 2012 for example, the Conference "requested a draft pamphlet (about non-believers and AA) or progress report be brought back to the 2013 Conference Committee on Literature."

We know what the 2013 Conference did.

And that brought to eight the number of times the General Service Conference dodged the publication of a Conference-approved pamphlet that would "assure non-believers that they are not merely deviants, but full, participating members in the AA Fellowship without qualification."

Mel C. was a delegate at the Conference in April. He represents Area 83 of Alcoholics Anonymous, which includes Canada's largest metropolitan area, the city of Toronto.

Mel had the great good fortune to attend his first agnostic AA meeting on Thursday, May 30th. He was at the Beyond Belief meeting in downtown Toronto, just above the St. George Subway Station on Bloor Street. Beyond Belief was the first agnostic AA group and meeting in Canada, with its first meeting on September 24, 2009. Joe C., one of the founders of the group and the author of the recently published book *Beyond Belief: Agnostic Musings for 12 Step Life*, chaired the meeting and he had asked Mel to be guest speaker.

The meeting room was packed, and Mel expressed his surprise at how many people were in the room (a classroom at the Ontario Institute for Studies in Education). There were between 30 and 40 people, from diverse backgrounds and cultures, with a wide range of continuous sobriety, from months to decades. In fact, in the sharing after Mel's talk, it turned out that two people were at their first-ever AA meeting.

Mel gave a great talk! It was enjoyed by all present. Somewhere during his sharing he spoke about the Conference and its decision to reject the publication of a Conference-Approved pamphlet about agnostics and atheists in AA. To be fair to Mel, he did not use the word "reject," and said that it had been deferred to next year's General Service Conference. But after seeing this behaviour repeated over a period of several decades, by the same – very same – AA organization, it's time for rigorous honesty, and to call a rejection a rejection.

Mel's role at the Conference is described this way, on the Area 83's website: "As voting members of the Conference, delegates bring to its deliberations the experiences and viewpoints of their own areas. Yet they are not representatives of their areas in the usual political sense; after hearing all points of view and becoming fully informed during Conference discussion, they vote in the best interests of AA as a whole."

In a conversation following the Beyond Belief meeting, Mel said he had read the proposed pamphlet, "AA – Spiritual not Religious." He clearly liked it and no doubt supported its publication. He indicated that the stories in the pamphlet about agnostics in AA in long term recovery were convincing and well-written.

"Why did the Conference reject it?" he was asked.

202

Mel did not offer an official answer. He did acknowledge that some could conclude that the behaviour of the Conference was a result of the Bible Belt origins of many of its members and/or the attachment of those present to their own conception of God and recovery.

The meeting room emptied slowly, as usual. People talked with each other, friends they had not seen for a few days or a few months. New friendships were struck. The newcomers were warmly welcomed. Laughter filled the air. It had been a very good evening. A lot of people had been inspired by the "experience, strength and hope" of Mel and the other men and women sitting around the table at Beyond Belief.

———

The decision of the General Service Conference not to publish "AA – Spiritual not Religious" raises a very disturbing question.

This is particularly true given that the mandate of the General Service Board and Conference – like every other AA organization – is one of "service." Surely this service is offered to those without a faith in an interventionist God. Surely agnostics and atheists were included in "anyone, anywhere" when those present at the 2013 AA Conference stood up and declared that the hand of AA is always to be there for "anyone, anywhere who reaches out for help."

It certainly is not evident in the actions of the Conference.

After four decades of being implored to publish a pamphlet that would make agnostics and atheists feel more accepted in AA, and after evidence of how damaging this refusal is not only to the non-believing alcoholic but also very much to AA as a whole, especially in terms of its ongoing relevance to a more diverse and ever growing non-Christian portion of the population, let us paraphrase the founder of Alcoholics Anonymous and once again ask the General Service Conference:

How much and how many more times will you fail them?

An AA Pamphlet for Agnostics – The 1970s

By Roger C.

A "Conference-approved" pamphlet for agnostics and atheists in AA was first proposed in 1975.

The proposal was the result of a letter from Al L., an AA member in Florida, who asked the trustees' Literature Committee to consider publishing such a pamphlet.

(The trustees of AA consists of 14 alcoholics and 7 non-alcoholics. These trustees are the principal planners and administrators of AA's overall policy and finances, which is about as high-level as it gets in Alcoholics Anonymous.)

This is what Al wrote to the trustees:

> I'm a happy non-belligerent agnostic. I feel that many non-believers miss the AA boat before they find out that they are also welcome. The 'God bit' frightens then off before they learn that their spiritual beliefs or non-beliefs need not deprive them of the blessings of AA.
>
> Is it possible for the "powers that be" in AA to publish a pamphlet designed specifically for agnostics? I don't mean the Big Book's version – Chapter IV We Agnostics – that doesn't make sense to me. Never did…
>
> Many agnostics believe at first that AA, with all of its "Let God Do It" and "That one is God, may you find him now" is really a thinly veiled attempt to shove "religion" down their throats. You and I of course know that isn't the case…
>
> I would not advise that such a pamphlet for agnostics imply or infer that "God" will get you sooner or later or that you will necessarily come to believe in the power of prayer or that you must "turn it over."
>
> My logic, common sense and dedication to AA keeps me sober – and I don't think the non-spiritual have been given a fair shake.

204

There's much of course in Al's letter that makes a great deal of sense. Nonbelievers in AA have definitely not been given a "fair shake" over the years.

After all, what does an agnostic do when an interventionist God appears a total of six times in the 12 Steps? What does he or she do when the AA meeting – in a church basement, no less – ends with the Lord's Prayer?

Welcome. Stay strong.

It is important to note that Al is asking for a pamphlet that lets go of the idea that God is necessary for recovery. The pamphlet would acknowledge straight out that agnostics and atheists can and, quite commonly, do get sober and maintain their sobriety within AA – and do that without God.

To its credit, the Literature Committee was open to the idea, at least initially. The trustees thought Al's proposal was important enough that in February 1976 they appointed a two-member subcommittee to study the issue and report back. "The Committee recommended that the preparation of a pamphlet for Agnostics be studied by a sub-committee consisting of Ed S. and Paula C."

We know nothing about Ed and Paula, except that they were obviously committed and hardworking. They completed their task in four months and in July 1976, they submitted a preliminary report strongly recommending the publication of this pamphlet. Here is what the report recommended, divided into three parts:

A. Reasons for the pamphlet. A pamphlet for the agnostic and/or atheist should be compiled and written using mainly existing AA material on this subject as a consequence of the following:

- This pamphlet is vitally needed to carry the message to both newcomers and old timers.

- Alcoholics Anonymous, despite first appearances, is neither sectarian nor religious, and is open to all alcoholics of every persuasion or non-persuasion. The number of nonbelievers in the program, or who need the AA program but are discouraged by its theism, may be more substantial than is probably realized.

- The chapter "To The Agnostic" in the Big Book is fine as a start but more material

- This pamphlet will probably also help the God believer in AA to understand his/her own spiritual values better, as well as to develop tolerance and understanding of many newcomers to AA.

- The pamphlet would affirm in clear and concise fashion that "the only requirement for membership in AA is a desire to stop drinking" and that our founders and the group conscience of the fellowship does not and has never considered an alcoholic's spiritual beliefs as necessarily relevant to the achievement of healthy and happy sobriety.

B. A draft should begin as soon as possible. The sub-committee will collect material from extant literature including the Grapevine. George Gordon (chair of the trustees' Literature Committee) and Al L. will serve as consultants on this project.

- If it appears that this pamphlet geared to the agnostic and/or atheist will not achieve the aims listed above, then it will be discontinued by the Committee at this time.

C. This type of pamphlet does not fall under the category "special groups of alcoholics" literature. Rather it concerns a more fundamental and worldwide problem that has resulted in much misinterpretation of the AA Fellowship.

This last point is very important.

What the subcommittee is saying is that the goal is not to make room for agnostics and atheists in AA in the way that there are groups and meetings specifically for young people or our LGBT friends. Instead, the subcommittee is saying that what AA needs to do with this pamphlet is affirm that sobriety is indeed possible in AA without an interventionist God. Ultimately, that is the only way that it is possible for agnostics and atheists to participate in AA as "full, participating members in the AA Fellowship without qualification." It is the recognition of the fact that "our founders and the group conscience of the fellowship *does not and has never considered* an alcoholic's spiritual beliefs as *necessarily* relevant to the achievement of healthy and happy sobriety."

Of course, try telling that to some of "our more religious members."

In August 1976, the trustees' Literature Committee reviewed the two-page report. It suggested that the subcommittee now write a new version of their recommendations in greater detail and present it to the 1977 Conference Committee on Literature before further action is taken on its preparation.

And here, unfortunately, is where light turns to darkness.

The committee reviewed the revised report in October of 1976.

And turfed it.

Moreover, the trustees Literature Committee did a ninety degree reversal and "decided not to ask the 1977 Conference Literature Committee to consider a pamphlet for agnostics/atheists."

(The Conference meets for a week once a year every spring. It consists of roughly 130 members: delegates from 93 Conference areas in North America, trustees of the General Service Board, and various directors and AA staff. It functions as the active voice and group conscience of the fellowship. All official AA literature must be "Conference-approved.")

To this day, even after "an exhaustive search," a copy of the subcommittee's final report has never been found.

What we do know, however, is that the effort to get a pamphlet for, about and by agnostics in AA continued on and on and on, into the 80s, 90s and continues in the new millennium.

In fact, the 2013 General Service Conference rejected such a pamphlet, called "AA – Spiritual Not Religious," and referred the matter to the 2014 General Service Conference.

Maybe they will get it right someday. After all, it's only been on – and off – the agenda for a mere forty years.

Stay strong.

This article is based entirely upon the following document: *History - Proposals to Create a Pamphlet for the Nonbeliever / Agnostic / Atheist Alcoholic.*

An AA Pamphlet for Agnostics – The 1980s

By Roger C.

In October, 1981, Ed S. wrote to the AA trustees' Literature Committee and asked that the idea of preparing and publishing a "Conference-approved" pamphlet for agnostics and atheists in the fellowship be reconsidered.

You see, he had tried to get such a pamphlet once before, and the idea had been rejected.

In the 1970s Ed had been a trustee – one of AA's 21 policy and financial administrators – and a member of a sub-committee of the Literature Committee.

He and Paula C. – the other member of the subcommittee – had recommended that AA compile and write "a pamphlet for the Agnostic and/or Atheist." In a report presented to the full Literature committee in July, 1976, they wrote that such a pamphlet "is needed to assure non-believers that they are not merely deviants, but full, participating members in the AA Fellowship without qualification."

At first, the Literature Committee was gung ho to proceed. In August it asked for more detail in a revised report that it would present to the General Service Conference, which would make the final decision.

(The Conference meets for a week once a year, every spring. It consists of delegates from 93 Conference areas in North America, the trustees of the General Service Board, and other directors and AA staff. It functions as the group conscience of the fellowship. All official AA literature must be "Conference-approved.")

Astonishingly, however, the Committee did a dramatic about face and in October of 1976 trashed the idea and "decided not to ask the 1977 Conference Literature Committee to consider a pamphlet for agnostics/atheists."

The reason for that reversal has never been made public.

Apparently Ed was not the kind of person who gives up simply because of adversity. His letter in October of 1981 read, in part:

Even though it would not be a best seller, could we have a pamphlet written by an agnostic or atheist for those who have trouble believing? Possible title: "Came Not to Believe."

In January 1982 "the committee declined to recommend the publication of a pamphlet intended for agnostics or atheists who have trouble believing."

Again, no reason was offered.

———

The idea of a pamphlet for those "who have trouble believing" finally made it to the General Service Conference in the spring of 1989.

At least some of the interest in such a pamphlet was generated by an article in the AA Grapevine in October of 1987 called: *Is There Room Enough in AA?* In the article, J. L. from Oakland, California writes about how, as an atheist with many years of sobriety, he feels muzzled in the rooms of AA:

> I hear so little from atheists in AA because those of us who do not believe in God keep quiet about it. I have done so partly out of timidity and partly to avoid the comment that the admission of atheism frequently brings: that I will someday believe or I will get drunk.

Does that sound familiar to anyone? For more on this you can read The *"Don't Tell" Policy in AA.*

At any rate, the article prompted a letter from Jack M. to the General Service Office dated February 1, 1989.

At the time Jack had some thirteen years of sobriety in AA, and one of his comments picks up on the theme of the Grapevine article:

> I can't understand why (believers) hardly ever tire of trying to convince or persuade non-believers to change, particularly in AA which is a program of attraction, because the thought of trying to persuade a believer to change never even enters my mind.

He goes on to say:

> There just doesn't seem to be any AA General Service Conference-approved literature written specifically for the non-believer. Is such a project under way? ...A collection of encouraging words would not have to be adversarial, antagonistic, cogent, defensive, patronizing or persuasive. A foreword could even be included which would explain the apparent conflict, at least

to some newcomers, between the statement in our preamble regarding AA not being allied with any sect, denomination, organization or institution and the fact that we all rise... and recite the prayer beginning Our Father at the close of each meeting. The foreword could also contain a clear statement that belief in a higher power is not at any time a requirement for membership or for getting and staying sober.

Another letter had also been written to the General Service Office in 1989 and that one was by Tom M. of Florida.

He writes of the many atheists who have gotten and stayed sober within the rooms of AA. "We believe," he says, "that we have accumulated experiences that can give hope, strength, and comfort to newly sober people in AA who are of the agnostic or atheistic persuasion."

He goes on to say:

> To declare your agnosticism or atheism at many meetings (at least in this part of the country) brings upon oneself knowing stares and sometimes repudiation from someone in the group. Now, I personally don't have this problem anymore. My longevity in sobriety is given respect, but I am still thought of as a paradox or oddball. I can handle that just fine, now. The question that bothers me, is that 'Can a newly sober agnostic or atheist handle being treated as an oddball?' Many cannot."

These letters, and others, were duly considered by the trustees' Literature Committee which made a recommendation "for some sort of spiritual literature in response to requests from atheists and agnostics."

Not a chance.

As noted above, the spring 1989 General Service Conference considered the request. And it blew the idea right out of the water. It "did not see a sufficient need to take action."

And so it goes. To put it mildly, the request for what is sometimes described as life-saving literature for the non-believing alcoholic was treated cavalierly.

Then. And in the previous decade, as we shared in an earlier article on AA Agnostica: *An AA Pamphlet for Agnostics – The 1970s*.

And in the years since.

Conference-Approved Literature

By Roger C.

Many of us are hopeful that the General Service Conference will one day approve a pamphlet that welcomes agnostics and atheists in AA and, in so doing, acknowledges that a God has nothing at all to do with our sobriety.

One of the names proposed for such a pamphlet is "AA – Spiritual Not Religious."

Let's be clear, though. We, personally, don't need that pamphlet. After all, we already know that we got sober in AA without the assistance of an interventionist deity. Nor do we rely on the Conference to tell us what literature will be helpful to us in either our short or long-term recovery.

Let me explain, starting with the second point.

———

The term Conference-approved, according to the General Service Office "does not imply Conference disapproval of other material about AA. A great deal of literature helpful to alcoholics is published by others, and AA does not try to tell any individual member what he or she may or may not read." (*Service Material from the General Service Office*)

Of course, as agnostics and atheists in AA we know that. Let me offer just two examples of non-conference-approved literature that have been found to be helpful in the rooms of AA.

The first is a book that was published two decades ago called *A Woman's Way Through the Twelve Steps*. Many women's groups across North America use readings from this book, written by Stephanie Covington, at their meetings. As Linda R. reports in her review on AA Agnostica:

> ...this book is focused on exploring different perspectives on the Steps, in order for alcoholics to create their own path of recovery. Using the Steps as guides, the book helps them discover or rediscover what they think, feel and believe and connect this to their actions and their relations with other people in the world around them.

Why is such a book necessary? Well, read the Conference-approved *Alcoholics Anonymous*. Women were, at best, ignored in the Big Book, their

211

roles understood as secondary to and supportive of the more important humans: men. Nor were the 12 Steps written with any understanding of a woman's experience or needs.

A much more recent book that is increasingly popular for alcoholics everywhere is Joe C's *Beyond Belief: Agnostic Musings for 12 Step Life*. It is a wonderful book of daily reflections. I watched Joe work at writing this book for over four years, and was shocked and delighted when he published it. As Carol M. asks in her review of the book, also on AA Agnostica, "Where else would you find Sam Harris followed by Mother Teresa, Bill Wilson followed with Anais Nin, a doctor's opinion by Dr. Seuss or a spiritual perspective from Albert Einstein?"

I am aware of Joe's book already being used at a number of agnostic AA meetings across North America. And why is this book necessary? Simply because of its diversity, the multiplicity and the richness of the viewpoints shared in it. Daily reflection books are important. Alcoholics and addicts buy roughly 800,000 of them every single year. Most of these books are religious, explicitly Christian. This is a secular daily reflections book, and now has a vitally important place in the recovery of alcoholics and addicts.

Now, here's the thing – neither of these books, and hundreds of others of inestimable value to those in recovery – will ever be "Conference-approved."

Why not?

Because the term "Conference-approved literature" is meant only to identify the books "solely owned, copyrighted and published" by Alcoholics Anonymous World Services (AAWS). As Barefoot's World puts it: "The statement Conference Approved in no way constitutes a list of any written documents of which an AA body approves or disapproves… What any AA member or group reads is no business of the GSO or of the Conference." (*What Conference Approved Literature Means*)

So, again, back to question.

Why would we care if there is a Conference-approved pamphlet for agnostics and atheists in AA if we have no personal need for such a pamphlet and if it's nobody's business what we read except our very own?

Because "Conference-approved" means censorship. "Conference-approved" has come to mean the non-inclusion and expulsion of groups using non-conference approved literature.

This is not new, but it is growing worse. The tendency was the subject of a talk almost thirty years ago by the former General Service manager of the GSO, Bob Pearson. Here is what he had to say at his eighteenth and last General Service Conference in 1986:

> If you were to ask me what is the greatest danger facing AA today, I would have to answer: the growing rigidity — the increasing demand for absolute answers to nit-picking questions; pressure for GSO to "enforce" our Traditions; screening alcoholics at closed meetings; prohibiting non-Conference-approved literature, i.e., "banning books;" laying more and more rules on groups and members.

Any of that sound familiar today?

In life-j's recent article, *Yet Another Intergroup Fight*, he writes that "a member of the god faction even countered with a motion that in order for a meeting to be listed it... only use AA approved literature. At this point even the moderates got scared that AA would move to something more rigid than what we had started with. It may yet."

Not it may yet. It already has in some places.

As reported in another article, *Booting the bastards out*, the Greater Vancouver Intergroup Society turfed two agnostic groups for "using non GSO conference approved literature."

The same thing is happening as we speak in Portland, Oregon. And in perhaps a dozen other cities across the United States and Canada.

Nevertheless, some of us believe that a "Conference-approved" pamphlet that might be called "AA – Spiritual Not Religious" could be a tiny step towards encouraging the more doctrinal and literalist members of our fellowship to be more tolerant towards those members of AA who don't believe there is a God out there in the cosmos preoccupied with helping them to not get drunk again.

I emphasize the word "tiny."

But it could indeed help the agnostic or atheist newcomer to AA: "Hey, friend, there's a pamphlet just for you on the literature table! Welcome!"

And if some Christian member said something remarkably asinine like, "You can't get sober without God," then a new option for a response is available: "That is not true. And it says so right in this Conference-approved pamphlet called 'AA – Spiritual Not Religious.' Here's a copy, Christian. Please be quiet and read it."

Or words to that effect.

And if you can't do those two things with it, then it is not a pamphlet for agnostics and atheists and it is of no value or interest to us.

We are admittedly only discussing a short term good. What ultimately has to go is the term "Conference-approved." Why not simply "Conference-published"? Or as Denis in Vancouver suggests, "Conference-developed"?

The term "Conference-approved" will always do far more harm than it does good. Anyone who gives it any thought at all will recognize that it is the perfect formula for censorship.

And that's exactly what is happening.

And that is not what the fellowship of AA is about.

IX. Controversy In The New Millenium

Indy We Agnostics Re-Listed

By Roger C.

The first nonbeliever's group ever to be booted off an "official" AA meeting list has been re-listed.

The Indianapolis We Agnostics group was actually de-listed twice. The first time was in November, 2010, when the group received a letter informing them that because "your group reads a changed version of the Twelve Steps... it is the judgment of the Indianapolis Intergroup's Service Committee that your group has decided it is not an AA group."

Without further discussion, We Agnostics was removed from the Indianapolis AA meeting list.

And later put back on.

And removed again – this time no reason was given – on May 8, 2011.

The issue simmered and festered over the summer and into the fall.

And it did a lot of damage within the AA community in Indianapolis.

Virginia R, the AA area delegate for southern Indiana reported: "The committee's action caused all sorts of collateral damage. Long-time friendships were affected and there was a general sense of simmering hostility from all corners of our local AA community."

Faced with an unprecedented backlash, the Intergroup Service Committee met again on Thursday, October 6, and voted to re-list We Agnostics.

At this point, "it got very twisted," according to Joe S, a founder of We Agnostics, as he described the whole process of re-listing his group.

The de facto lawyer for the Service Group and the author of the article Indy AA remains undiluted in the July issue of the Indianapolis Intergroup newsletter, Stephen U, argued on Saturday, October 8, that the vote to re-list We Agnostics was "null and void."

Something to do with proper notice of the vote not having been provided.

A day later, on Sunday, October 9, a general membership meeting of the Indianapolis Intergroup was held.

At that meeting representatives of AA groups in Indianapolis expressed their lack of confidence in the Service Committee and voted ("something like 112-72," according to Donna) against the decision to delist We Agnostics.

The following Thursday, October 13, the Service Committee met in a special meeting and voted, for a second time, to re-list We Agnostics.

Proper notice must have been provided this time because the next day – more than six months after having been delisted – We Agnostics was back on the meeting list on Intergroup's website.

It was a gruelling experience for all involved.

Joe, who is the first to acknowledge that his own behaviour was not always impeccable, says that he is exhausted as a result of the controversy. "I have been detoxing from it for weeks," he said.

The area delegate, Virginia, says, "The whole ordeal was physically, emotionally and mentally exhausting. Glad to be done with it."

And the final outcome?

According to Joe, the Service Committee has now taken the position that "if anyone complains about a meeting, they will be told to go to another meeting."

Let the Wood Burn

"Let the wood burn, ladies and gents. It will all be ashes soon. Remember we haven't done anything wrong, which means we don't have (anything) to fix."
Joe C.

By Roger C.

Joe C. celebrated 35 years of continuous sobriety on a Saturday night – December 10, 2011 – at the Beyond Belief meeting in downtown Toronto.

It was a special occasion. About 50 people came from the four corners of the earth – well, Pickering and Richmond Hill – to join in the celebration. Joe was one of the founders of Beyond Belief, the first agnostic group in Canada. Its first meeting was held on September 24, 2009.

Beyond Belief, along with the We Agnostics group, was "de-listed" by the GTA AA Intergroup on May 30th of this year, ostensibly for using a nonbeliever's interpretation of the 12 Steps of recovery, which were described by Bill W as a suggested program of recovery in the Big Book in 1939.

A motion to put the two Toronto groups back on the official list of AA meetings was presented at the GTA Intergroup meeting at the end of November. There was much talk of "compliance," of what the two groups would have to do or stop doing in order to conform to the demands of a majority of the groups in the organization.

Representatives were to go back and determine what their groups felt about these agnostics and their wayward steps and ways and whether or not they were fit to be considered bona fide members of the fellowship.

The debate has sometimes been heated, the volume amped up.

This left some members of the agnostic groups a bit anxious and wondering what to do. And this is where Joe came in. "Remember we haven't done anything wrong, which means we don't have (anything) to fix," he said.

It was a startling message, which some ignored. When someone is shouting at them, the first question people often ask is: "What have I done wrong?"

Nothing, says Joe. No rules broken. Nothing to fix.

217

There are, of course, those in AA who just want agnostics to go away.

It has ever been thus. Jim Burwell, one of the original members of AA, was a "self-proclaimed atheist, completely against all religion." At one point, his group, which met at Bill W's home in Brooklyn, held a prayer meeting to decide what to do with him. "The consensus seems to have been that they hoped I would either leave town or get drunk," Jim reported.

If the agnostic and her group won't go away, how about if she and it are seen but not heard?

When the two groups were booted off the AA meeting list, a few AA freethinkers started a website called AA Toronto Agnostics. The goal was to fulfill the AA responsibility declaration so that the suffering alcoholic – including the non-religious alcoholic – would be aware of and have the option of attending a freethinker's meeting.

There will no doubt be some in the rooms of AA who will be upset at the thought of agnostics AA members having their own website.

For all to see.

But, if we pay attention to Joe, that too is not a problem.

"I honestly think that moving from being ridiculed to violently opposed is evolutionally positive (if that's a word)," he wrote, the day before his birthday celebration.

And it is, in a sad but hopeful way, a marker of progress being made by agnostics in AA. Those who want to make the rooms of AA comfortable for all must not flinch, according to Joe, simply because the volume is being amped up and the language now more harsh.

"Remember we haven't done anything wrong."

Back at the Beyond Belief meeting, Joe accepted a 35 year medallion. A wonderful accomplishment and an inspiration to others.

When you think about it, being one of the founding members of an agnostic AA meeting could not have been easy. But Joe stuck with it, through the easy glides and the rough rides.

Let the wood burn, ladies and gents.

Is Listability the New AA?

By Joe C.

It's January 2014 and Vancouver is in the news: the city is winner of the 2025 AA World Conference. Congratulations are in order.

There is also controversy brewing in Vancouver, with two agnostic groups having been removed, at least temporarily, from the official Intergroup roster of AA meetings. This coming Tuesday (21 Jan 2014), Vancouver Intergroup will vote on whether or not agnostic groups are to be deemed "*listable*" on the Greater Vancouver AA meeting list.

This plays into a bigger drama about AA's growing pains as more and more atheists come into the rooms. Tolerance and inclusiveness are being tested on both sides – that's nothing new to AA, as we'll discuss.

The 2014 Winter Olympics are in Russia in the next couple of weeks. It was just four year ago that, again, Vancouver played host to the world for the 2010 Winter Games. I remember a 2010 controversy when city officials either jailed or relocated a lot of the city's undesirables. The plan was to ensure that every picture taken by every fan, athlete or dignitary would only show squeaky-clean Vancouver.

Al-Anon, a refuge of sober second thought, some time ago adopted a three-fold filter that Socrates is credited with offering us: Is it true? Is it fair? Is it useful? I know that not all of the people of Vancouver were ashamed of their homeless population nor did they feel threatened by them. If the decision went through the Socratic filter, it may have been concluded that it was not true that these people posed any threat to visitors, that it was not fair to disrespect the human rights of one class of people for the pleasures of another and as for was it useful – I expect there are still hard feelings in Vancouver, four years later.

Maybe Intergroup is unconsciously going through the same urgent clean up. Why let controversies go unchecked, while preparing to impress the world? If the problem-cases are small enough, eliminate them.

So, who are these groups and are they scapegoats or have they violated the rules of fair play in AA? Two groups in Vancouver, like another hundred or so groups in North America, don't see belief in, or obedience to, "God as we understand Him" as being a requirement for AA-style sobriety. While belief in

219

a prayer-answering God is popular in AA, it isn't a prerequisite for membership. The groups read a version of the AA Twelve Steps without the phrase "God as we understood Him." None of this is news for the core AA Agnostica reader but please bear with us while we bring newer readers up to speed.

According to an 18 page report from the new Vancouver Intergroup Manager the groups had to be eliminated from the meeting list and their voice silenced without delay – it wasn't the manager's self-will, it was argued; it was the result of a sense of duty. The groups aren't real groups; they aren't *listable* and should not have been welcomed in the first place.

These agnostic AA groups unabashedly say, "Hey, we're not asking permission. AA gives us the right to autonomously run our meeting as we see fit. AA isn't a popularity contest, if you don't like it, don't come, that's fine. We're not doing anything wrong – in fact, we're doing what our founders would have us do, carry the message of hope to still-suffering alcoholics that come to AA through an ever-widening gateway."

"No way," says the Vancouver Intergroup; "not so fast. Every group is autonomous, 'except in matters affecting other groups or AA as a whole.' We are autonomous as an Intergroup, too – and we are going to recommend that our popular groups vote on what constitutes a listable group."

Is an agnostic group bad for AA or a confusion to newcomers?

Is artistic liberty a good thing like the slogan "Live and let live" suggests to us? And what about the other Traditions? Our co-founder, Dr. Bob said this about our Traditions. "Honesty gets us sober (Step One) but tolerance (Tradition One) keeps us sober." Tradition Two specifically says "we do not govern." How do we tell a trusted servant from a twisted servant who has gotten drunk on dogma? Tradition Three has one and only one membership requirement – and it's not a willingness to believe in or pray to God, is it? Who's to bless and who's to blame here?

Let's apply the Socratic test to the Vancouver Intergroup's arguments. Socrates is known for his contributions to modern society's ability to be both reasonable and virtuous. Personally, I am not certain that we can reason people out of a corner that emotion has painted them into. As our co-founder Bill W. has cautioned us, fear and intolerance are highly emotional catalysts that can destroy Alcoholics Anonymous. Our Traditions were fashioned to defend us from our own emotional slips. [1]

So let's put the Vancouver Manoeuvre up against the Socratic test: is it true; is it fair; is it useful?

First, it is argued, you can't change the AA Steps. If you interpret them, you can't call yourself an AA group.

Here is the "authority" that anti-agnostic members draw from. Bylaws of the General Service Board, Inc., page S111 of the AA World Service Manual has this turgid little offering:

> The General Service Board claims no proprietary right in the recovery program, for these Twelve Steps, as all spiritual truths, may now be regarded as available to all mankind. However, because these Twelve Steps have proven to constitute an effective spiritual basis for life which, if followed, arrests the disease of alcoholism, the General Service Board asserts the negative right of preventing, so far as it may be within its power to do so, any modification, alteration, or extension of these Twelve Steps, except at the instance of the Fellowship of Alcoholics Anonymous.

On its own, without context, we might conclude that there it is – no changing the Steps. But who does this limit apply to and who is the enforcer? That's not confusing when we read the entire Service Manual. This bylaw applies to the annual General Service Conference of Trustees, Delegates and employees that approve and conduct the business of AA each year. It is the Board that does the enforcement. In no way does this apply to AA groups or members. This has been so since 1957.

But maybe while technically the General Service Board (or any Intergroup Office) should never govern nor punish groups, is it possible that the spirit of Twelve Step sacredness should be observed by every group? Not according to the Twelve Step author, Bill Wilson. AA Comes of Age was published in 1957 also. Here, for the record, Bill tells a story in the Chapter on Unity about the first known group ever to take God out of the Steps. He defended this group without reservations.

On page 81 he talks about how AA was growing around the world. Buddhists said that they would like to be part of AA, but also would like to replace the word "god" with "good" so that the practice of the Steps would be compatible with their non-theistic belief. Bill Wilson writes:

> To some of us, the idea of substituting 'good' for 'God' in the Twelve Steps will seem like a watering down of AA's message. But here we must remember that AA's Steps are suggestions only. A belief in them, as they stand, is not at all a requirement for membership

among us. This liberty has made AA available to thousands who never would have tried at all had we insisted on the Twelve Steps just as written.

So it is simply **not true** that agnostic groups that read an agnostic interpretation of the Twelve Steps are breaking our Traditions or even go against the spirit of them – according to the guy who wrote both.

And as far as reading anything that the group deems to be fair, true and useful, in an effort to attain and maintain sobriety, the General Service Office reminds us "Conference Approved Literature" doesn't suggest that either GSO nor the Conference is in the business of banning or disapproving any literature that a group or member might find helpful. [2]

Next up, an Intergroup email to group representatives states, "In January there will be discussion about this submission and a decision made as to what constitutes a '*listable*' group."

If you are searching your Service Manual, the Intergroup Guidelines or the pamphlet, The AA Group, for the world *listable*, you won't find it. It's a made up word. But we all know what is meant. We can't have anyone calling themselves an AA group without ensuring they follow THE RULES. Check the Appendices at the back of Alcoholics Anonymous or look in the AA World Service Manual for "the Rules" and you can't find them either. What we find in the Manual is Warranty Six (Concept XII) where, if Bill Wilson had any second thoughts about defending groups reading God-free Twelve Steps, he could have mentioned it here. Instead he celebrates the liberties afforded members and groups and assures that no punishment, judgment, nor demand for conformity ever be imposed on an AA group by AA itself. [3]

"There are no emergencies in AA," Ward Ewing told me in 2011 when talking about what he learned while Chairman of the Board of AA. General Service – a four year term. It was a learning curve for Reverend Ewing as a non-alcoholic Trustee. A sense of urgency was something he brought to AA but we taught him, as he told me, good decisions – spiritual decisions – were never made in haste, anger or apathy.

Have AA groups in Vancouver broken Traditions? No. Is it Vancouver Intergroup's right to set aside our Traditions and create their own "listable" requirements for AA groups? Sure – but don't lie to yourselves or others. *It's not the groups that are changing Vancouver AA, it's Intergroup. In the AA that our co-founders left us, a group is a group if the group says so*. Trusted servants accommodate; we do not judge.

If Intergroup passes judgment on unpopular groups, in AA we call that tyranny of the majority. If the minority groups demanded that all of AA conform to their wishes and change everything, that would be wrong, too – that's tyranny of the minority. But the groups aren't asking AA to change for their sake. What they are asking is to be treated with the same unifying love and tolerance that others are accorded.

Vancouver, if you go down this road, and especially if you want to use Toronto as an example, consider the law of unintended consequences. Agnostic AA membership is up – Toronto agnostic groups saw a surge in popularity after being tossed from Intergroup, not a drop in popularity. Contributions to Intergroup from the remaining groups is "below budgeted expectation" according to the latest Greater Toronto Area Intergroup minutes. Maybe that's a coincidence and maybe that's what Bill W. calls "the power of the purse." Maybe Toronto is still a story in the making.

Vancouver hasn't discovered a new and dangerous trend; deviating from the norm has been part of AA longer than most of us have been alive. This is what makes our society so special. We all have our own opinion but we all have to work from the same facts. Vancouver reminds us of our history; if we don't know our history, we are damned to repeat it. When Bill, Bob and our other pre-baby-boomers faced these same fears about artistic liberty (the right of the group to interpret the Steps for their purposes), they asked what they were afraid of? "Naturally, we began to act like most everybody does when afraid. After all, isn't' fear the true basis of intolerance. Yes we were intolerant. How could we then guess that all those fears were to prove groundless?"[4] Tolerance and inclusion require the opposite of fear—courage and whatever it is we have faith in.

So, group representatives, as you consider the proposal set forth by the Central Office Manager of the Greater Vancouver Intergroup Society, please be courageous and ask yourselves as you read, discuss and vote on the issue of the *listability* of groups other than your own:

Is it true; is it fair; is it useful?

---

[1] From Page 17, AA Tradition – How It Developed:

> The number of membership rules which have been made (and mostly broken!) are legion... The way our "worthy" alcoholics have sometimes tried to judge the "less worthy" is, as we look back on it, rather comical. Imagine if you can, one alcoholic judging another.

223

At one time or another most AA groups go on rule-making benders... Newcomers argue that they aren't alcoholics at all, but keep coming around anyway... Others refuse to accept all the Twelve Steps of the recovery program. Some go still further, saying that the "God business" is bunk and quite unnecessary. Under these conditions our conservative program-abiding members get scared. These appalling conditions must be controlled, they think, else AA will surely go to rack and ruin. They view with alarm for the good of the movement!

At this point the group enters the rule and regulation phase. Charters, bylaws and membership rules are excitedly passed and authority is granted committees to filter out undesirables and discipline the evildoers. Then the elders, now clothed with authority, commence to get busy. Recalcitrants are cast into utter darkness; respectable busy-bodies throw stones at the sinners.

[2] Conference-Approved Literature.

[3] Warranty Six from AA Service Manual: Combined with Twelve Concepts for World Service by Bill W.:

> In preceding Concepts, much attention has been drawn to the extraordinary liberties which the AA Traditions accord to the individual member and to his group: no penalties to be inflicted for nonconformity. . . Because we set such a high value on our great liberties, and cannot conceive a time when they will need to be limited, we here specially enjoin our General Service Conference to abstain completely from any and all acts of authoritative government which could in any wise curtail AA's freedom under God. . . . Therefore we expect that our Conferences will always try to act in the spirit of mutual respect and love—one member for another. In turn, this sign signifies that mutual trust should prevail; that no action ought to be taken in anger, haste, or recklessness; care will be observed to respect and protect all minorities; that no action should ever be personally punitive, . . our Conference will ever be prudently on guard against tyrannies, great or small, whether these be found in the majority or in the minority.

[4] Twelve Steps and Twelve Traditions, p. 140.

Booting the Bastards Out

"It does me no injury for my neighbor to say there are twenty gods or no God. It neither picks my pocket nor breaks my leg."

Thomas Jefferson (Notes on Virginia, 1782)

By Roger C.

Out they went

"We booted the bastards out," D said. "They wanted to water down AA and they tampered with the Steps."

D was a representative at the Greater Toronto Area (GTA) Intergroup. He was speaking immediately after the vote in May of 2011 to remove the meetings of Beyond Belief and We Agnostics, two agnostic groups, from the official GTA AA meeting list.

The Greater Vancouver Intergroup Society (GVIS) will soon decide on whether or not to list the agnostic meetings of two AA groups, We Agnostics and Sober Agnostics, on the regional AA meeting list and to include – or not – representatives of these groups in their monthly Greater Vancouver Intergroup Society meetings.

What many in AA don't understand is that these agnostics and atheists are neither trying to water down AA or tamper with the fellowship's program of recovery, as D so passionately put it.

And in the end we are not the foes of anyone in AA.

Appendix II: Spiritual Experience

As we all know, the Big Book – *Alcoholics Anonymous: The Story of How More Than One Hundred Men Have Recovered From Alcoholism* – was first published in April, 1939.

What we don't always know is that it immediately caused some real problems for some of those one hundred men and for other readers of the book.

And so in the second printing two years later in March, 1941, *Appendix II: Spiritual Experience* was added to the Big Book.

The appendix, just under four hundred words in length, is an effort to define more carefully and clearly the nature of recovery from alcoholism as it was

225

understood by the majority of the men in the fellowship at that time. It is also more inclusive in its presentation of getting sober and living a life of sobriety.

In the appendix, sobriety is described as the result of a "personality change sufficient to bring about recovery from alcoholism."

Moreover, that recovery is described as a path that usually takes time, sometimes lots of time. It is an educational journey involving change, learning and growth.

You can almost hear the sigh of relief when those of us who are a tad short of a belief in a divine and miraculous salvation read these words, simply because they so well reflect our own stories of "what it was like, what happened, and what it's like now." It acknowledges the often-times hard work of recovery from alcoholism. For us there is and was no interventionist God involved and "our experiences are what the psychologist William James calls the 'educational variety' because they develop slowly over a period of time," as it is so very well put in the appendix.

Another valuable thing Appendix II does is redefine a "higher power" as an "inner resource." Here it is: "Our members find that they have tapped an unsuspected inner resource which they presently identify with their own conception of a Power greater than themselves." We don't have to look up into the clouds and stars for this higher power. Instead we can look within ourselves to find new insights into the nature and demands of our own lives and the absolute necessity, for us, of continuous sobriety.

The appendix still explicitly includes "God" as a higher power and a part of recovery for many alcoholics. Agnostics and atheists have no trouble with that, as a rule. Nor do we try to tell "our more religious members" that they should give up their faith and embrace agnosticism. What is extraordinarily disturbing – and sometimes amounts to bullying – is that the reverse is not true. Some believers never stop insisting that agnostics and atheists drop their own world views and adopt the believer's God-based understanding of "how the world works." Creepy to many of us, especially in a program that is meant to be based on attraction and not promotion.

Finally, the appendix embraces inclusivity, a hallmark of the guiding principles of AA. It acknowledges that the "personality change sufficient to bring about recovery from alcoholism has manifested itself in many different forms."

"In many different forms."

This phrase invites us to welcome the fact that there are different paths to recovery. We should not in AA suggest there is only one way – "my way, the way I did it" – to get sober and maintain our sobriety. Because if we look around us honestly, that's clearly not the truth.

Tampering with the Steps

The argument used to boot the agnostic groups out of the GTA Intergroup and its list of regional AA meetings is that we have "tampered" with the Steps.

Agnostic groups sometimes use alternative versions of the Steps.

Appendix II of the Big Book makes a distinction between two types of AA members. There are those who believe and those who do not. For instance, when describing the importance of an "inner resource" or a "Power greater than ourselves" in recovery, the appendix points out that: "Our more religious members call it 'God consciousness.'"

Quite correct. And our least religious members don't. A commonly shared version of Step Three goes as follows: "Made a decision to turn our will and our lives over to the care the collective wisdom and resources of those who have searched before us."

Many don't relate to or find meaning in the word "God," and the ideas that it represents. And many cannot engage in the mental gymnastics of saying "God as we understood Him" in order to please "our more religious members."

Why don't we just fake it 'til we make it? For one thing, being a hypocrite about one's beliefs is the exact opposite of "rigorous honesty," which is generally recognized as a crucial factor in recovery.

We are of course told, repeatedly and incessantly, that this deity of our understanding can be anything we want, a Good Orderly Direction or a Group of Drunks. So what's wrong with reaching out to the "collective wisdom" of those who have searched before us?

Is the problem that this version has been written down?

It can be used because it's the key to recovery "as we understand it" but it shouldn't be written down? It can't be shared in a group? It's supposed to be a secret?

Or we get the boot?

Honestly?

Two things.

The Steps – even as originally written – are "suggestions" only. It says so on page 59 of the Big Book.

An AA member doesn't have to do the Steps if that is her or his decision. Indeed, no one has ever been booted out of AA for not doing the Steps.

They are suggestions, not an order. Nowhere does it say, "To be a member of AA you must do the 12 Steps – and you must do them exactly as written."

That's not our fellowship.

AA is about unity, not uniformity.

The reality is that many agnostics and atheists in AA fully accept the premise that their sobriety depends upon "a personality change sufficient to bring about recovery from alcoholism." That's why some of us have a commitment to the 12 Steps. For many, the Steps can bring about that change. And we understand that change is possible without "Him." Without an interventionist "God." And so many of us have our own versions of the Steps – based upon the original Steps – that allow us to access the resources that will bring about that change and help us to grow as we nurture and bolster our ongoing and continuous sobriety.

As members of AA, we also recognize that the Steps are suggestions only. If someone feels that the Eightfold Path of Buddhism is more helpful as a program of recovery, then that is fine too.

We are not here to tell another person what to do, but to support her or him in recovery.

That is AA, as we understand it.

The last thing the Steps were ever meant to be was an excuse to boot suffering alcoholics out of the door of the fellowship, even if the Steps were ignored or if versions different from the original Steps were used and shared. The person who wrote the Steps summed all of this up quite perfectly:

> We must remember that AA's Steps are suggestions only. A belief in them as they stand is not at all a requirement for membership among us. This liberty has made AA available to thousands who never would have tried at all, had we insisted on the Twelve Steps just as written. (Alcoholics Anonymous Comes of Age, p. 81)

A final thought on the Steps. We do not want to change the official and original AA Steps. No vote need be held by the General Service Conference. The various versions that are sometimes shared at agnostic groups are not meant to change the original 12 Steps but are solely for the use of the group, based upon the conscience of its members. Besides, these groups no more require their members to use any version of the Steps than does AA as a whole.

AA and Inclusivity

AA was always meant to be an umbrella under which any suffering alcoholic could find support. Any alcoholic. Any group of alcoholics. Practicing that is not watering down AA.

Tradition Three (long form):

> Our membership ought to include all who suffer from alcoholism. Hence we may refuse none who wish to recover. Nor ought AA membership ever depend upon money or conformity. Any two or three alcoholics gathered together for sobriety may call themselves an AA group, provided that, as a group, they have no other affiliation.

Some have argued that agnostic groups are affiliated to an outside issue, the ideology of agnosticism or atheism. That is really quite silly as non-theism is as much an ideology as not stamp collecting is a hobby. It would be a lot more legitimate to say that groups that end their meetings with the Lord's Prayer are affiliated to the Christian Church, an outside issue and one of the few things forbidden by our Traditions and promised in the AA Preamble: "AA is not allied with any sect, denomination…"

The affiliation accusations against agnostic groups are simply not worth any further discussion.

And just in case the wording of the Third Tradition is not clear enough, in an AA Grapevine article published in 1946, appropriately titled *Anarchy Melts*, Bill Wilson wrote:

> So long as there is the slightest interest in sobriety, the most unmoral, the most anti-social, the most critical alcoholic may gather about him a few kindred spirits and announce to us that a new Alcoholics Anonymous Group has been formed. Anti-God, anti-medicine, anti-our Recovery Program, even anti-each other — these rampant individuals are still an AA Group if they think so!

Forced by the facts to admit that agnostic and atheistic groups are not in violation of Tradition Three, some of our "more religious members" then resort to the argument that these alcoholics are trying to change AA and that

that is a violation of Tradition Four: "Each group should be autonomous except in matters affecting AA as a whole."

Do agnostic groups affect AA as a whole?

Not at all.

Certainly, if asked, most non-believers in AA are of the opinion that there ought to be room for all under the big tent of the fellowship. Our understanding is that AA is inclusive, and accepts everybody with a desire to stop drinking, regardless of belief or lack of belief. But that's not new: it has always been AA's message and its primary purpose.

Historically, agnostics groups have trundled along quite unnoticed in AA. Just two examples of this are the *Quad A groups in Chicago* which have been in existence since 1975, and the groups in California which started with the first group called "*We Agnostics*" in 1980 in Los Angeles. You can read about one of the founders of that group in the article, *Father of We Agnostics Dies*.

This peace is only disturbed when agnostics and atheists and their groups are crudely and unexpectedly attacked, as happened in Toronto. Then there is exactly what can be expected: an explosion of unseemly controversy and unwanted publicity.

Most agnostics and atheists in AA want the fellowship to be what it was originally meant to be: inclusive of everybody! We are not trying to change AA, we are hoping that AA will be and do what it was meant to be and do in the first place, when it was first founded.

The attacks on agnostics and atheists in AA most often display an intolerance towards others, and a disrespect for the beliefs of other alcoholics.

It drives people away.

As Bill Wilson wrote in another article in the Grapevine, *The Dilemma of No Faith*, in 1941: "In AA's first years I all but ruined the whole undertaking... God as I understood Him had to be for everybody. Sometimes my aggression was subtle and sometimes it was crude. But either way it was damaging – perhaps fatally so – to numbers of non-believers."

The "subtle and sometimes crude" aggression towards agnostics and atheists in AA, and their groups, ought to stop. The damage is too real, and much too serious, to far, far too many people. Proselytizing and/or attacking simply don't belong in our fellowship.

Decision time

Decision time is at hand in Vancouver.

The Greater Vancouver Intergroup Society (GVIS) is in the process of deciding on whether or not two agnostic groups shall be "deemed as AA groups" and "be allowed to be listed in the directory and on the GVIS website."

How that decision is made is currently unclear. It may be a decision made by the Operating Committee or it may be put to a vote by group representatives at a regular monthly meeting of the GVIS.

As things now stand, the agnostic groups stand accused of "altering and/or modifying the literature of AA" and "using non GSO conference approved literature."

Now, even the GSO will tell you that using literature that is not Conference-approved should never be considered a criminal act in AA, exposing a group to an ousting: The term Conference-approved "does not imply Conference disapproval of other material about AA. A great deal of literature helpful to alcoholics is published by others, and AA does not try to tell any individual member what he or she may or may not read." (*Service Material from the General Service Office*)

And as for "altering and/or modifying" the 12 Steps – because that is really the issue here – well, we have dealt with that at length above and neither has that ever been a crime in the AA fellowship.

It's one alcoholic talking to another alcoholic. It's a fellowship of support. It has a "suggested" program of recovery.

It's not about censorship. It's not about rules. It's not a "my way or the highway" kind of institution. That just isn't AA.

Are those principles that hard to follow and respect?

One of the things that was shocking at the time the agnostic groups were booted out of the Greater Toronto Area Intergroup was the incredible hostility towards these groups by some of the people in attendance, some of the reps.

D's reference to "booting out the bastards" was not that atypical, sadly.

It begs the question: Why is there this sometimes rampant hostility towards the non-believer?

Appendix II - a final reference to this wonderful addition to the Big Book - reminds us, all of us, that "Willingness, honesty and open mindedness are the essentials of recovery. But these are indispensable."

Open mindedness: "A willingness to respect views and beliefs that differ from one's own. Open minded people have views but know that their views do not have to be held by everyone." (Urban Dictionary)

For the record, we agnostics and atheists in AA are not, at least for the most part, bastards. We are sons and daughters, brothers and sisters, moms and dads.

We are, come to think of it, exactly like every other member of the AA fellowship – the anyone's, anywhere who reach out for help.

And who want the hand of AA always to be there.

Our beliefs and non-beliefs hurt not a single person in AA.

As Thomas Jefferson, the third President of the United States, put it: "It does me no injury for my neighbor to say there are twenty gods or no God. It neither picks my pocket nor breaks my leg." (*Notes on Virginia*, 1782)

The Greater Vancouver Intergroup Society has a wonderful opportunity to demonstrate and support the very spirit and purpose of the fellowship of AA.

Or it can boot the two groups, We Agnostics and Sober Agnostics, off of the official regional AA meeting list and out of Intergroup.

One Alcoholic Judging Another

"The way our 'worthy' alcoholics have sometimes tried to judge the 'less worthy' is, as we look back on it, rather comical. Imagine, if you can, one alcoholic judging another!"
Bill W.

By Roger C.

Vancouver Intergroup went on a bender of self-righteousness last Tuesday.

There were apparently 80 or 90 people in attendance at the meeting. They were given orange ballots which did not address the question of whether or not to list the two Agnostic groups in question; rather the ballot asked the delegates if Intergroup should "continue to discuss the issue of whether or not to list the Agnostic groups in the meeting directory." Yes or No.

People filled in their ballots. Four or five different people collected the ballots. Then they left the room. They came back three or four minutes later to announce the results: forty-seven delegates apparently voted No and twelve apparently voted Yes.

A woman, almost in tears, said she could not understand how the the vote ended the way it did in view of tradition three and AA's commitment to be inclusive rather than exclusive. But it was over and the issue decided. Members of the banned agnostic groups were never given the opportunity to defend their rights within AA and the matter was closed.

In a comment about the controversy created by Vancouver Intergroup, and referring to the efforts of AA Agnostica and the women and men committed to inclusivity within AA, Ernie Kurtz, the author of *Not-God: A History of Alcoholics Anonymous*, had this to say:

> As happens to just about every historical phenomenon, "AA" in places has betrayed and fallen from aspects of its essence, and not only in regard to God and the Steps. This will, necessarily continue: it is a virtual law of history. There is all the more need, then, for the prophetic vision that calls the fellowship back to its own program, to its own true story. For now, the present moment, AA Agnostica is supplying that vision and voice. All who truly love the fellowship and its program can only be grateful to you, for you. The role of the prophet is never smooth nor easy, so many who do believe in God

233

pray that your courage continues. We all need the honesty of your vision.

Joe C. is the author of *Beyond Belief: Agnostic Musings for 12 Step Life*. Joe is also one of the co-founders of the first agnostic group in Canada and it was booted off the official Greater Toronto Area AA meeting list on May 30, 2011.

Joe talks about that experience:

> I was crushed by Toronto Intergroup's decision. I grew up in AA. I have been sober since I was a teenager. I have always been outrageous. I have always pushed the envelope. I have always been tolerated and loved. When I was told that I was no longer welcome here it was an innocence lost that I cannot properly express. It was like having my family tell me to leave and never come back. For weeks, I was flabbergasted. I was angry and I was hurt and I thought very little of AA culture.

Joe goes on to quote the German philosopher, Arthur Schopenhauer: "All truth passes through three stages. First, it is ridiculed. Second, it is violently opposed. Third, it is accepted as being self-evident."

Most of us who are a part of the ever-growing agnostic and atheist contingent within the fellowship of AA will most certainly agree with Joe's conclusion: "Maybe we are at the important second step here. We must be moving towards the third. My heart goes out to you, Vancouver."

The Vancouver Intergroup rule-making bender brings home the meaning and relevance of Tradition Three and the Responsibility Declaration, both of which summarize the very essence of the vision and mission of AA.

And in the spirit of AA, I support Vancouver Intergroup, not in its decision, of course, but in its right to be wrong. "Every group has the right to be wrong," Bill Wilson wrote. (12 and 12, p. 47)

And the "Greater Vancouver Intergroup Society," as it calls itself, isn't the first group to exercise that right within our fellowship. Nor will it be the last. Guaranteed.

Yet Another Intergroup Fight

By life-j.

Laytonville, where I live, is a small coastal mountain valley village of about 2000 on Northern California's Highway 101, about 3 hours north of the Bay Area. This is a sparsely populated area. The next, smaller village is 25 miles north, the next, bigger one 25 miles south. Our local metropolis of 20,000 people, the seat of our local Intergroup, is 50 miles away. Laytonville is where I decided to start a Freethinkers meeting. There is good reason to think that this Freethinkers meeting could have gone practically un-noticed by the world, and AA, forever.

I had been thinking about doing it for a while, but when a newcomer came to our regular Laytonville Fellowship hall meeting, and introduced herself as an agnostic, it felt like it was time to act.

On the first Sunday in April of 2013 I approached Mendocino County Inland Intergroup with the idea of starting a freethinkers meeting. As I wrote to the chairman beforehand:

> I'm toying with the idea of making a freethinkers meeting here in Laytonville. I presume you have heard of the group in Toronto that got excommunicated from intergroup for taking god out of the steps for the purposes of their freethinkers group, but otherwise kept the steps to be worked as always. Just want to explore whether we will get excommunicated too, or whether we're sufficiently freethinking here in Mendocino County to have a meeting without god. Or should I just quietly put it on the schedule, and not stir up any shit?

This was an Intergroup which up to this point had functioned quite well. I was going into my second year as a representative for my local fellowship, had served a term as co-chair, and had worked on a couple of things, including updating the bylaws.

So I got to introduce the issue, not as any old recovering alcoholic showing up at the meeting to petition, but as an actual voting member of Intergroup. My fellowship had supported my idea of making such a meeting, though they were reserved about my idea of changing the steps, and therefore eventually I decided to make it a separate group.

Some people had done service in intergroup for many years, pretty much the folks that cared about making it function, while many groups and individuals until now hadn't considered it worth the effort and had no representative.

Well, it didn't go so easy. After discussion in April, it was brought up for vote in May. It was tied, 4-4, with one person who claimed to be in favor abstaining, and the chairperson abstaining from breaking the tie, though she was in favor too, but a little concerned about causing trouble for herself. Back to more discussion.

What happened next was that the god focused faction went and rallied their forces. They denied this of course, but it is odd that they managed to line up representatives from all the hitherto un-represented groups, that all were on their side.

We were now busy getting polarized, focusing on "uniformity" instead of "unity".

I heard it said in the AA Agnostica chat room the other night: "Any argument that begins with "What if" is a fear based argument." And plenty of fears were voiced about how this group would be the doom of AA.

I guess I had really been quite innocent about the whole thing. I thought it would simply have been treated as a business item. On the back of our schedules it said:

> Meetings included in the schedule are listed at their own request. A schedule listing does not constitute or imply approval or endorsement of any group's practice of the traditional program of Alcoholics Anonymous.

That the schedule says so must mean something, right? There must be some kind of meeting which is not endorsed, but is still listed – but doesn't look like it is ours.

A couple of times we approached a re-vote. But by now some of us were concerned that the god faction had gathered enough force to defeat listing the meeting, so we dragged our feet a bit. One of the more level-headed members suggested that we amend the bylaws to include:

> This Intergroup shall have no control over the internal affairs, the management or conduct of any member group; complete independence of each group must be preserved.

AA Group defined: Any two or three alcoholics gathered together for sobriety may call themselves an AA group, provided that, as a group, they have no other affiliation. (Tradition Three, Long Form)

But it was drowned out in discussion. One member of the god faction even countered with a motion that in order for a meeting to be listed it had to use the original 12 steps, and only use AA approved literature. At this point even the moderates got scared that AA would move to something more rigid than what we had started with. It may yet. That motion is still floating around, but has not been voted on.

I finally countered with another motion. I confess it was real crafty, bordering on the devious, but all it really did was to say things as they are, that Intergroup now wants to control things:

> Up to this point Intergroup has been a service organization with no actual authority, and has listed groups on its schedule at their own request based on AAs philosophy that our leaders are but trusted servants, they do not govern, and that of group autonomy. We propose that Intergroup must take it upon itself from simply being trusted servants to become a governing body which evaluates the worthiness of individual groups, and decide which groups should be listed in the schedule, and which ones can't be. If this motion fails we will keep doing things the way we always have, list meetings at their own request.

> This being an important policy issue, it should pass with substantial unanimity, that is 2/3 majority.

Let's make a long story short: This first Sunday of February 2014 we finally voted on my motion. The chairperson, supposedly otherwise supporting my position spoke out vehemently against the motion and its deviousness, but a motion is a motion, it was made and seconded, and voted on. One in favor, two against, about 10 abstaining. So it failed, which means the meeting now gets listed, right?

Not at all. The chairperson decided that it needs to be discussed at the next meeting.

At this point I resigned from Intergroup. After one vote in the beginning where we had a solid majority, but wasted the opportunity, (apparently also out of some people's fear) and another vote which is simply being discounted, what else could I do? I don't know what they are going to do now.

I got to be the bad guy, especially with this motion. If the meeting had been listed after a carrying vote in the beginning, maybe the god people would still have rallied their forces and tried to rescind the vote 6 months later, but at least then they would have been the bad guys, not me.

Looks like all I can do at this point is to move on, focus my energy on making our Freethinkers meeting work, go around to meetings in the area and announce it, put my energy into the AA Agnostica chat room, and other measures to help the agnostic newcomer. For the time being it looks like our local Intergroup is a lost cause.

I hold it as an axiom of the expression of thought that, except in cases where a person may have lost their faculties at a later stage – when a person expresses thoughts, and then later expresses other thoughts that to some degree contradict the earlier thoughts, and provided we can assume that these thoughts are expressed after reasonably careful consideration – that the later, contradicting thoughts bear witness to that the person expressing them has evolved in some manner, and has modified their point of view, and that the latter expressions therefore carry more weight than their previous, earlier thoughts, in some cases considerably more.

Bill Wilson wrote the Big Book with what, five years of sobriety? When therefore he kept writing all through his later years we ought to pay special attention to that. He never really rescinds his position that having a god is essential to recovery, and that sooner or later we will all "get it," but he does attain a certain humility about it, most famously in the piece *The Dilemma of no Faith* from the April 1961 Grapevine which I won't quote here, but I highly recommend reading it, and he increasingly speaks out in favor of inclusivity, against rigidity and dogmatism.

About Tradition 3 he writes:

> In fact, our Tradition carries the principle of independence for the individual to such an apparently fantastic length that, so long as there is the slightest interest in sobriety, the most unmoral, the most anti-social, the most critical alcoholic may gather about him a few kindred spirits and announce to us that a new Alcoholics Anonymous Group has been formed. Anti-God, anti-medicine, anti-our Recovery Program, even anti-each other – these rampant individuals are still an AA Group if they think so! (July 1946 Grapevine)

About Tradition 4 he writes:

With respect to its own affairs, the group may make any decisions, adopt any attitudes that it likes. No overall or intergroup authority should challenge this primary privilege. We feel this ought to be so, even though the group might sometimes act with complete indifference to our Tradition.

One argument we hear is that the formation of a group with altered steps influences AA as a whole. Bill Wilson does clarify what sort of thing he considers will "injure AA as a whole":

> For instance, no group or inter group could feel free to initiate, without consultation, any publicity that might affect AA as a whole. Nor could it assume to represent the whole of Alcoholics Anonymous by printing and distributing anything purporting to be AA standard literature. (March 1948)

So where does this all leave us? With a dogmatic AA that increasingly subscribes to ideas like those expressed by the "White Paper." With, it appears, a backlash of more christianity. Even in my home fellowship. We abolished the Lord's Prayer a number of years ago, and stuck with the serenity prayer. Here recently someone asked that we started using it again. Didn't go over so well with me, of course, and they eventually modified it to that the secretary could ask a member to close with the prayer of their choice. That sounded real good, and practically everyone bought it. You know what that means, though: OK, not the LP ending every meeting, the SP still used a bunch, and a whole lot more of the 3rd, 7th, and 11th step prayers. All in all, more god focus.

———

As I was finishing this tale of my woes with Intergroup I heard that the WAFT conference slated for Santa Monica in November was going to ban non-conference-approved literature at the convention. Initially the FAQ on their website said: "Because we are a part of AA... the steering committee (SC) has decided not to allow any non-conference-approved literature at the convention." They went back and forth on it, first saying no non-conference-approved literature, then saying the question was under consideration, then no again, and, after more objections, they replaced the "no" with a dash after the question "Will there be non-conference-approved literature at the convention?" Presumably the dash meant either "we're thinking about it" or "we're avoiding dealing with it." Finally, after a couple of weeks of hemming and hawing the FAQ now says that the steering committee will "make this literature available in a separate, clearly defined location."

Why the debate at all? Why all the reluctance to include literature that hasn't been published by the GSO?

Look at the trail of this debate. In the first FAQ on this subject, the steering committee said "Because we are a part of AA..." and then went on to "not allow" non-conference-approved AA at the convention. The committee is succumbing – knowingly or unknowingly – to the fundamentalists' vision of AA. Their reason for keeping the non-conference-approved literature "separate and clearly distinct" is so that it will not be confused with the "true" AA, the definition of which is found, according to the fundamentalists, in selected conference-approved literature (God, powerlessness, surrender, etc., as in the Big Book), and which some Intergroups are increasingly insisting upon, and this certainly not in service but in an attempt at governance. [1]

Let's look at a quote from the recent New York Times article, *Alcoholics Anonymous, Without the Religion*:

> "AA starts at its core with honesty," said Dorothy, 39, who heads the steering committee for the We Agnostics and Freethinkers International AA Convention. "And how can you be honest in recovery if you're not honest in your own beliefs? If you don't believe in the God they're praying to, that's not honest practice."

Couldn't have said it better myself.

How can you honor your own beliefs if even at an agnostic convention you are still only allowed to use the same old books filled with god? The convention needs to especially be the place to share alternative literature to supplement the conference-approved AA literature we already know. If we can't even be honest at "our very own convention" where can we? Are we going to have to not only fight the intergroups, but now even our own people?

All this fear of the god people seems to know no end. Come what may, we need to stand up for what we (don't) believe in. For almost seventy-five years now we have tried to placate the people bent on the "God bit," as Jim Burwell put it, and what is the result? Things have gotten worse instead of better over the last decade. We agnostics and atheists need honest practice, now, at every level.

If this convention is to mean anything it must be a place where we can honestly share with each other what is working for us – not just as individuals, quietly in the convention corridors when we hope no AA police are listening - but openly, as a group, from the podiums, around the tables, in all the meetings and workshops, from the books we use to the alternative versions of the steps that we are trying on for size in meetings all over the continent.

———

I did start the Laytonville Freethinkers meeting on August 22nd at the local Grange, and I have registered it with World Service. People come in from 50 miles away to support it. And here we are, a half dozen people at this little meeting out in the middle of nowhere, aware of the grave threat we pose to AA's future, but somehow we manage to remain calm and composed about it.

---

[1] The document that comes closest to an official definition of AA is the AA Preamble, which is also conference-approved literature. It makes no mention whatsoever of God or a Higher Power or even the 12 Steps and is ignored by those obsessed with the "God bit" and the Intergroups that succumb to their persuasion. Here it is:

> Alcoholics Anonymous® is a fellowship of men and women who share their experience, strength and hope with each other that they may solve their common problem and help others to recover from alcoholism. The only requirement for membership is a desire to stop drinking. There are no dues or fees for AA membership; we are self-supporting through our own contributions. AA is not allied with any sect, denomination, politics, organization or institution; does not wish to engage in any controversy, neither endorses nor opposes any causes. Our primary purpose is to stay sober and help other alcoholics to achieve sobriety.

> Copyright © by The AA Grapevine, Inc. Reprinted with permission.

A full background on this document, prepared by the General Service Office, is available here, *The AA Preamble: Background Information*. The Preamble appears at the very beginning of the *AA Service Manual*, before the Table of Contents.

Never Fear Needed Change

By Joe C.

As the Christian calendar rolled over yet again, another AA member asked me why I thought AA was no longer growing. Like me, he remembers the 1970s and 1980s when perpetual population growth in AA was expected. AA's population, which had always been growing, doubled from the 1970s to the 1990s. The fellowship's population peaked just after 1991 and in the last 20 years we have never reached beyond 2.2 million members worldwide. AA language was cutting edge for the 1940s. Seven decades later the same old tune doesn't sound so funky. The world is changing and AA can change too, but resists.

As we seek understanding about the 20-year growth drought, clues might present themselves when we look at the problems at the Intergroup office in Toronto, Canada. A changing of Canadian demographics tells a story of why, in Canada anyway, our fellowship may not be keeping pace with the larger community we say we are committed to, namely everyone with a desire to stop drinking.

The facts about a changing Canada

In 1991, Canada had 26.9 million people and 83% were Christian. In 2001 population grew 10% to 29.6 million while the Christian population dropped to 77%. The Christian population (like the AA population) stayed almost flat over the decade (1.5% increase) while the Canadian population increased by over 2.5 million people.

Over that decade, Protestants are down 8%, Catholics are up 5%. The second largest religious population is no religion at all. The non-religious have increased 44% from 3.4 million to 4.9 million Canadians.

Of the non-Christian religious, Jews remain flat at 1% of our population and predominantly eastern religions have exploded. Collectively, Muslims, Buddhists, Hindus and Sikhs have doubled in population in Canada at the end of the 20th Century from 721,130 Canadians to 1,455,605 Canadians. For the record, people who fall into none of these categories are also on the rise. The "other" classification increased 72.5% from 1 million to 1.9 million Canadians.

To accommodate the Islamic faith in AA not only would we allow the replacement of the phrase, "God as we understand Him," with Allah but the male pronoun, "He" has to go. There is no gender or plural "Higher Power" in the Muslim faith. Muslims who may be finding Allah "doing for them what they could not do for themselves" in AA are but a sliver of the non-Judeo/Christian Canadian population.

Buddhists, some of whom would not define Buddhism as a religion at all, and have no interfering or intervening god, had a 88% growth rate from 1991 to 2001 in Canada from 163,000 to over 300,000. In one decade the total non-theistic population surge in Canada went from 4.5 Million in '91 to 6.8 Million, a 51% increase.

Twelve per cent of the world population are atheists, absolutely sure there is no interfering god listening to prayer or granting sobriety to AA members. Many are proud AA members, using the Twelve Steps to get sober and considering their own success proof of the non-existence of god. Most nonbelievers have no axe to grind with believers about whether they should or should not believe. They simply want to be treated as equals and be able to communicate without censorship.

According to a 2006 Stats Canada report, the 16% of Canadians who claimed to have no religion in 2001 had quadrupled from a mere 4% in 1971. Is this a short term trend? Not if youth is our future. In Canada fewer than half of 15 to 30-year-olds have religious belief or practices. We know 15 to 30-year-olds drink; some of them get sober. When this Millennial generation reaches the average AA member age of 47 years old, with half the country not believing in God, how many will be finding their sobriety from AA, if we don't start expressing our principles in a language they understand?

Data shows that in 2011, USA members are up slightly and Canadian membership is down for another flat year (of less than 1% change).

The facts about a stagnating Alcoholics Anonymous

What we know about 2011 is that this was the year that Toronto Intergroup started forcibly reducing the number of groups instead of increasing the number. Specifically, Intergroup is going against the longstanding AA tradition (since 1975) of embracing agnostic AA groups and instead is discriminating against them. Groups that are deemed AA by the General Service Office (GSO) are nevertheless excluded from having a voice on the Greater Toronto Intergroup floor and being listed as a meeting for newcomers or visitors.

While GSO is looking forward to talking about diversity and change as the catalyst of AA growth at the 2012 General Service Assembly, Toronto is voting against diversity or change. AA members in Toronto want the Twelve Steps for people who don't believe in god. A divided Toronto Intergroup is saying, "Not in our city."

There is no rule against a group posting, reading or distributing agnostic steps in AA. But Toronto group conscience employs the narrowest possible view towards preserving AA integrity. A suburban Intergroup rep expresses a shared sentiment when he says, "It's OK for members to be agnostic but they shouldn't be allowed to have their own groups."

Is that fair? Is that true? Is that legal? It has been pointed out to the Intergroup Chair that some of the AA members in the agnostic community of Toronto have felt harassed since the Intergroup action and that according to the Ontario Human Rights Commission website, Intergroup is violating the law by not accommodating minority rights in AA. As far as I know, this information, this letter to the Chair, was not shared with other Intergroup reps.

According to the Ontario Human Rights Commission, agnostics in AA have the right to accommodation when using a non-theistic version of the Twelve Steps for their own purposes. Neither harassment of minorities based on theistic belief nor systemic discrimination is legal in Canada:

> It is the OHRC's position that every person has the right to be free from discriminatory or harassing behaviour that is based on religion or which arises because the person who is the target of the behaviour does not share the same faith. This principle extends to situations where the person who is the target of such behaviour has no religious beliefs whatsoever, including atheists and agnostics, who may, in these circumstances, benefit from the protection set out in the Code.

> In either situation, creed must be involved – either because the person who is the subject of the discrimination is seeking to practice his or her own religion, or because the person who is harassing or discriminating is trying to impose their creed on someone else. In both cases, creed must be involved.

> Discriminatory practices that fail to meet any statutory justification test are illegal and will be struck down.

The fact that Toronto AA doesn't have a human rights policy, a procedure for managing complaints or accommodating creed, race, gender or sexual orientation needs just speaks to how AA is not in step with the society it claims to serve in Ontario, Canada.

Since 1991, the Greater Toronto Area has more than doubled in population to over 5.5 Million people. Visible minorities collectively have eclipsed residents of European descent in a city that answers 911 calls in 150 languages.

Outside the rooms of AA, Canada's population is very different than it was in the 1970s. Inside AA's rooms we look and behave pretty much the same now as we did then – predominantly Caucasian 40+ males of Judeo/Christian descent. Stagnant demographics are a tell-tale sign that systemic discrimination is present in an organization like ours.

Canada is growing. So is alcoholism. But AA is staying the same. Assuming that the laws of nature abhor a vacuum, are we more likely to grow or decline if we refuse to accommodate the needs of today's alcoholics?

In 1965 Bill W wrote in the AA Grapevine:

> Let us never fear needed change. Certainly we have to discriminate between changes for worse and changes for better. But once a need becomes clearly apparent in an individual, in a group, or in AA as a whole, it has long since been found out that we cannot stand still and look the other way.
>
> The essence of all growth is a willingness to change for the better and then an unremitting willingness to shoulder whatever responsibility this entails.

Change is risky – what if it doesn't work out for the better? AA is self-correcting. When we try something and it doesn't work, it goes away all by itself – be it god's will or natural selection. AA has never needed to enforce rules or govern meetings or members. Many feel we would no longer be AA if we did draft and enforce rules for members or groups.

Once there was a man. He had a message. The message started a movement. The movement created a monument. If the fluid, flexible message becomes a reified, cast in stone monument, growth is impossible. The movement starts to decay. The next stop is the mausoleum, where our children will learn about AA in the museum.

X. Moving Forward

Making a Case For Atheist/Agnostic Groups in AA

By JHG

The idea that atheists and agnostics have the right to take part in the AA experience and fellowship does not involve either a subtle or complicated mental juggling act.

The third tradition explicitly says, "The only requirement for AA membership is a desire to stop drinking." Virtually no one in AA would outright slam the door shut and ban atheists and agnostics from becoming members, but there is more to actually including us than begrudgingly accepting our right to be members. Anyone who has ever been in a typical AA meeting knows that there is plenty of de facto exclusion. It often hurts to be an atheist in AA. All the god talk and the repeated claims that it is impossible to get sober without a Higher Power present significant obstacles for atheists and agnostics.

And closing meetings with the Lord's Prayer doesn't help.

Being allowed to join AA doesn't mean a thing if my experience causes me to not want to come back. I don't have to like everything I hear, but unless my experience gives me a glimpse of something I want, AA will be of very little use to me. It's a program of attraction. I have to want it in order for it to work. It is not enough to be able to sit meekly and silently in the back row. And it is insulting to be magnanimously tolerated if it comes with being told, "Keep coming back. Eventually, you will either find your Higher Power or you will get drunk."

The true fulfillment of Tradition 3 rests on whether anyone who wants to stop drinking can feel at home in AA and participate fully. Being relegated to a marginalized position does not constitute membership in any meaningful sense.

It is natural that those who need to find a way to get sober without having to embrace the concept of a higher power would want AA groups where who we are and what we stand for is accepted.

However, contrary to AA's slogan, "Live and let live," many AA members strenuously challenge the legitimacy of these groups. Even though no one is seeking to eliminate God from the AA program altogether, devotees of the "god of love" heap ridicule and contempt on everyone associated with atheist/agnostic groups. In spite of the inarguable fact that addicts are dying because of AA's intolerance towards those who do not accept that an interventionist God is responsible for their sobriety, many members of "the last house on the block" thwart the life-saving inclusivity of these groups by snubbing them and refusing to list them in local meeting schedules.

When AA's Twelve Traditions were crafted, one of the main guiding principles was a shrewd avoidance of a top-down organizational model. Tradition 2 is very explicit. Leaders don't govern. Instead, they assume the role of "trusted servants." The allusion in Tradition 2 to a "loving God" may be anathema to atheists, but this god is a nonessential ingredient in the process. The mention of God in this Tradition is intended to empower and liberate rather than bind. It is a deliberate move to discourage rather than promote any sort of religious or political orthodoxy. It is not referring to the almighty, sovereign god of the Abrahamic religions but instead imagines a commonality and a beneficence that is experienced through the "group conscience," a bottom-up process that encourages the expression of divergent viewpoints.

The rejection of top-down thinking is also explicit in Tradition 9, which enjoins AA against becoming "organized," and in Tradition 4, which grants the groups autonomy. AA's bottom-up center of authority not only establishes a network that is able to function with very little administrative structure, it also enables and encourages maximum creativity, flexibility, and adaptability at the group level.

The heart of the traditions is Tradition 5, which outlines the "one primary purpose" of an AA group, which is "to carry its message to the alcoholic who still suffers." The idea that the group has a distinctive message, "its message," stands in sharp contrast to the twelfth step's "this message," but the fifth tradition's implied notion that each group's message is pliable and unique is consistent with the second and fourth traditions. The fifth tradition says what the group's purpose is, to carry its message. The second tradition specifies how the group goes about shaping its message, through the group conscience. And the fourth tradition empowers the group to carry out the dictates of the group conscience without unnecessary interference.

To summarize the goals and intent of these Traditions: AA aspires to provide a solution that will work for anyone who wants to stop drinking, but recognizes that there is no one-size-fits-all formula that can achieve that.

There's a saying in AA, "For every nut who walks in the door there's a wrench that will fit them." One of the main ways that AA is able to custom fit the solution to individual needs is the group. AA groups are crucial in fostering vital one-on-one relationships and in providing a sense of belonging. Different AA groups have different strengths. AA groups are in a position to craft a targeted message better than anybody else. Anything that interferes with a group's ability to carry its message puts lives in jeopardy. Thus Tradition 4 says, "Each group should be autonomous except in matters affecting other groups or AA as a whole."

The intent of the fourth tradition is very clear. The creativity of individual AA groups is not to be curbed in any way unless it involves "matters affecting other groups or AA as a whole." The reason for the exception clause is not to protect the AA "brand" or to insist on any sort of orthodoxy. The goal is maximum effectiveness at every level of the AA organization. AA as a whole and AA groups are supposed to complement each other. The service structure that makes decisions on behalf of AA as a whole only exists to support the real work of AA, most of which occurs at the group level. AA as a whole is restrained from interfering with what a group deems effective, and the group is restrained from anything that would jeopardize AA's general effectiveness.

The burden of proof is always on anyone who would restrict the autonomy of a group. Most AA members get that – thus the saying from AA folk wisdom, "All you need to start an AA group is a coffee pot and a resentment." This is of course a humorous reference to the fact that many AA groups are founded by disgruntled former members of existing groups, but it is also a true reflection of the conscious intent of Traditions 2, 3, and 4. The long version of the third tradition explicitly states, "Any two or three alcoholics gathered together for sobriety may call themselves an AA group, provided that, as a group, they have no other affiliation."

That the existence of atheist/agnostic groups is controversial is very hard to understand, given that they seem like perfect examples of precisely the kind of responsiveness to the needs of its members that the fourth tradition is explicitly designed to encourage and support.

Those who would deny their legitimacy need show that there is something about them that infringes upon "matters affecting other groups or AA as a whole." What do atheist/agnostic groups do that adversely affects AA? They do not turn theists away. They are not allied with any "related facility or outside enterprise." Their purpose is not to promote or endorse atheism or any belief system that is alien to or in conflict with the primary purpose of AA groups. The sole reason for the groups' existence is to fulfill the traditions' explicit aim to carry the message of recovery to individuals who would otherwise fall through the cracks. Period. Full stop.

But what about the claim that the meetings misrepresent what AA is about and/or that they undermine AA unity?

Honest people can disagree about what would constitute a misrepresentation of AA. However, a good starting point for understanding what an accurate representation looks like is conference-approved AA literature.

Appendix II in the big book says, "Most emphatically we wish to say that any alcoholic capable of honestly facing his problems in the light of our experience can recover, provided he does not close his mind to all spiritual principles... We find that no one need have difficulty with the spirituality of the program."

If we take these words at face value, we could even say that those who say that finding a Higher Power is necessary are the ones who are misrepresenting what AA is about. Atheist groups don't promote atheism, but there is blatant promotion of religious ideas in many AA groups. No one ever suggests that meetings whose members flagrantly endorse religious beliefs be banned from AA or removed from the schedule – unless there is some kind of obvious and formal affiliation with a particular religion.

There is no question that the storm surrounding atheist and agnostic meetings is a threat to AA unity, but it is important to look objectively at the question of who or what is actually causing the disunity. Truly understanding the traditions generally starts with self-examination. Does AA's first tradition require atheists and agnostics to set aside our own personal needs for the sake of putting the common welfare first? Clearly, the very presence of atheists and agnostics is a disruption of AA's status quo, but do atheists and agnostics owe AA unquestioning docility? Do we just need to not rock the boat and adopt the stance of going along to get along? It is easy to put the blame on atheists and agnostics, but where is the actual fault? Atheists and agnostics are not imposing anything on anyone. We just want to find a way to stay sober without having to abandon our own core values and understanding. Is AA unity so fragile that it can't survive the admittance of a small handful of non-theists?

The paradox of AA unity is that it is strengthened rather than imperiled by the fellowship's diversity. "We are," the big book says, "people who normally would not mix." Joining together with people whose political views and social values might well be abhorrent to me demands somehow getting beyond or putting to one side my own perspectives on the world. As in the well-known folk story about the blind men and the elephant, none of us has the complete picture.

The peaceful coexistence of radically different viewpoints with regard to everything except one common goal, staying sober, is what AA unity is about.

Maintaining a balance between having confidence in my own approach and being open-minded with regard to other approaches often requires a considerable amount of work. That each of us is sometimes going to err on the side of our own obsessions is predictable. My life depends on having a "design for living" I know I can count on. My way may not be "the right way," but I should be thoroughly convinced that it is absolutely the right way for me; otherwise, my commitment will wither when I need it the most, in times of crisis.

That there is no one right way doesn't change the fact that my own sobriety depends on finding the right way for me and committing to do what it requires, no matter how uncomfortable it might get. There is wisdom in the AA truism, "If your home group is not the best group in the world, you need to find a new home group." Most people know enough to realize that this is meant wryly rather than literally. The point is that finding a right way that feels exactly right for me is not too much to demand. The difference between an imaginary right way for everybody and a necessary right way for me can be difficult to keep in mind, especially if finding a proven solution I can count on feels like a matter of life and death.

But if AA unity is not about enforced uniformity, what is it about? Unity that is entirely open-ended is meaningless. Viable communities are grounded in shared values. There is ultimately more to unity than glossing over irreconcilable differences.

Even though there is no one right way to recover from addiction, arriving at something of a consensus regarding the core of what holds us together is crucial. AA is a "we" program. Recovery is not a solitary undertaking. Personal freedom cannot come at the expense of the we of the program. The greatest threat to sobriety is for the recovery community to be at cross-purposes with itself. The first tradition says, "Our common welfare should come first; personal recovery depends upon AA unity." And in the aptly titled chapter, "There Is a Solution," the Big Book says, "We have a way out on which we can absolutely agree, and upon which we can join in brotherly and harmonious action."

There are two basic components to the kind of unity upon which personal recovery depends. First, there is the absolute empathy and support that comes out of having survived the life-threatening affliction of alcoholism. Second, there is the willingness, no matter how deep our differences, to "join in brotherly and harmonious action." Our agreement is possible because we have discovered a spirit of brotherly and harmonious action anchored in the shared experience of having come through the harrowing challenge of a disease that wanted us in an institution or dead. The operative word in the phrase "on which we can absolutely agree" is "can." It does not say "must." It leaves the onus on us to reach out in a spirit of love and tolerance.

For most of us, our sobriety and our very lives depend on ultimately being able to put aside our differences and open ourselves to the unparalleled personal transformation that comes with the identification and support of "one alcoholic talking to another alcoholic." The solution for us is in being a part of a community whose shared identity is deeper than our differences, deeper even than what can be put into words, and certainly deeper than banner-carrying, slogan-quoting and quasi-religious conventionality. Attempts to define or circumscribe our collective identity always leave something out. Focusing on anything that excludes or divides, like theological assertions, puts lives in jeopardy.

Unity is paramount, but it's a both/and proposition, both united around a single purpose and multi-faceted in its particulars, allowing for a diverse set of individual needs. There is a shedding of our "terminal uniqueness" but, at the same time, an embracing of "to thine own self be true," a principle which is not solely for use on medallions.

Realistically, it is inconceivable that the prevalence of god talk in AA is going to go away any time soon, but neither is the dilemma presented by atheists and agnostics showing up at AA. The number of persons needing an approach to sobriety that does not rely on a higher power is on the rise.

The only real solution is to work toward building a culture that can accommodate the needs of both theists and non-theists.

Theists may be uncomfortable with atheist/agnostic meetings, but there is far more real harm – not to mention the violation of AA principles and traditions – involved in needlessly placing obstacles in the path of an atheist who wants to get sober than is involved in ruffling the feathers of those with an apparently messianic zeal for God.

The true spirit of AA is to ensure that the hand of AA is always there to help anyone, anywhere get sober and maintain their sobriety. That is the unique and ultimate purpose of our traditions. Let us not amid the current brouhaha let anyone or anything cause us to lose track of that.

JHG lives in a part of Texas where The Bible Belt is somewhat softened by conservative Roman Catholicism. A long while back, he went to church to get clean and was miraculously transformed from a pot smoking heathen into a Christian alcoholic. His idea then of a promising geographic cure was to go to seminary, after which, he spent a number of years as a Methodist minister. Unable to control his drinking, he eventually arrived at what the Big Book calls "the jumping off place," the inability "to imagine life with or without alcohol." His introduction to the idea of finding his own higher power ultimately led to atheism. JHG learned the traditions the hardest way possible, by trying to get other people to follow them, an approach that somehow has nevertheless produced valuable insight into his own motives and designs. He has an atheist sponsor and is currently married to another atheist whom he met in AA.

The Only Requirement Group

By Reed H.

When I first joined the AA program in 1999, I was willing to do whatever it takes to stay sober. That included getting on my knees and praying to a higher power.

I never had much of a conception of a higher power prior to entering the program. I never went to church growing up and I never prayed. So when my first sponsor told me to get on my knees, hold his hands and pray, it felt strange, to say the least.

For years, I took the advice of AA members and prayed at night and in the morning. Although it didn't do any harm, I never really felt comfortable doing it. As much as I tried, I was unable to develop a concrete conception of a higher power. Yet, AA encouraged me to continue to seek.

I took that encouragement to heart and searched and searched. In the end, I finally made a discovery: there is no supernatural higher power or paranormal overlord watching and influencing my every move. And there certainly is no "better place" than the one I'm in now.

This discovery, which ironically I credit to AA and the search for a higher power, suddenly made it more and more difficult to fake my way through the prayers and God talk at AA meetings. I felt like a hypocrite.

I also started to realize how religious AA really can be, despite its insistence that it's not. That concerned me. In particular, I started to understand how AA could turn off newcomers, especially during a meeting with repeated droppings of the G-word.

Eventually, I left my home group, which is old school when it comes to reciting prayers, and I joined an excellent 12th Step Meditation group that de-emphasizes AA's religious aspects. At the same time, I did some Internet research to see if there were any agnostic AA groups around.

I discovered that there are many such groups including Beyond Belief in Toronto, the city where I first got sober. I made contact with group member Stan R. and he gave me some great advice on how to start a group. He also warned me about some of the inevitable resistance that would arise in Halifax if an agnostic group were to form.

With this in mind, I decided to reach out to other AA members. I put a notice in the area newsletter asking if there were other atheist or agnostic AA's who would like to get together and chat. I quickly received responses from three members, Allan G., Judi M and Arch M., all whom were quite eager to get together.

We met for coffee and it was like four long lost friends reuniting for the first time. We all shared some of our frustrations as non-believers in AA and had a few good laughs along the way. We were relieved to find others of the same ilk and immediately began the process of starting a new group.

Within a couple of weeks, we had a time slot at a local community centre. At our first meeting on November 23, 2011, we were joined by a few more members. Word had spread.

At that meeting, we decided on a name (The Only Requirement) and a format (a "topic" meeting). The next thing we decided on were the readings. Wanting to be true to our goal of creating a secular AA meeting, we decided on reading the *Agnostic Preamble* and the *Agnostic 12 Steps*, which Stan had graciously passed along.

We all sensed that choosing these readings would ruffle some feathers, particularly in light of what happened in Toronto – we had all read the article in the Toronto Star about how the Beyond Belief and We Agnostics groups had been turfed from Intergroup because of the Agnostic Steps.

Regardless, starting in early December, we forged ahead and began to have regular meetings on Wednesday evenings.

But it hasn't been all smooth sailing. The meeting has not been well received by members of the old guard who are protective of tradition and concerned about change. Some of those members sit on the board of Central Service, Halifax's answer to Intergroup.

The rumours we heard about the board's displeasure were confirmed when I asked the newsletter editor to put a notice in the February edition about the group. The first time I requested a notice, the editor was very accommodating. This time, not so much.

As it turns out, he had been instructed by the board not to put anything in the newsletter about the group. Since we read the Agnostic 12 Steps, the board felt the meeting could "affect AA as a whole," he said, and because of this, in their eyes we are not an AA Group.

We suspected this might happen. We could perhaps drop the reading of the Agnostic 12 Steps in order to be added to the fold. But that likely won't happen. It seems many of us are simply tired of making compromises in spite our beliefs (or lack thereof).

Meanwhile, attendance has been solid fluctuating between 10 and 15 members. More importantly, the meetings have featured great discussion, great sharing and great sobriety.

The agnostic meeting has been warmly embraced by AA members who have hidden for too long and have faked their way through countless AA meetings. Members who choose to call their higher power "God" have also attended our meeting and have made great contributions to our discussions.

If you're ever in the Halifax area, please be sure to drop by our meeting.

Two New Agnostic Meetings

By Russ H. and Denis K.

Over the past several months there has been an upsurge of interest in starting meetings for agnostics and atheists in AA.

Some people have gone ahead and done so, having discovered that all it takes is a few other interested AA members, a room that is available once a week, and a coffee pot.

Today we are going to hear about two of those new agnostic AA meetings, one in Canada and one in the United States.

We Agnostics – Lafayette, California

Mondays 5:30 – 6:30 PM
Little League Hut
711 St Mary's Rd.
Founding meeting: Monday, July 8, 2013

By Russ H.

A group of 29 very enthusiastic AA members turned out to the inaugural meeting of We Agnostics in Lafayette, California.

As I am writing this, an email message just came in from Dede S., an old friend whose appearance at the meeting was a delightful surprise. She writes "It was a grand meeting and I was very moved when I got home and walked the dogs. I cried because I took a deeply, emotional and spiritual feeling home from that meeting. Isn't that what AA gives us when it is just right?" I think Dede speaks for many of the people who were there.

As you will see in the attached materials, we are neither for nor against any particular religious or philosophical point of view. We aim to conduct a meeting where the religious/nonreligious dichotomy is kept in perspective and freedom of expression is the most important consideration.

Impetus for starting this meeting actually began to develop a couple of years ago. My friend, Connie O., brought my attention to the controversy in the Toronto area surrounding the removal of two groups from the official list of AA group meetings. She also sent me a link to *AA Agnostica*. For the first time, I became aware of AA meetings around the world that are dedicated to providing an alternative to the heavily Christian ethos that permeates mainstream AA. One outcome was that I began to receive periodic email notifications of postings made on the AA Agnostica website.

A few weeks ago one of those postings announced plans now underway for the We Agnostics and Free Thinkers (WAFT) International AA Convention (IAAC) in Santa Monica late in 2014.

A contingent of at least six of us will be at the WAFT IAAC planning meeting in Santa Monca at the end of August. Everywhere I go with the WAFT convention flyers I am greeted with delighted responses. At one meeting when I passed out some of the flyers a man sitting next to me had tears of joy in eyes.

While attending agnostic meetings, Dorothy, Pam and some other people supplied me with meeting formats and other materials which could be used for an agnostic AA meeting.

All of this made the next step very easy to take. Encouraged by several AA friends, I rented a spot in one of our local meeting places, typed up a meeting format (which includes two readings from the Big Book: *More About Alcoholism* and *Into Action*) and announced the time and place of the meeting. Our "We Agnostics" group is now meeting weekly.

On a more personal note:

It is often said that the essential experience in Alcoholics Anonymous is simply one alcoholic talking to another about their common problem. In the process, a message of recovery is often transmitted that transforms lives. I know that my own recovery occurred that way.

When I "came to believe" it was not to a belief in God. It was to the belief that I really could lead a clean and sober life. That belief was inspired by recovered alcoholics who looked right at me, with the unmistakable demeanor of people who are telling the truth, and said "Come to lots of AA meetings and don't drink or use drugs in between. If you do that, one day at a time, chances are good that one day you will discover the desire to drink and use will have vanished." That's what I did in the summer of 1995, and that's what happened.

From the beginning I have listened to people insist that AA is a spiritual rather than a religious program. At first I really didn't care very much one way or the other. I saw clean and sober people all around me in AA. I wanted what I saw in them – to be clean and sober – more than I had ever wanted anything in my life. So, I concentrated on the "don't drink or use" advice. I heard people talk about "doing the work." Yet my own experience was that being

257

sober was not (and is not) something that I do. It is something that was given to me. It is now something that I am.

I've attended thousands of AA meetings at dozens of locations in the U.S. and abroad. My perception is that well-intentioned people in AA often unwittingly stifle meetings and repel newcomers with their religious (a.k.a. "spiritual") zeal. I know the views expressed on AA Agnostica and by those working to put together the convention for agnostics, atheists and free thinkers in AA represents a minority opinion in AA at this time. But I am delighted to discover that it is a larger minority than I thought, and even more delighted to have connected with all of you finally.

Sober Agnostics – Vancouver, British Columbia

Tuesdays 7:00 p.m.
Holy Trinity Anglican Church
1440 West 12th Avenue
Founding Meeting: Tuesday, May 7, 2013

By Denis K.

At the first meeting of "Sober Agnostics," May 7th, there were nine people present; four women and five men. The meeting started with a little awkwardness as many of the people had never met before, that reservedness was soon overcome.

Mike D. chaired the meeting by simply reading the agnostic preamble and then the passage for that day from Joe C.'s book, *Beyond Belief: Agnostic Musings for 12 Step Life*. Those at the meeting then shared what they wanted, when so moved to do so. It took a few awkward moments of silence for the first person to speak but everyone present spoke to the topic. There were some great insights and honest sharing and plenty of genuine laughter.

It was suggested to try this format for a couple of months then review it for changes. Sober Agnostics is now underway as a Tuesday night destination; some people are not there every week due to vacations, business travel etc. but we have a weekly attendance of 12 or more.

Here is how it all began, for me…

Halfway through my sobriety, some nineteen years ago, I had to admit to myself and to a couple of close fellowship friends that all this stuff about an intervening god made no sense to me at all, that in fact I had never believed in any causal agent in the first place; it simply made no sense in my world.

258

Since then I have continued to attend AA meetings, and I have shared my disbelief in god with a few trusted and long term AA friends. We collectively shared new ideas we had discovered in various books and on the internet but never expressed these ideas at meetings in order to avoid the uproar we had seen when people did in fact speak out about their lack of belief.

We silently suffered the dogma and the rituals that have taken over many of the local meetings. Things like ending the meetings by holding hands and then the chair calls out "Who's the boss?" and then everyone recites the serenity prayer or worse yet, the Lord's Prayer. When someone reads the "Promises" and when it gets to the question, "Are these extravagant promises?" some or many members chant "We think not." These practices/rituals are not only sophomoric to many of us, they are downright offensive and carry an almost cultish feel to them.

Over the years I met many fine people at AA meetings who have dropped out and gone their own path.

Encountering many of them from time to time has shed light on their decision to leave our fellowship. Most have told me they were simply tired of the gossip, the boring and repetitive dogma, the unearned familiarity from some people, the religiosity and in many cases the cult-like atmosphere that has overtaken so many meetings. These people aren't normally complainers; they seem to a barometer of what many of us have endured to belong and remain in our fellowship. All who I have spoken to agree membership in AA should not be an endurance test nor a test of one's sensibilities.

A couple of years ago several of us decided to form a discussion group based on what we were reading on the AA Agnostica website. Each Monday we would print and discuss the previous day's posting. This led to having our discussions around *The Little Book, Beyond Belief* and *Living Sober*.

The Monday night discussions are always no holds barred, open and from the heart leading to some interesting insights reflecting the depth of commitment these men have related to the AA fellowship and their personal recovery.

We took the step of registering our Monday evening meeting, a men's discussion meeting, "We Agnostics," with Vancouver Intergroup and are now in their meeting directory. When I approached the Intergroup office I was concerned our meeting might be rejected. Happily the fellow who took our application was supportive of what we are doing.

When the new and latest group and meeting, "Sober Agnostics," registered, the same man commented that it was about time this type of group came to fruition.

Thank goodness for open-minded people!

Through the AA Agnostica website we received several inquiries from people looking for an agnostic AA meeting here in Vancouver. A decision was made to keep our existing group a closed men's discussion group and start the new mixed group. These members are now announcing the group at other AA meetings, which has created a great deal of curiosity.

It is natural for these agnostic groups to attract some attention, and not all of it is positive.

When approached by members who are questioning our style of meetings or are hostile and demeaning of our efforts we simply refer them to the AA Agnostica website for investigation prior to more contempt.

We are here to stay folks, get over it!

The upshot of all this is that agnostic meetings have a foothold here in Vancouver and will continue to grow as word gets out to other agnostics in the AA community. Yes we will be criticized by the people who have always criticized something new in AA.

I can recall the seventies when the first gay groups were getting started and the outrage that was shared. We then heard much the same stuff when the doctors and lawyers and judges formed their own groups: The sky was falling. Then came the children of the sixties and seventies who were users of both alcohol and drugs. Somehow many of these people stayed sober and in our fellowship in spite of some groups attempting to enforce an "alcoholics only" requirement for AA meetings.

In spite of all the current turmoil I believe the AA Agnostica community will continue to grow and attract many like-minded people who will serve to widen the AA gateway for all still suffering alcoholics.

Heathens, Spies, Websites, Water-boarding & Carrot Cake

By Bob K.

Chapter 4 of the Big Book, We Agnostics, is less than satisfying for many non-believers. Six months ago I went undercover so that I might investigate these devious agnostic creatures. It was my hope to discover what it was in Chapter 4 that they found objectionable.

Disregarding a tremendous amount of personal danger, I was able to infiltrate Toronto's two agnostic AA groups, starting with the second anniversary party of Beyond Belief. They had an interesting speaker from New York City who opened his talk by saying that he believed AA to be a spiritual programme. I was shocked, as I am sure all are, to hear the word "spiritual" at such a meeting. Seemingly, the guile of these strange unbelieving entities was even beyond what I had expected.

I must report that, as a group, they were quite ordinary in appearance, albeit the "nerd quotient" was undeniably above the norm. Anxious to appear to fit in, but with great trepidation, I sampled some foodstuffs from a rather elaborate buffet. The fare of the agnostics was shockingly similar to our own, and they had lots of it. The species dines well.

Early on in the course of my investigations, a third group was formed in Richmond Hill. I investigated this meeting, and also the second downtown meeting, blatantly called We Agnostics. All of these gatherings were shockingly unshocking. Using cunning and subterfuge, I ingratiated myself with the head heathen, and all was going well, until it wasn't. Anyway, more later about my capture, water-boarding and subsequent indentured servitude.

Interestingly, our Big Book does not define "alcoholism" or "alcoholics," but rather provides "descriptions." As in paragraph one of the We Agnostics chapter – "If, when you honestly want to, you find you cannot quit entirely, or if when drinking, you have little control over the amount you take, you are probably alcoholic." Geez, I remember expecting something a little more harsh in the qualifications – at least some DTs, extreme withdrawal, 60 ouncers, vodka on cornflakes and a minimum of one pink elephant. It occurs to me that "The Days of Wine and Roses" starring Jack Lemmon and Lee Remick was filmed AFTER the writing of the book. Ca explique beaucoup.

I have some observations about agnostics and atheists, gleaned from twenty plus years of seeing these creatures at regular meetings.

1. Among newcomers to AA, there are very few 'real' atheists. The vast majority of those proclaiming "When I got to AA I was a total atheist" will later tell of tragic or unfair events which led to their resentments against God. They are much like the angry four year old who screams the ultimate punishment at his mother – "You're not my mommy any more…" A good many others pursue a life-style of hedonism and self-centeredness, possibly in complete opposition to a religious upbringing, and fear some very dire consequences IF there is a God. They optimistically wish for no God but, beaten down by alcohol, reactivating belief is not terribly difficult. This first group also can come to God via the fourth step of the program.

2. About half to two thirds (by my perception) of those new arrivals to AA who would designate themselves 'agnostic' have, like the folks described above, merely dodged the issue. These groups are the people for whom this chapter was written and there were plenty of them at the time Bill wrote the Big Book. Our 12-Step recovery process reduces both fear and resentment, formerly blocking these folks from a relationship with God. Not a giant stretch for those whose roots of disbelief do not run deep.

3. But what about the real agnostic or atheist? Here is the fellow who has been puzzling you, especially in his lack of belief. These folks have given these matters serious consideration and are often more well-versed than most on religious matters.

And indeed, such are the members of the downtown groups – agnostics, Buddhists, humanists, atheists, wanderers and seekers. Many achieved sobriety through regular AA, assisted by the liberality of Bill Wilson, and the concessions granted to the atheists and agnostics of the 1930s. The Spiritual Experience Appendix added in 1941 allows a pursuit of psychic (spiritual!) change, and one's own "God as we understood Him" (courtesy of the early atheist, Jim B.) has truly provided a "widening of the gateway."

Sadly, for an unknown quantity of other still suffering alcoholics, the gateway is not wide enough. Freedom to choose one's own spiritual path, one's own concept of God, is contradicted for them by AA's pitbull-like adherence to the King of Christian prayers. Several have without doubt found a workable path to sobriety among the non-believers, and within the non-religious atmosphere of these "unconventional" groups.

Back to my infiltration of the agnostics: all was going well.

I befriended these strange creatures and gained their trust, even writing a few blogs for their heathen website. No one suspected a thing, and then one day someone sneezed. The "God bless you" was out of my mouth before I could pull it back. It hung in the air like a mushroom cloud. The room was deadly silent.

Then of course came the water-boarding. George W. claimed it wasn't torture. My experience was different. Hour after hour it went on, and the SAME questions over and over and over again: "Is there a God?" "Do you have an immortal soul?" "Do heaven and hell exist?" I would have done anything to make it stop. Not being an agnostic myself, I did NOT know that the answer that these heathens were satisfied with was a simple "Maybe."

Bob K

While brainwashed, I was FORCED to write a blog, *God as We Understood Him: AA in the 1930s*, for the heathen website. May all who believe forgive me and may God have mercy on my soul !!

Two Years Old!

AA Agnostica is now two years old! Launched in the summer of 2011, it was originally called AA Toronto Agnostics and its purpose was to let people know about the times and locations of two agnostic meetings, after they had been removed from the official AA meeting list by the Greater Toronto Area Intergroup.

A year later it morphed into AA Agnostica and since that time has described itself as "a space for AA agnostics, atheists and freethinkers worldwide." It is indeed a place where those from absolutely anywhere on the planet who do not profess to a belief in an interventionist deity – a portion of the population growing at an incredible pace – may share their "experience, strength and hope" as they tread the wondrous road to recovery.

And share our stories we have! Over the past year, there have been a total of 46 brand new posts on the website, one every Sunday morning. These have been written by 26 people from three different countries: the United States, Canada, and Great Britain. Another six have been reprinted from the AA Grapevine, for a grand total of 53 posts.

Let's break those numbers down even further.

Twenty-six of them were written by Canadians, but these numbers are a bit misleading since ten of those were written by yours truly, Roger C., and another six by the wonderful writer from Whitby, Ontario, Bob K. That skews the math rather badly. Bob's most recent piece, as usual, involved a good bit of research: *Anonymity in the 21st Century*. Another sixteen were written by Americans and, of those, there is a decided tilt towards the west coast, with half a dozen coming from California. That's no doubt because Frank M., the Hollywoodian, has shared three marvellous pieces on AA Agnostica. Frank now has the honour of having the most viewed post on AA Agnostica: *An Atheist's Guide to 12 Step Recovery*. And it's a pleasure to report that five posts were written by folks from Great Britain. Again these numbers do not include reprints from the AA Grapevine.

Everybody will have their own favourite posts, which appear in several categories on AA Agnostica.

One of our more popular categories is the 12 Steps. Seven articles were written on that topic, two by Gabe S. from London, England. His first was *A Higher Power of My Understanding*. Canada has a few western provinces, and a fellow from Alberta, just west of Saskatchewan, wrote *Personalizing the 12 Steps*, which has turned out to be a popular post on the website. I wrote an historical piece, *The Origins of the 12 Steps*, largely because I needed to include this history in *The Little Book: A Collection of Alternative 12 Steps*, which was published in February.

Reviews. We also do book reviews on AA Agnostica and some wonderful books were reviewed over the past year. One book, written by Joe C., a founder of the first agnostic AA group in Canada, was reviewed by Carol M., *Beyond Belief: Agnostic Musings for 12 Step Life*. One of my favourite reviews is of the book by Stephanie Covington, *A Woman's Way through the Twelve Steps*. Linda R. wrote that review almost a year ago.

History and AA. We enjoy our history on AA Agnostica! Over the past year, 16 posts fell into that category. John L. from Boston wrote a classic piece with his *Washingtonian Forebears of Alcoholics Anonymous*. There is much to be learned in John's piece. Our Bob K. wrote an outstanding biography of *Edwin Throckmorton Thacher (Ebby)* that connects a lot of people from Wikipedia to AA Agnostica. And the story of Girl Scouts by Frank. M., *A Lesson for AA from our Betters*, is brilliant.

The Lord's Prayer. We've only had one post in this category over the last year, but it could be argued that it is a must-read: *The Lord's Prayer and the Law*.

And our second favourite category is **Experience, Strength and Hope**. There were some lovely posts on this topic over the last year. Let's just mention a few of them. After being sober for 59 years, Ivan K. wrote *The Bird in Your Hand* for AA Agnostica. That was followed by *My Name is Marnin*, written by Marnin M. who, with 42 years of sobriety, two few weeks ago started a "reformed" AA meeting in Hobe Sound, Florida. And finally we have the marvellous post by Megan D. She and Charlie P. founded the first AA meeting ever to be called "We Agnostics" in Los Angeles in 1980.

———

Where do we go from here?

Well, there is only one proper answer to that: "Onwards and upwards!"

The traffic to AA Agnostica is increasing at a truly impressive rate. Since January 2012, when the website was moved to a private server, the number of visitors has increased every month. Certainly there is a great deal of interest in the message found at AA Agnostica and that is exactly as it should be: the 26 people who contributed articles over the past year were from an astonishing array of backgrounds and what they shared with us was often startling, compelling, disturbing and, sometimes, an inspiration. Just what we have come to expect in AA.

We invite all who are reading this – you – to consider writing a post to be shared on AA Agnostica.

We will continue to post a new piece every Sunday. These will follow the themes and categories that have been used over the past two years. And we will add a brand new category, called "*Many Paths*," where we will have posts about other recovery programs and organizations. As one path simply will not work for everybody, it's important to have choices and this category will celebrate the many paths of recovery.

The raison d'être of AA Agnostica will continue to be to provide agnostics, atheists and freethinkers with an opportunity to share our experience, strength and hope, to encourage the fellowship of AA to be more accommodating towards non-believers and to affirm that, as Bill White put it in the Foreword to *The Little Book*, "all pathways of recovery are cause for mutual celebration."

AA's entry into the twenty-first century is not an easy one. But the effort within the fellowship to meet the challenges of the twenty-first century is a worthy one, if we place any value at all in the principles expressed in the Responsibility Declaration.

AA Agnostica is not about what we want others in AA to do, an approach which would come with an unbearably high dose of belligerence and negativity. It's about what we do, and how we go forward.

And so the We Agnostics and Freethinkers International AA Convention. And so more agnostic AA meetings and groups. And so our continued celebration of the many paths of recovery. And so this website. And so our support for all in recovery and especially, in our case, given our own understanding of the need, the non-believing alcoholic in AA.

"Onwards and upwards."

An AA Convention for We Agnostics

An interview with Pam W.

Roger: Thank you Pam for agreeing to do this interview. You're a member of the steering committee that is now hard at work planning a We Agnostics and Free Thinkers (WAFT) International Alcoholics Anonymous Convention. I understand the planning for the convention is in the early stages. First, where and when will it be held?

Pam: The convention will be held in Santa Monica, California, Thursday through Saturday, November 6 – 8th in 2014. We found a lovely location at the Unitarian Universalist Community Church in the center of Santa Monica, only a couple of miles from the beach. It has a courtyard with a BBQ and enough classrooms for several workshops and marathon meetings. The UU community is very embracing of non-believers and it has a special place in our history as the location of Chicago's Quad A's first meeting in 1975. It is a perfect place for this historic event. [1]

Roger: Tell us a bit about yourself, Pam? What is your motivation for wanting this Convention?

Pam: As a teen I discovered alcohol, and I had no control from the very beginning. By my late 40s, I couldn't go a day without coming home from work and polishing off a bottle or two of wine. Weekends were filled with emotional negotiating over how much time I would spend running errands before I could get home and start drinking, to purge my feelings and distress. I was an alcoholic. Finally, fearfully, I stepped into an AA meeting in June 2008.

It happened to be an agnostic AA meeting. I found an immediate and overwhelming acceptance in that meeting and started to attend two of the Hollywood We Agnostics meetings. I never experienced the evangelical overtones at these meetings that I discovered in other meetings. I don't like to be preached at EVER and here was a place that I could learn how to be in recovery without that distraction or distress.

That is my biggest motivation for wanting the convention. To make others aware that there is a solution in AA for them, no matter their belief systems.

Roger: I take it that reflects the motivation of the steering committee that is organizing this convention. How did you connect with the members of the steering committee?

Pam: I met the other two members of the steering committee, Dorothy H. and Jonathon G., at the We Agnostics meeting in Hollywood which Charlie P. and Megan D. first started in 1980. [2]

Dorothy and I were talking one weekend about how often newcomers walk into our group and sigh with relief that they have found us. We decided we needed to put together a convention to help support each other and to reassure agnostics, atheists and freethinkers that we are not alone in the program of Alcoholics Anonymous. Jonathon, Dorothy and I believe that we can best be of service by letting others know of this wonderful alternative within the framework of AA's Traditions by organizing this convention.

Roger: I don't have to tell you that there is some controversy surrounding agnostics and atheists in AA. I personally belong to an agnostic group, Beyond Belief, that was booted off the official AA meeting list for taking God out of the Steps. [3] Will those with a belief in God be welcome at this Convention?

Pam: Absolutely. As it says in the preamble used at many agnostic meetings: "We do not endorse or oppose any form of religion or atheism. Our only wish is to assure suffering alcoholics that they can find sobriety in AA without having to accept anyone else's beliefs or having to deny their own." Where we fail in the program, and in life, for that matter, is when we push our beliefs on others or deny our own.

Our hope is to share this embracing theme and to remember that this program is about recovery and helping the newcomer achieve a "personality change sufficient to bring about recovery from alcoholism." We are all about inclusivity. And inclusivity means working to make everyone feel welcome, not deciding who is in and who is out.

Roger: Tradition Eleven says that AA's public relations policy ought to be based on attraction rather than promotion. Aren't you promoting a certain form of belief or, perhaps more accurately, non-belief?

Pam: Not at all. At the first AA Convention in Cleveland in 1950, Dr. Bob said, "So let us never get such a degree of smug complacency that we're not willing to extend, or attempt to extend, to our less fortunate brothers that help which has been so beneficial to us." We are not promoting anything. We are merely responding to the need to make AA more inclusive, to let people know that there is an option WITHIN AA. We are making sure that the hand of AA is there for our less fortunate brothers and sisters, including the agnostic, the freethinker and the growing number of those of diverse, non-Christian backgrounds. We are heeding Dr. Bob's counsel and not being complacent.

That first international convention led to many others and has led directly to this We Agnostics and Freethinkers International AA Convention. In what would turn out to be his farewell talk – he died just a few months later – Dr. Bob also "simmered" the 12 Steps down to two words, "love" and "service." Our convention is not about promotion but follows in the fine tradition of "love and service" that Dr. Bob so wonderfully described at the very first AA convention in 1950. [4]

Roger: Along the lines of my last question, Tradition Four says that a group is autonomous – can do what it wants – except when what it does affects other groups or AA as a whole. Your very goal is to affect AA as a whole. Are you not then in complete violation of this Tradition?

Pam: Only if inclusion is a violation of Tradition Four. We are only asking for more accommodation for the individual who needs to find a safe home group where her or his spiritual beliefs or non-beliefs are never, ever, treated as an obstacle to recovery and a life of sobriety. There is no question this is for the betterment of AA. Freethinkers, agnostics and atheists have been a part of AA since Jim B. And Hank P. created the compromise of the Higher Power concept. We are opening wide the doors to shed a brighter light on this program as an embracing solution that can work for anyone. That is being a responsible member of AA.

Roger: Okay, back to the Convention. What will be the format of the convention? How long will it last? Will there be workshops? What kind of workshops?

Pam: We are so excited for this convention! All the details aren't ironed out as yet, but we just had our most pivotal planning meeting on June 8th, where we had attendees from as far away as Hawaii. The convention WILL stretch over three days, with activities from 9 a.m. to 5 p.m. On Thursday, there will be the traditional opening ceremony to welcome our fellow We Agnostics and Freethinkers (WAFTs). This will be when we have our featured keynote speaker to start off our celebration!

In the afternoon there will be a few more featured speakers. These will be shorter shares, likely 30 minutes each, where we hear more inspirational stories of sobriety from our fellowship. This will set the tone for the first We Agnostics and Freethinkers International AA Convention. That first evening

269

we'll wrap up early to allow for mingling and socializing at either a dinner or a barbeque. It's California after all, so there will HAVE to be a barbeque!

Over Friday and the first half of Saturday, there will be marathon AA meetings as well as a variety of workshops.

We will have one dedicated room for back-to-back marathon-style meetings. We have asked our fellow agnostic groups to provide their formats and host these meetings, allowing us to "travel" to their meetings in New York, Chicago, Boise, etc., without having to leave the room. It will be fulfilling to experience other non-religious styled meetings and share our different paths to recovery in the program.

As for the workshops, this is one of the more exciting parts of the event. Our workshop topics will come from everyone! We are asking for suggestions and ideas from the community with which we are connecting in our outreach. We have heard from almost all of the 22 states that have agnostic-style and freethinker themed meetings so far. We even made connections in Tokyo and England and, of course, your home town there in Toronto. We believe that the strength of the agnostics and others in our fellowship will create lively and worthwhile discussions. These will be planned ahead of time, so we are hoping to get those suggestions in the works over the next several months.

On the evening of the second day, we are looking into having a beach bonfire.

After lunch on our final day of the convention, Saturday, we will have another panel of speakers, who will have very different spiritual backgrounds. Let's just say it will probably be our more spiritual day, and, I am sure, one filled with a great deal of emotion on the part of the steering committee, as we come to the conclusion of sharing our experience, strength and hope with each other at an event we put together in the spirit of unity and celebration.

Roger: Sounds absolutely fantastic! There is, obviously, a great deal of work to be done. Pam, what are the crucial next steps?

Pam: Oh, my goodness. There is so much to do! The steering committee is talking every day and we are getting such a great response from all over... The website committee is working on the website... We are getting established as a not-for-profit organization... We have to identify our keynote and guest speakers... Some of us are focused on compiling lists of activities for visitors to do outside of meetings as well as putting together lists of hotel accommodations for convention attendees... We need to get our fundraising going...

One of the unique qualities of this convention is how much inclusion we are able to establish by using the tools of the internet. Our next planning meeting will be held at the Santa Monica Library on Saturday, August 31st, and everyone who wants to can participate! The library has the resources which will allow us to do an internet connection to our fellows around the world. As we get closer to the date, we will provide the time and information on how people can log in and be a part of the process. In the meantime, contact us at the address above. Please!

And, of course, there is continuous outreach. I think Dorothy, our steering committee head, is set on reaching every possible supporter of WAFT in every corner of the world. She wants to make sure that we don't leave even one AA rock unturned!

Roger: My final question, Pam. As you go forward, over the next year and a half, what do you want the message of this Convention to be? What is the theme of the convention?

Pam: Over the days leading up to our June 8th planning meeting, we were brainstorming different themes and we had about twenty or so variations. I was personally hung up on the idea of "A Bridge Towards Unity" because I thought it really spoke to the idea of inclusion and unification. One of our fellowship, Angela from Boise, responded to an email on the topic and poignantly stated that she felt that anything with the words "bridge" or "build," even though they emphasize tolerance, would perpetuate the divide, the differences. Rather, she argued, it was time to celebrate the fact there are many paths to recovery, a reality always keenly appreciated within the fellowship of AA.

Well, we shared her opinion during the planning meeting. Others in the meeting voiced similar concerns and ideas, and, by a nearly unanimous vote, the convention theme was decided: "Many Paths to Recovery."

In that moment, it seemed as if a new momentum stirred in the room. It was not only a more concise vision of the WAFT International AA Convention, but a statement of what a bright future this convention has for us going forward. We are reaching out to all of the fellowship and becoming connected in a way that is securing the unity we have in AA. I think this is an amazing testament to the program and what it has to offer us in sobriety. Our paths may be different but our experience, strength and hope are what bind us. And, through this act of service in providing an international forum to help bring about recovery for the alcoholic who still struggles, we are surely following in the path of the founders of AA.

Roger: I can't think of a better way to conclude, Pam. Thank you for taking the time to do this interview. Obviously we wish you the very best. And we here at AA Agnostica, and I'm sure others in AA from around the world, will do our part to make this Convention a wonderful success, a true landmark in AA's modern and ever-evolving history.

---

[1] The involvement of the Unitarian Universalist community in the first Quad A (Alcoholics Anonymous for Atheists and Agnostics) is recounted in the e-book, *A History of Agnostic Groups in AA*.

[2] Megan D. wrote an article which you can read here in this book, *Megan D.* A very touching account of Charlie P. is also shared, *Father of We Agnostics Dies*.

[3] *Does religion belong at AA? Fight over 'God' splits Toronto AA groups* (Leslie Scrivener, Toronto Star, June 3, 2011).

[4] *Dr. Bob's Farewell Talk* (From his remarks on Sunday, July 3, 1950, at the First International AA Convention in Cleveland, Ohio).

We Are Not Saints

By Roger C.

My name is Roger and I am an alcoholic.

It was snowing on Friday evening, the last day of November, in downtown Toronto. I didn't know that until I hauled my bicycle out of the porch and onto the driveway.

It made me a bit nervous. I would have to ride almost three kilometres (two miles, for those south of the border). It didn't matter though; it was an important meeting and I very much wanted to be a part of it.

It was after 7 p.m. and dark. I attached lights to the front and back of the bike, a flashing red one on the rear fender. Snow flakes slapped against my face as I began to peddle my way. There weren't many people on the streets as I wheeled the bike past Danforth Avenue, through Monarch Park, and under the railroad tracks onto Gerrard Street. When I got to the Unitarian Universalist Congregation on Hiawatha Road I could see Chuck waiting at the door.

"Hi Chuck," I said.

"Hi Roger. The door locks automatically so we need someone to keep it open for others."

"I'll be the greeter then," I said. "Am I the first?"

"Yep," he said.

The first to arrive after me were Joe and Lisa. Then Denis. The next pair were Brian and Naomi.

Joe brought me a coffee. Starbucks! We chatted. Both Joe and I are on the verge of publishing books on recovery from alcoholism and addiction and we are, well, pretty excited.

Chuck was lugging chairs from the second floor down into the basement. He had taped a sign to the top of the stairwell:

We Are Not Saints
AA Meeting
Downstairs

Next to arrive were Kevin, then Ed, Eric, another Joe, Greg, Jackie, Larry, Julie and Frank.

Joe replaced me as greeter (Larry would take over later) and I went into the church basement to the meeting room. It was small. And it looked like a basement. There was a table with a pew against the wall and then the chairs that Chuck, and now Eric, were lugging down from upstairs. Some people were already sitting in a circle around the table, with a couple of rows on one side. I grabbed a spot on the pew. I hadn't sat on one of those since I was a child. I felt, well, at home. With friends and safe, is how I felt.

More people arrived: Frank, Bob, and Duncan. The last three were Wayne, Dianne and John.

It was 8 p.m. and Chuck started the meeting, on time. "Good evening," he said. "I want to welcome you to the first meeting of 'We Are Not Saints,' an agnostic AA group in Toronto."

I could feel the pulse of energy in the room. I took another look around the table. Twenty-one people in all: sixteen men and five women. Mid-twenties to mid-sixties. There was a flush of pride on people's faces, a glow in the eyes, a smile on lips. Those present were participating, after all, in a noteworthy event in AA.

As the meeting started, the Minister of the Congregation, Wayne Walder, informally leaned into the room and welcomed those present, a courtesy appreciated by all.

Chuck read the Agnostic AA Preamble:

> AA agnostic meetings endeavour to maintain a tradition of free expression, and conduct a meeting where alcoholics may feel free to express any doubts or disbeliefs they may have, and to share their own personal form of spiritual experience, their search for it, or their rejection of it. In keeping with AA tradition, we do not endorse or oppose any form of religion or atheism. Our only wish is to ensure suffering alcoholics that they can find sobriety in AA without having to accept anyone else's beliefs, or having to deny their own.

As is customary at meetings, Lisa then read "What is AA?"

> Alcoholics Anonymous is a fellowship of men and women who share their experience, strength and hope with each other that they may solve their common problem and help others to recover from alcoholism. The only requirement for membership is a desire to

274

stop drinking. There are no dues or fees for AA membership; we are self supporting through our own contributions. AA is not allied with any sect, denomination, politics, organization, or institution; does not wish to engage in any controversy, neither endorses nor opposes any causes. Our primary purpose is to stay sober and help other alcoholics to achieve sobriety.

The respect for privacy at AA meetings does not allow me to say much more, nor would I wish to. Suffice it to say that the first meeting of the agnostic AA group "We Are Not Saints" was an open meeting and three topics were discussed, in a lively and engaged fashion, by those present.

The meeting ended, as agnostic meetings invariably do, with the responsibility declaration. On November 30, 2012, a Friday evening in a UU church basement in Toronto, twenty-one atheists, agnostics and freethinkers held hands and said the declaration together, out loud, reciting it with pride and conviction: "I am responsible. When anyone anywhere reaches out for help I want the hand of AA always to be there. And for that I am responsible."

As is the case in AA, there was much fellowship after the meeting.

I had a lovely discussion with Duncan, a visitor from a small town in rural Ontario. Turns out Duncan was contemplating starting an agnostic group in his community, and looking for advice and information.

I chatted at some length with Julie. She had once taken a Mindfulness Based Stress Reduction (MBSR) program and I wanted to know more about it. And my friend, Bob! In the summer (long forgotten now!) he had taught me how to play golf. Bob had come all the way from Whitby in order to show his support to the folks in the room. And I chatted with Eric who had walked by an "old haunt" from his drinking days on his way to the meeting. How his life had changed in AA! And I chatted some more with Joe, first about Bill W, the co-founder of AA, and then about e-readers, like the Kindle, Nook and Kobo.

Oh the fellowship! How I love the fellowship of AA!

Eventually, I made my way back outdoors. A lot of snow had fallen during the meeting. The streets were white. "Winter is here," I thought. I didn't much care though. As I pedalled home, mostly uphill on the way back, there was a celebratory spark in my soul as I contemplated the fact that there were now five agnostic AA groups in the Toronto area. And I was so, so very happy at the thought of next Friday evening's meeting of "We Are Not Saints."

Conclusion

There are no doubt some who, having read this book, will wonder if it is the goal of agnostics and atheists to "change" Alcoholics Anonymous.

The fundamental answer to that question is "no."

It might even be: "No, not at all. Our goal is to help AA realize its unquestioned primary purpose, which is to lend a helping hand to the suffering alcoholic, all suffering alcoholics."

So let's take a few moments to deal with the quasi-criminal accusation leveled at us by some that agnostics and atheists want to change AA. We will do so by looking at three things: the individual agnostic in the rooms, agnostic groups and alternative versions of the 12 Steps.

The individual agnostic and atheist

A person does not have to believe a thing to be a member of AA. That goes from the day he or she enters the rooms of AA until forever. This declaration of individual freedom is contained in the Third Tradition: "The only requirement for AA membership is a desire to stop drinking."

That tradition is often attributed to Jim Burwell, a "self-proclaimed atheist, completely against all religion." He was one of the very first members of the fellowship and got sober in the late 1930s with Bill Wilson in New York. He was well respected within AA and started AA groups in Philadelphia, Baltimore, and San Diego. He died an AA member – and a sober atheist – on September 8, 1974.

Agnostic groups

What about groups, though? Can you have agnostic groups in AA? Of course you can. Here's the long form of Tradition Three:

> Our membership ought to include all who suffer from alcoholism. Hence we may refuse none who wish to recover. Nor ought AA membership ever depend upon money or conformity. Any two or three alcoholics gathered together for sobriety may call themselves an AA Group, provided that, as a group, they have no other affiliation.

That's pretty clear, right?

Well, amazingly enough, sometimes it is not.

And sometimes it will be suggested that agnostics and atheists have "affiliations" to a website, or a Facebook Page, or a philosophy, or maybe even to science. So absurd. Those who make those accusations should be careful, especially if they hold their meetings in church basements and end them with the Lord's Prayer.

And then there are those in AA who will either ignore the Tradition or, for their own purposes, attempt to interpret it with conditions.

The author of the Traditions, Bill Wilson, recognized this and so in an effort to fully explain Tradition Three he expanded on it in an article in the Grapevine:

> So long as there is the slightest interest in sobriety, the most unmoral, the most anti-social, the most critical alcoholic may gather about him a few kindred spirits and announce to us that a new Alcoholics Anonymous Group has been formed. Anti-God, anti-medicine, anti-our Recovery Program, even anti-each other — these rampant individuals are still an AA Group if *they think so!* (Anarchy Melts, AA Grapevine, July 1946)

Nobody can misunderstand that.

But it can be – and sometimes is – ignored, and there are those whose interests and beliefs are best served by pretending they are unaware of the meaning of this Tradition.

Rigidity is setting in in some parts of Alcoholics Anonymous. Moreover there is a canonization of the early AA literature, as though Bill and the handful of alcoholics who put the Big Book together were the equivalent of Moses coming down the mountain with the Ten Commandments.

Which leads us rather naturally to our next topic.

Alternative versions of the 12 Steps

The "true crime" for many is that agnostics and atheists – and particularly their groups – sometimes use an alternative version of the 12 Steps.

This has repeatedly been the excuse for barring or expulsing groups from AA regional meeting lists and Intergroups.

Two or three thoughts come to mind.

First, thanks to our friend Jim Burwell and a lively discussion at the time *Alcoholics Anonymous* was written, the Steps are "suggestions" only.

It says so right in the Big Book.

And again the author of the Steps was clear about what that means:

> We must remember that AA's Steps are suggestions only. A belief in them as they stand is not at all a requirement for membership among us. This liberty has made AA available to thousands who never would have tried at all, had we insisted on the Twelve Steps just as written. (Alcoholics Anonymous Comes of Age, p. 81)

Moreover – and this is where it starts to get bizarre – from the very first day we enter the rooms of AA we are told that we can interpret the Steps as we wish. "God as you understand Him," don't you know. Some then decide their higher power is going be Good Orderly Direction and others will say it's their home group of AA. So what's wrong with entrusting "our will and our lives to the care of the collective wisdom and resources of those who have searched before us" as is suggested in a secular version of the third Step?

Nothing. Nothing at all, according to the long-standing practice within AA.

Except for some people who don't understand, or who are confused, or who are just downright belligerent and insist upon equating Bill Wilson with Moses and the Twelve Steps with the Ten Commandments.

Or who are just a tad lacking in love and tolerance towards nonbelievers in AA.

Then there are those who will insist that the alcoholic will be confused if he or she comes into the fellowship and there are different versions of the Steps.

This fear of multiple versions of the Steps is highly exaggerated and over-dramatized.

For one thing, the newcomer, instead of feeling confusion, might very well feel a sense of freedom and liberation.

Besides – and some need to write this down somewhere – agnostics and atheists are not trying to change the original 12 Steps. Secular alternatives are not meant to replace the 12 Steps originally published in the Big Book, but are solely for the use of individuals and groups who may find them helpful.

Again, all in accordance with long-standing practice within AA.

Now, as we approach the end of this book, here's a thought that might be worthy of consideration within all of AA.

And the thought is this: maybe agnostic groups are exactly what is needed in AA.

Maybe it's not just a matter of tolerating our stubborn refusal to find a prescribed Higher Power, and of reluctantly acknowledging that we are alcoholics with a desire to stop drinking and so perhaps AA ought to find some way to accommodate us, even if only reluctantly and in the back rooms, so to speak.

Instead, maybe agnostic groups should be welcomed and encouraged by our fellowship.

Here's why.

Increasingly these days AA is viewed as a religious organization. It's hard – if not impossible – to avoid coming to that conclusion.

Meetings are held in church basements. There is usually a huge plaque beside the podium covered with the Twelve Steps, and the word "God" (or "Power" or "Him") appears six times in those Steps. Moreover AA meetings have become increasingly scripted, and thus meetings now often include someone reading "How it Works" which claims that God – "if He were sought" – can and will solve a person's problem with alcohol. Enough religion yet? There is more to come. Many North American AA meetings end with the Gospel of Matthew from the New Testament, Chapter 6, Verses 9 to 13, universally known as "The Lord's Prayer."

As a result of this, everyone of sound mind agrees that AA is religious. Indeed, the Courts in the United States over the last decades have repeatedly, consistently and unanimously decreed that AA is a religious program.

And as long as agnostic groups are booted out of regional Intergroups for sharing versions of the Steps without the God bit, that opinion is reinforced. It is proven to be true, in fact.

But now what would happen if the opposite were true and agnostic and atheist groups were welcomed and encouraged in AA?

Well, that's a new ball game. That would "widen the gateway," as Bill Wilson put it, and perhaps significantly alter the way AA is understood, both publicly and within the fellowship.

It might even be the true beginning of AA as a "spiritual not religious" program.

Ironically, agnostic groups may prove to be the very salvation of the fellowship of Alcoholics Anonymous.

Nor should we be surprised by that. The only goal of any and all agnostic groups is to help AA realize its unquestioned primary purpose and to lend a helping hand to the suffering alcoholic, all suffering alcoholics.

In order to access the value inherent in agnostic groups in AA and for the fellowship to move forward as a contemporary force, however, we have to once and for all drop the "Don't Tell" policy in AA. We need to discuss the place of agnostics and atheists, and our groups, in AA in an open, honest and intelligent way.

And that's what this book has, proudly, been all about.

AA Agnostica

AA Agnostica is meant to be a helping hand for the alcoholic who reaches out to Alcoholics Anonymous for help and finds that she or he is disturbed by the religious content of many AA meetings.

AA Agnostica is not affiliated with any group in AA or any other organization.

Contributors to the AA Agnostica website (aaagnostica.org) are all members of Alcoholics Anonymous, unless otherwise indicated. The views they express are neither their groups' nor those of AA, but solely their own.

There is an increasing number of groups within AA that are not religious in their thinking or practice. These groups don't recite prayers at the beginning or ending of their meetings, nor do they suggest that a belief in God is required to get sober or to maintain sobriety. If the readings at their meetings include AA's suggested program of recovery, then a secular or humanist version of the 12 Steps is shared.

If you asked members of AA who belong to these non-religious groups about their vision of the fellowship, they would probably describe it this way:

> **ALCOHOLICS ANONYMOUS** is a fellowship of men and women who share their experience, strength and hope with each other that they may solve their common problem and help others recover from alcoholism. The only requirement for AA membership is a desire to stop drinking. There are no dues or fees for membership: we are self-supporting through our own contributions. AA is not allied with any sect, denomination, politics, organization or institution: neither endorses nor opposes any causes. Our primary purpose is to stay sober and help other alcoholics to achieve sobriety.

AA Agnostica does not endorse or oppose any form of religion or atheism. Our only wish is to ensure suffering alcoholics that they can find sobriety in AA without having to accept anyone else's beliefs or having to deny their own.

We can be reached by email at **aaagnostica@gmail.com**.

51309040R00175

Made in the USA
Lexington, KY
19 April 2016